The New Lives of Teachers

The New Lives of Teachers provides a new research informed and evidence-based framework to investigate and understand teachers' lives. Using a range of contemporary examples of teaching, the authors demonstrate that it is the relative success with which teachers manage various personal, work and external policy challenges that is a key factor in the satisfaction, commitment, well-being and effectiveness of teachers in different contexts and at different times in their work and lives. The positive and negative influences upon career and professional development and the influences of school leadership, culture, colleagues and conditions are also shown to be profound and relate directly to teacher retention and the work-life balance and wellbeing agenda. The implications of these insights for teaching quality and teacher retention are discussed.

This book will be of special interest to teachers, teachers' associations, policy makers, school leaders, and teacher educators, and should also be of interest to students on postgraduate courses.

Christopher Day is Professor of Education at the University of Nottingham, UK. His previous books include *A Passion for Teaching*, also published by Routledge. **Qing Gu** is an Associate Professor at the University of Nottingham, UK.

Teacher quality and school development series
Edited by Christopher Day and Ann Lieberman

With the continuing concerns of governments worldwide about teacher quality, raising standards and student wellbeing and citizenship, the series will provide coherent, authentic, thoughtful and communicative portraits of the contexts and conditions for understanding and enhancing teacher quality and school development. The aim of this series is to bring together, disseminate and communicate original and authoritative experience and research which will 'speak to' teachers, teacher educators, other researchers and other research user communities (e.g. teacher associations and policy making/implementation organisations). This major series will be written by highly reputable scholars from different countries and all authors will ensure that they provide an international context for their work.

Forthcoming titles:
High Quality Teaching and Learning
International perspectives on teacher education
Ann Lieberman and Linda Darling-Hammond

The New Lives of Teachers

Christopher Day and Qing Gu

Routledge
Taylor & Francis Group

LONDON AND NEW YORK

First edition published 2010
by Routledge
2 Park Square, Milton Park, Abingdon, Oxon OX14 4RN

Simultaneously published in the USA and Canada
by Routledge
711 Third Avenue, New York, NY 10017

Routledge is an imprint of the Taylor & Francis Group, an informa business

Typeset in Galliard by Wearset Ltd, Boldon, Tyne and Wear

British Library Cataloguing in Publication Data
A catalogue record for this book is available from the British
Library

Library of Congress Cataloging-in-Publication Data
Day, Chris.
The new lives of teachers / Chris Day and Qing Gu. – 1st ed.
p. cm.
Includes bibliographical references.
1. Teachers–In-service training. 2. Teachers–Training of.
3. Education–Biographical methods. 4. Teachers–Vocational
guidance. I. Gu, Qing. II. Title.
LB1731.D39 2010
371.1–dc22   2010000861

ISBN10: 0-415-48459-6 (hbk)
ISBN10: 0-415-48460-X (pbk)
ISBN10: 0-203-84790-3 (ebk)

ISBN13: 978-0-415-48459-6 (hbk)
ISBN13: 978-0-415-48460-2 (pbk)
ISBN13: 978-0-203-84790-9 (ebk)

Contents

PART III
Conditions for success   **125**

Figures

Tables

Acknowledgements

We wish to acknowledge the researchers and teachers who participated in the original VITAE project, especially Professors Gordon Stobart and Pam Sammons and Dr Alison Kington. We also wish to thank Hayley McCalla, who committed herself with great skill and patience in attending to the production of the manuscript through all phases of its development. Finally, we wish to dedicate this book to the many teachers across the world who continue to commit themselves daily to teaching to their best, in order to make a difference to the quality of the education of children and young people.

Preface

Many years ago, as a novice teacher in a growing area near Los Angeles, I got my first teaching assignment as a sixth-grade teacher. I had 46 students. Needless to say, I was overwhelmed. I had three children of my own, with one in the sixth grade. To get to work, I drove 35 miles over two mountain ranges. But I was fortunate to go to work in a carpool with two other teachers in my school. There was always a buzz in the air as we helped each other, not only to cope, but to learn together how to become good teachers. Our principal was new, but very supportive. After the first year I was given the honour of teaching my first gifted class, for which I had to transfer to another school. My new principal left the school every afternoon, before any of the teachers, to go ride a dirt bike in the mountains.

We all felt abandoned! No one cared what we did, the problems we were having, nor how we might learn from one another. There was a blanket of sadness in the school as we all struggled mightily against the indifference of our principal. I drove home day after day feeling unwanted and unloved, despite the fact that I was working hard to connect with my students.

The New Lives of Teachers teaches us *why* all these personal, emotional, organisational and intellectual ideas matter. But more than that, it helps us understand how the current context has expanded the pressures under which teachers must now teach. New views of accountability, new policies that often restrict what teachers have learned through education and experience, as well as new understandings of learning, now further complicate teaching work. *New Lives* educates us in a way that not only illuminates, but, perhaps for the first time in years, has teachers speaking for themselves, explaining to us all the complexities that make up the lives of teachers who commit themselves to teaching young students. We learn the importance of the school context and its effects on teachers' commitments and sense of identity; how recognition, motivation and efficacy, particularly in the early phases of teaching, matter. And we see the powerful effects of teachers' personal lives on sustaining or constraining their commitment to their work.

Government policies that thwart teachers' ability to be creative and engage with students play a part, as does weak leadership. Teachers' problems in their personal lives can erode their commitment to their students as they seek a balance between their lives in school and their lives at home. This has always been difficult to explain to people, but in *New Lives* we experience the complex lives teachers have, and how these affect their work effort. The work context, the leadership, colleagueship and the students, as well as the governmental context, all provide a part of the backdrop for how teachers experience their teaching assignment. And it is all here, discussed by teachers in different phases of their teaching lives, highlighting the current contexts in which they teach. How leadership responds to mandates matters. How colleagues support one another makes a difference. How a school sees itself affects how teachers feel about each other and their students. All of this we learn about through the eyes of teachers, as well as through the deep analysis of the authors.

Especially when teachers are novices, they care deeply about developing a sense of their professional selves. They struggle with many classroom conditions. Portraits of a number of teachers make manifest the importance of in-school support, good relations with colleagues and students, personal events and school leadership. Few professions are so dependent on external social and organisational factors and internal critical influences. We learn *why* support from school leaders is so important and *why* and *how* colleagues can influence one's sense of wellbeing.

Creating a work–life balance turns out to be a critical factor in teachers' continuing to be resilient, despite difficult working conditions. Teachers need their professional lives to be individually motivated, relationally connected and organisationally supported. Commitment involves not only a combination of emotional and intellectual work – it is fuelled by the passion of caring about one's students as whole people, as well as learners. And it is the delicate balance of all these factors that supports or diminishes a teacher's sense of commitment and compassion for their students.

New Lives describes teachers in different phases of their teaching life, thus distinguishing different needs at different times. Novice teachers developing commitment need support from their colleagues in a different way to those who have spent their entire career in teaching. Experienced teachers are challenged by sustaining motivation and excitement in teaching. Teachers in the middle phases of teaching seek support and recognition, which for them is critical in sustaining and increasing their motivation and self-efficacy.

The portraits in *New Lives* not only humanise what we come to learn about teaching and learning, but also show the impediments (poor leadership, restrictive government initiatives, tough students) and motivators (making a difference in a student's life, getting a leader who values teachers, interested students) that make a difference.

We finally have a book that gives us a lens through which we can look inside school cultures and that helps us understand *why* and *how* teachers live in schools, some merely surviving, but many thriving. We no longer need to say that teaching is complicated, we learn what that means.

Now I know why I felt so sad in my second school. I understand how it made me feel when my first principal supported *me*, rather than an irate parent who did not want her daughter to learn about the United Nations (the district curriculum) as it didn't go with her politics. I see how important the drive home over the two mountain ranges was, as I shed my teacher role and became a mother worrying about what we were going to have for dinner. I see how my first principal supported us novices with a pat on the shoulder, an occasional unannounced treat, a smile, lunch discussions and words of care and concern. And you will understand too – as a reader of this fine piece of work – how teachers' professional work and personal lives are connected, and how passion fuels the commitment of teachers to manage this complexity. And you will understand how the current context complicates, even more, the 'lives' of teachers and what it takes to support resilience, commitment and the passion to teach.

Ann Lieberman
Stanford University

Introduction

Many teachers in schools across the world enter teaching with a strong sense of vocation, a 'passion' for teaching. Yet, whilst some survive and flourish, others fall by the wayside. In reporting on the results of a survey of 1,000 teachers with up to five years' experience in American schools, Sonia Nieto (2005: 3) observed that:

> 96% said that they loved teaching and 72% declared that contributing to society and helping others was paramount to them. In most cases, they became teachers out of a sense of mission, for love more than for money. Their responses, taken together, define an idealistic group of people who share at least one significant quality: They have a passion for teaching, a quality that, according to the report, is, 'palpable, vastly unappreciated and a valuable asset that money can't buy'.
>
> (Farkas *et al.*, 2000: 36)

This book is about the work and lives of teachers in primary and secondary schools in the twenty-first century. It is the first since Huberman's seminal work (Huberman, 1993) that investigates the highs and lows, the challenges and trials, tribulations and rewards of beginning, mid-career and veteran teachers who work in a variety of schools and in what has been described as the United Kingdom's most stressful occupation (*Guardian*, 2009).

The book is the first of its kind to present a holistic perspective of what it is like to be a teacher in changing and challenging times. Drawing on a range of international research and using previously unpublished empirical findings from a unique, large-scale, four-year mixed-methods research project.[1] It will show how teachers need more than specialist content and pedagogical knowledge if they are going to teach to their best and make a positive difference to the lives of children and young people over the span of their working lives. They need passion, commitment and resilience in work that is becoming more, rather than less, complex. The book will also show that how teachers build and sustain – or do not sustain – the quality of their work in classrooms may be influenced not only by their sense of vocation, but also the broader social and policy contexts, the quality of in-school support from colleagues and school leaders, and events and experiences in their personal lives.

The portraits of teachers presented in this book challenge traditional notions that expertise and effectiveness are necessarily a function of age and experience. They suggest that it is unwise to rely only upon teachers' initial sense of vocation if standards in schools are to be raised; and they reveal the importance to quality teaching of commitment and resilience. They also show, unequivocally, that commitment over time is influenced by a range of anticipated and unanticipated personal, workplace and broad policy influences, which affect teachers in different ways according to their particular professional life phase.

The organisation of the book into parts and the sequencing of the chapters reflect these themes. In Part I, 'The contexts of teaching', Chapter 1, 'The new teaching environments', provides an international, research-informed view of the uncertain economic, social and technological contexts in which teachers work in the twenty-first century, and which have caused governments across the world to intervene in unprecedented ways into the governance, curriculum and classroom life of schools. Beginning with a brief history of change, it finds that in England and elsewhere, trust in teachers' professional judgements about what and how to teach has been diminishing over the last two decades. The development of new systems for student assessment, school inspection and teacher surveillance are examples of how policy makers have used a series of interventionist strategies in their attempts to ensure that standards of student academic achievement are raised as a means of increasing national economic competitiveness in the new global economy. Alongside this, evidence of increasing disharmony in society has caused teachers' previously informal roles in students' social, emotional and citizenship education to become more formal and more demanding. Some claim that a so-called new age of 'post-professionalism' (Ball, 1993) has developed, in which teachers succeed only by satisfying others' narrowly conceived definitions of their work. The final part of Chapter 1 places teaching in five particular contexts which influence teachers and teaching:

1   the rise of emotional uncertainty among students;
2   changes in workforce demands;
3   the effects on teaching of the telecommunications revolution;
4   the 'Every Child Matters' inclusive social agenda; and
5   the emerging new demography of the teaching workforce.

Chapter 2, 'The person in the professional: learning, identity and emotional wellbeing', discusses contexts and conditions which impact positively and negatively on teachers' lives. It focuses especially upon three influences:

1   Organisational learning cultures – variations in teachers' experiences and competencies to manage the realities of teaching, together with the differences in the levels of workplace support, are associated with particular sets

of organisational conditions that affect their teachers' learning and development and, through this, their capacities to sustain the good teaching and management of successful student learning.

2   Professional identity – teachers need to have a stable sense of self as a person and a teacher.

3   Emotional wellbeing – teachers need to have a positive sense of emotional wellbeing in their work in order to bring their whole selves to the task of teaching.

Part II, 'The professional lives of teachers', presents key factors which critically influence the capacities of teachers to teach to their best. Each of the four chapters is built around the realities of teaching experienced by 18 teachers. Drawing upon previously unpublished qualitative empirical data in the VITAE project (Day *et al.*, 2007), the chapters reinforce and provide graphic examples of the influences on teachers in the new environments in which they work.

Chapter 3, 'Critical influences on teachers' professional lives', provides a conceptual overview of patterns of influence upon teachers across different professional life phases. The chapter draws upon data which reinforce and extend the non-linear development of many teachers identified in Huberman's (1993) seminal research and the work of David Hansen (1995), which distinguishes a 'vocation' from a 'career'. The chapter uses the term, 'professional life phase' as a means of providing new insights into the lives of teachers who work in different contexts and who are in different phases of their teaching experience. The first part of the chapter presents distinctive phases in teachers' professional lives in which groups of teachers demonstrate similar professional concerns. It focuses upon their positive and negative commitment trajectories, both over a 'real time' three-year period and historical turning points in their professional lives, through the use of backward mapping, 'critical incident' techniques. It extends the traditional conceptualisation of critical incidents in the existing literature on teachers and teaching by identifying the nature and patterns of their influences on teachers' sense of commitment and resilience, and their ability to manage these over the course of their professional lives.

The second part of the chapter demonstrates four distinct critical influences – personal, pupil, workplace and policy – on teachers' commitment, resilience and professional identities, and reveals that it is not only the influences themselves, but their combinations and relative intensity that matter. Teachers' abilities to manage these are critical to their capacity to teach to their best over time. The final part of the chapter presents stories of teachers in early, middle and later professional life phases, and discusses implications of the findings for teachers, school leaders, policy organisations and teacher educators.

Chapters 4, 5 and 6 provide extensive illustrations of teachers in each of three broad professional life phases as a means of unpacking the complex influences that affect their sense of commitment, wellbeing and resilience. Chapter 4, 'Portraits of beginning teachers: schools matter', focuses on teachers whose experiences demonstrate different trajectories in the early phase of their work. It is in this phase, historically, that many teachers either change schools or drop out of teaching altogether. As Cherubini (2009: 93) states, 'How the novice first sinks or swims and second adapts to the respective culture, and it to them, significantly influences their professional and social stability.' The chapter underlines the importance of school cultures and colleagues who nurture these teachers' positive sense of self and sense of belonging during their socialisation into the profession and particular school community.

Chapter 5, 'Managing tensions and transitions in the middle years of teaching: teachers at the crossroads', reveals that, contrary to Huberman's (1993) findings, the middle years of teaching represent an important watershed as teachers begin to make decisions about, for example, the balance of work–life commitments, whether to remain as classroom teachers primarily or to pursue further career advancement that might involve them increasingly taking leadership roles outside the classroom. The evidence from teachers in this phase shows that, although most remain committed, tensions caused by the growing demands of bureaucracy, deteriorating pupil behaviour and changes in personal life circumstances placed them at a crossroads of commitment.

The final chapter in this part of the book, 'Veteran teachers: sustaining commitment, exercising resilience', focuses upon teachers in the later phases of their working lives. A lack of consensus and clarity in the current notions of 'veteran' teachers tends to imply a professional homogeneity within this group of teachers. This chapter, however, demonstrates that teachers with 24 years' experience have differentiated professional concerns and identities from those in the final phase of their professional lives (31+ years of experience). It also shows that as teachers grow older, the challenge of maintaining the energy needed for the complex and persistently challenging work of teaching children and young people increases. What it is that keeps them believing and demonstrating daily that they can and do 'make a difference' to the lives of those they teach is, therefore, of huge importance to heads, colleagues and, more importantly, children and young people.

Part III, 'Conditions for success', consists of four chapters and presents a more extensive discussion of the issues arising in Part II. The first three chapters discuss: the relationship between teacher commitment and success; school leadership effects on teachers' lives; and the importance of resilience. These three themes, we suggest, are at the heart of teachers' capacities to teach to their best. The final chapter focuses upon what being a 'good' teacher really means in the schools of the twenty-first century.

Chapter 7, 'Teacher commitment: a necessary condition for success?', identifies commitment as a critical factor in the progress and achievement of pupils. It discusses commitment as a part of professional identity, and the effects of changes in personal, workplace and external policy and social contexts which may cause this to wax and wane over a professional life span.

Chapter 8, 'Leadership effects', focuses upon the contributions made by school leaders to the professional and personal wellbeing, job satisfaction and effectiveness of teachers through their own passion for care and achievement of staff and students, their nurture of cultures of high expectations, a positive sense of efficacy, and their development of individual, relational and organisational trust among all members of the school community.

Chapter 9, 'Resilience counts', builds upon the evidence of international research, with illustrations drawn from the experiences of the teachers in this book, that resilience is important in sustaining commitment. This chapter conceptualises resilience as both a psychological and a socially constructed concept, influenced by organisational and personal factors and determined by individuals' capacities to manage combinations of personal, professional and context-specific factors. Teaching to one's best over time and in different circumstances has always required resilience. Yet, as the work of teachers becomes more complex and thus more demanding, nurturing and sustaining resilience – the capacity to bounce back in adverse circumstances – has become more central to the roles of school leaders, teachers themselves and all those who have a stake in retaining teachers who are fully committed to their work in the emotional worlds of schools and classrooms. The chapter concludes that resilience is not an option, but a necessary quality that all teachers need to have if they are to resist the challenges to their morale and sense of wellbeing that may be posed by policy, pupils, the workplace and life experiences.

Chapter 10, 'Teachers who make a difference: new lives, old truths', brings together the principal issues raised in the preceding chapters and asks whether the lives of teachers in the twenty-first century really are so very different from those in the last century. The chapter begins by focusing on the difference that research reports claim can be made to children and young people's achievement by 'high-quality' teachers in comparison to those who are not; and follows by identifying what 'quality' means. If they are to manage their new lives successfully, teachers need to possess:

1   a combination of technical and personal competencies, deep subject knowledge, empathy and passion. Who teachers are as people cannot be separated from who they are and what they do as professionals. It is a concern for both care and achievement of pupils that identifies teachers who are committed;
2   a strong sense of moral purpose and positive emotional professional identity and agency are crucial to teachers' own motivation and capacity to teach to their best;
3   the ability to understand and manage emotions within themselves and others;
4   commitment; and
5   resilience.

Whilst school leaders and colleagues play key roles in supporting teachers in the increasingly complex, challenging and stressful policy and social contexts in which they work, it is their support for their wellbeing and achievements, the quality of their relationships with pupils, their care, courage and hopefulness, their emotional identities and their passion which count the most in the new environments in which teachers work.

There are five key messages from this book for national and local policy makers, teacher educators and heads who are focused on raising teaching and learning standards and enhancing pupils' wellbeing and achievement in schools:

1   attention needs to be paid to the physical, psychological, emotional and social conditions of teachers' work;
2   teachers' work and lives are inextricably connected;
3   teacher commitment is a key ingredient of good teaching by teachers and successful learning by pupils, and is a necessary condition for their success;
4   teacher resilience is associated with a sense of individual and collective well-being, self-efficacy, agency and professional identity; and
5   different life events, relational and organisational contexts, especially those which pose personal and/or professional challenges, influence teacher commitment and their capacity to exercise resilience.

Understanding how and why teachers manage to remain committed to their work, then, is key to forging their capacity to teach to their best. The importance of doing so is illustrated vividly in the words below:

> It's a logical question. At the time I had not thought it through in detail. So I ad-libbed an answer, which I think is in the right direction. 'Go around to your friends and ask them just one question: "Who are your favourite teachers?" Then make a list of those teachers and go out and take their courses – no matter what they are teaching, no matter what the subject.' It doesn't matter whether they are teaching Greek mythology, calculus, art history, or American literature – take their courses. Because when I think back on my favourite teachers, I don't remember the specifics of what they taught me, but I sure remember being excited about learning it. What has stayed with me are not the facts they imparted but the excitement about learning they inspired. To learn how to learn, you have to love learning – or you have to at least enjoy it – because so much learning is about being motivated to teach yourself. And while it seems that some people are just born with that motivation, many others can develop it or have it implanted with the right teacher.
>
> (Friedman, 2005: 310)

Part 1

The contexts of teaching

Chapter 1

The new teaching environments

Introduction

> The quality of teaching is determined not just by the 'quality' of the teachers – although that is clearly critical – but also the environment in which they work. Able teachers are not necessarily going to reach their potential in settings that do not provide appropriate support or sufficient challenge or reward.
>
> (OECD, 2005: 9)

The schools in which teachers teach and the historical, social and policy contexts which mediate these, have always been important influences on their purposes and practices, their willingness and capacities to perform and to continue to perform to their best. This chapter examines changes in these broader contexts through the lens of economic, social and technological changes, and the effects of these upon teachers' work.

A brief history of change: the drive for quality in an age of compliance

There are a number of key events that have changed forever the post-war environment in which teachers teach and students learn in England and Wales. Supported by claims of falling standards relative to those in competitor nations which were deemed to be incompatible with the need to increase economic competitiveness and social cohesion, successive governments have attempted to re-orientate the strong liberal-humanist traditions of schooling, characterised by a belief in the intrinsic, non-instrumental value of education, towards a more functional view, characterised by competency-based, results-driven teaching (Helsby, 1999: 16), payment by results and forms of indirect rule from the centre (Lawn, 1996). As part of this, they are said to have placed new limits on teachers' autonomy. Under policies of decentralisation of the management of budgets, planning, staffing, student access and curriculum and assessment (Bullock and Thomas, 1997), they have reconfigured the conditions under which teachers work, putting into place a system that rewards most those who successfully comply with government directives and who reach government targets, and punishes those who do not.

Ball (2001) has described this central drive for quality and improvement as being embedded in three technologies – the market, managerialism and performativity (Lyotard, 1979) – and placed them in distinct contrast to the post-war, public welfarist state. Teachers, it is claimed, now work in a world where 'being good' is more important than 'doing good', and where trust in their professional judgements has been diminished, 'in incremental steps over the past two decades, in inverse proportion to the rise in popularity of standardised testing, "objective" assessment and the codification and quantification of teachers' knowledge and practice via professional standards' (Groundwater-Smith and Mockler, 2009: 9).

Prior to this new work order in England and elsewhere, a compact had existed between government, parents and schools in which, by and large, teachers were trusted to do a good job with minimum direct intervention by government in matters of school governance, the school curriculum, teaching and learning, and assessment. Quality assurance (a term that didn't exist in the 1970s) was provided by Her Majesty's Inspectors (HMI), a relatively benign group of ex-teachers and lecturers who had become civil servants and who were charged with monitoring and maintaining standards through their connoisseurship judgements on quality. Local education authorities (LEAs) (recently renamed as local authorities (LAs), the equivalent of school districts) were still responsible for curriculum and professional support, and employed either school advisers or school inspectors – consisting, like HMI, of ex-heads and senior staff – to achieve this and monitor schools. Apart from a minimalist core curriculum, LEAs and schools were able to exercise considerable freedom with regard to the balance of the curriculum taught (although most secondary education conformed to a university-entrance-driven national examination system for students aged 16–18), and this was reflected in different opportunities for students who lived in different LEAs. Colleges of education, responsible for providing the bulk of new teachers – through four-year education degree courses – also exercised choice in their pre-service work, as did universities in their post-graduate one-year courses. Significantly, continuing professional development (CPD) opportunities were largely left to the choice of individual teachers; 'teacher development', rather than the ubiquitous 'training' descriptor, was a term widely used; and the curriculum in schools was 'taught', not 'delivered'. Curriculum developments in schools were initiated and managed locally or by a national 'Schools Council', funded by government but governed by a partnership between teachers' professional associations and government. 'Value added', 'targets', 'accountability', 'training', 'performativity', 'audits' and 'performance management' were not yet even twinkles in the eyes of policy makers. The nation's primary (elementary) schools were the envy of the world and heads were the power in their own kingdoms, free to govern as they wished.

In 1988, all this changed:

> Following the Education Act 1944 the only curriculum areas under central-
> ised curriculum control in state-maintained schools in the UK used to be
> physical education and religious instruction, as well as the daily act of
> worship. The rest of the curriculum was a matter to be left to the judge-
> ment of the individual headteacher ... advised ... by the local authority ...
> and by a governing body. Since the Education Act 1988 all that has now
> changed. There is in its stead a state-dictated curriculum ... progress and
> achievement in all subjects are ... monitored and assessed at regular
> intervals.
>
> (Aspin, 1996: 55)

The new agenda

Why, then, did the relatively stable worlds of schools change? In responding to
this question, it is important at the outset to recognise that what has happened
to education is part of a larger ideological debate on the costs, management and
cost effectiveness of the public services in general. Education as a public service
in England has been a test bed for a raft of radical reforms that were born in the
mid-1970s out of political, 'new right' 'neoliberal' ideology and economic prag-
matism through which the post-Second World War monopoly of wisdom held
by professionals in education, health and the social services was challenged.

A new ERA (Educational Reform Act) dawned in 1988.

> This landmark piece of legislation represented the first substantial challenge
> to the system constructed at the end of World War Two, introducing to it
> such concepts as a national curriculum, local management of schools, grant
> maintained status and city technology colleges.
>
> (Chitty, 1992: 31)

Not only did this significantly change the education system of England and
Wales, but in doing so it cut a swathe through existing 'progressive' practices
and those who had used them. The progressive 'dinosaurs' of the post-war generation were systematically slaughtered or put out to pasture as new policies for
the entitlement of all children and public accountability of schools and teachers
were developed. The closures of Risinghill School in the mid-1960s and William
Tyndale School in the mid-1970s in England came to symbolise the end of so-
called progressive education (King, 1983), and signalled the beginning of root-
and-branch changes to the relationship between schools and government that
were to permeate all aspects of teachers' work. Since then, schools have learnt to
adapt to the new educational environment in which curricula and teaching
conform more closely to the requirements of the market and national policy
guidelines.

A 'new public management' (Clarke and Newman, 1997: ix) was identified in which schools were opened to market pressures, given greater financial autonomy and expected to improve on a yearly basis in terms of both teacher and pupil performance. Such improvements (or otherwise) were, and still are, judged through independent external inspection; national testing of pupils at ages 11, 16 and 17, and, until 2008, national testing of pupils at age 14 in English, maths and science; and annual performance management reviews of individual teachers. 'School effectiveness', 'school improvement', 'target setting', 'monitoring' and 'continuous (rather than continuing) professional development' have become the new watchwords. League tables of results are now regularly featured in the media; parents are encouraged to choose the school to which they send their children; and school governors have been given more responsibilities as schools have become locally managed and centrally accountable.

To ensure that schools comply with these innovations they are now monitored by School Improvement Partners (SIPs); are locally set targets for pupil achievement within a national framework of targets; and undergo regular school inspections by Ofsted (The Office for Standards in Education), with its judgements based upon a national assessment framework and in the context of a self-evaluation form (SEF), which is produced annually by every school. There is a 'naming' and 'shaming' of schools that are categorised as being under 'notice of improvement' or in 'special measures', a status meaning schools are under notice of closure, with a limited time to demonstrate improvement. Successful schools and their heads are awarded 'National Educational Leadership' status and given more resources. Moreover, the recently introduced 'Every Child Matters' agenda (2004) has ensured that schools are now formally charged with improving the citizenship, 'wellbeing' and academic achievement of all their pupils. Little wonder that some teachers have become cynical about change.

In the United States a high-stakes testing regime has been established in order to ensure that schools engage in a state-determined improvement agenda for all students to meet a prescribed level of achievement on state-authorised tests. The message there, as in England, is clear: improve or be taken over or closed down. In a wide-ranging, three-year evaluation of the effects of such high-stakes testing on high schools in Texas and Kentucky, New York and Vermont, Siskin and her colleagues (Siskin, 2003) found that, although they had provided a new tightening up of the curriculum in certain areas and a new sense of purpose in teaching, the net effect had been the massive growth of expensive measures of testing and curriculum validation of traditional core subjects at the expense of those which were not. Whilst teachers and teacher unions had welcomed the introduction and development of new standards for curriculum and teaching, they were reported to have been dismayed by the quality and applicability of the new tests that form the basis for judging the value of their work. Moreover, not all agreed that these high-stakes testing measures, as in England, had contributed to improvements in pupil achievements, especially those in areas of socio-economic disadvantage. Indeed, in England, the claims by government that standards of pupil attainment have risen as a result of their reforms continue to be disputed by academics, who point to variations of less than 1 per cent in the performance of 11-year-olds once external factors are accounted for – such as prior attainment and family income (*Teachers' Educational Supplement* (*TES*), 2006; Tymms *et al.*, 2008); and, in the case of 15-year-olds once change of intake and the exclusion of 'difficult' pupils before they take the examinations (Gorard, 2006; *TES*, 31 March 2006) are taken into account. Despite an increase from £38 billion in 1998 to £82 billion in 2008, and a total expenditure in education of £650 billion between 1998 and 2008, it was reported in 2009 that one in six pupils left full-time compulsory education 'without a single worthwhile qualification', with 100,000 'without even one C grade in GCSE exams and, if English and Maths were included, more than half (850,000) without five good grades (A* to C) as judged by the government's own benchmarks' (Randall, 2009: 10).

In a recent retrospective review of government policy in England since the Education Reform Act of 1988, Shirley Williams, a widely respected former education secretary (1976–9) and Leader of the Liberal Democrats Party in the House of Lords (2001–4) commented:

> Combining league tables with detailed central government prescription of the national curriculum gradually drove creativity and the joy of learning out of education.... This relentless regime, testing children more than any-where else in the western world, is associated with a high fall-out rate. At 16, 24% of English children leave education. This is the highest proportion of any country in the European Union.
>
> (Williams, 2009: 7)

She went on to note that, despite a 'substantial' spending increase of 29 per cent per pupil since 1995, comparative standards in reading, maths and science placed the United Kingdom 'a little' above the OECD averages. She concluded with this telling remark about teachers' work and lives: 'Teachers have been compelled to conform to a ceaseless flow of directions, regulations and notes for guidance. Not only has their professional autonomy been undermined; their morale, attested to by the annual inspectors' reports, is persistently low' (ibid.).

The 'new' age of professionalism

These regimes have changed what it means to be a teacher as the locus of control has shifted from the individual to the system managers, and contract has replaced covenant (Bernstein, 1996). The emphasis on corporate management that many reforms produce has, it is claimed, resulted in a sea change in the nature of professionalism. Each teacher must now be:

[a] professional who clearly meets corporate goals, set elsewhere, manages a range of students well and documents their achievements and problems for public accountability purposes. The criteria of the successful professional in this corporate model is one who works efficiently and effectively in meeting the standardised criteria set for the accomplishment of both students and teachers, as well as contributing to the school's formal accountability processes.

(Brennan, 1996: 22)

This new age is what Stephen Ball (2003) has called post-professionalism, in which teachers and other public service workers succeed only by satisfying others' definitions of their work. The ethical professional regimes that were dominant in schools are, he suggests, being replaced by entrepreneurial-competitive regimes (ibid.).

Other researchers have pointed to the proleterianisation, intensification and bureaucratisation (Campbell and Neill, 1994; Helsby, 1996, 1999; Ozga, 1995) of the teaching profession, referring to the extent to which teachers' work has been affected by external prescriptive policy interventions which result in less control or autonomy of classroom decision making and a diminished sense of 'agency' (Gilroy and Day, 1993).

Andy Hargreaves has presented the development of professionalism as passing through four historical ages in many countries: pre-professional (managerially demanding but technically simple in terms of pedagogy); autonomous (marked by a challenge to the uniform view of pedagogy, teacher individualism in, and wide areas for, discretionary decision taking); collegial (the building of strong collaborative cultures alongside role expansion, diffusion and intensification); and post-professional (where teachers struggle to counter centralised curricula, testing regimes and external surveillance, and the economic imperatives of marketisation) (Hargreaves, 2000: 153). Essentially, his work and that of other researchers (Helsby and McCulloch, 1996: Robertson, 1996; Talbert and McLaughlin, 1996) illustrates the growth of challenges from governments to teachers' agency and a contestation of control of curriculum content, pedagogy and assessment historically associated with teacher professionalism.

Yet being – and behaving as – a professional in the more traditional sense of exercising a degree of autonomy and demonstrating considerable commitment to the education of all aspects of their pupils is still an expectation placed upon teachers. Professionalism in this sense continues to be associated with having a strong technical culture (knowledge base); service ethic (commitment to serving clients' needs); professional commitment (strong individual and collective identities); and professional autonomy (control over classroom practice) (Etzioni, 1969; Larson, 1977; McLaughlin and Talbert, 1993).

The extent to which the raft of government reforms in England and elsewhere, and the associated pressures of increased transparency, contractual accountability, results-driven curricula and burgeoning bureaucracy have affected teachers' morale, professional identity and sense of agency remains a matter of debate among academics, and between academics and policy makers and those responsible for policy implementation. What is clear, though, is that, for education and the public services, what we are witnessing is 'a struggle among different stakeholders over the definition of teacher professionalism and professionality for the twenty first century' (Whitty *et al.*, 1998: 65).

Teachers in many countries across the world are experiencing similar government intervention in the form of national curricula, national tests, external inspection and standardised criteria for measuring the quality of schools in order to raise standards and promote more parental choice. Although schools are able to mediate the impact of the intensification and refocusing of work that is a consequence of such reforms (Apple, 1986) through efforts led by their heads, their persisting effect has been to erode schools' autonomy and challenge teachers' individual and collective professional and personal identities. Furthermore, reforms of this kind are being reinforced by changes in pre-service teacher training, through which students now must meet the measurable requirements of prescribed curricula and sets of narrowly conceived, instrumentally oriented competencies in order to succeed.

Beyond a minimum competency

Ironically, despite the development and increased monitoring of teaching standards at all levels, the need for teachers to teach beyond basic levels of competence is particularly relevant at this time in the history of school education, when schools and their teachers face an increasing number of challenges from the changing nature of the society from which their pupils are drawn, and from governments concerned about their economic competitiveness. Four recently published research reports demonstrate graphically the continuing educational and life disadvantages experienced by children and young people in the United Kingdom, and the importance of schools in contributing to the impact of these (Child Poverty Action Group, 2009; Day *et al.*, 2009; DCSF, 2009; The Sutton Trust, 2009). In their landmark report, *A Good Childhood*, for the Children's Society in the United Kingdom, Layard and Dunn (2009: 156–157) asserted:

> Schools have a key role. They should promote not only academic skills but also help children to develop *happy, likeable and pro-social personalities....* In too many schools, the ethos is one of struggle between teachers and children and discipline is poor.... It is essential that children in deprived areas are taught at least as well or even better than elsewhere.

These and other similar accounts (Lindsey, 2007; McLaughlin and Clarke, 2009; New Economics Foundation, 2009) represent not only an indictment of UK society and its values, but a real and present challenge to teachers in their efforts to educate. Here we outline five of these that we believe are ever present in many of our schools today, and are likely to become more intensive as this century progresses:

1   emotional uncertainties among young people;
2   changes in workforce demands;
3   the telecommunications revolution;
4   the 'Every Child Matters' agenda; and
5   the portfolio teacher.

I The rise of emotional uncertainties

Children and young people in every country live within contexts of profound social and economic change and emotional uncertainty. In the twenty-first century, information technology has played its part in simultaneously providing greater access to information worldwide and to cultures of gaming, whilst at the same time diminishing face-to-face interactions. The family unit has become fragmented as the number of children now living with one parent has increased. According to the United States Census Bureau (2005), for example, the percentage of children under the age of 18 living with both parents has dropped from 85.2 per cent in 1970, to 76.7 per cent in 1980, and then to 67.3 per cent in 2005. The situation in the United Kingdom is no better. Only 60 per cent of children aged between 12 and 15 lived with both parents in 2009, in contrast to approximately 75 per cent in 1990 (*Daily Mail*, 2009). Moreover, according to the earlier results of the *A Good Childhood* inquiry:

> While average incomes in the United Kingdom have doubled in the last 50 years, people are no happier today, on average, than people were 50 years ago. In fact, for young people in particular, there is evidence to suggest that the opposite is true: that improved economic conditions seem to be associated with increasing levels of emotional problems. Depression and anxiety have increased for both boys and girls aged 15–16 since the mid-1980s, as have what are called 'non-aggressive conduct problems' such as lying, stealing and disobedience.
>
> (www.goodchildhood.org.uk)

Over half (58 per cent) of young people surveyed were worried about their exams at school, and almost half (47 per cent) said that they often worried about their school work. It is a truism to state that the circumstances of the children we teach are continuing to change. For example, in early 2007 UNICEF's comprehensive report on the lives and wellbeing of children in 21 of the world's richest countries showed that in the United Kingdom, children suffer, 'greater deprivation, worse relationships with their parents and are exposed to more risks from alcohol, drugs and unsafe sex than those in any other country in the world'

(*Guardian*, February 2007: 1). The United Kingdom was ranked twenty-first out of the 21 countries in the study – followed by the United States – for five of the six dimensions reviewed, including material wellbeing, educational well-being, family and peer relationships, behaviours and risks, and subjective well-being. In terms of experience of school education, the United Kingdom was positioned seventeenth. Although at the age of 15, pupils at British schools scored relatively well on reading, maths and science, more than 30 per cent of 15–19-year-olds were reported as not being in education or training and, 'not looking beyond low-skilled work' (ibid.: 2). In terms of health and safety, almost 36 per cent reported having been bullied recently and almost 31 per cent reported having been drunk on two or more occasions. The United Kingdom also has the highest teenage pregnancy rates among European countries.

The World Health Organisation's (2008) statistics on primary health care add to the causes for concern about the conditions in which children live in the United Kingdom. Approximately one in three 15-year-olds have main meals with parents less than 'several times a week', and 13 per cent of children aged 11–15 are overweight. Close to 3 per cent of women aged 15–19 give birth per year, in contrast to 1 per cent in other western European countries, and 22 per cent of young people in the same age range are not in education. Last, but not least, 19 per cent of children admit that they have used cannabis in the last 12 months.

Taken together, then, the evidence suggests that children may become more sophisticated, especially in relation to technology, but that they are also more vulnerable, uncertain of their values and, paradoxically, may lack motivation, self-esteem and self-confidence in school-centred learning. This has implications for the recruitment, preparation and in-service support of teachers. In their *A Good Childhood* report, Layard and Dunn (2009: 10) emphasise that children need good schools to flourish, 'where they can acquire both values and compe-tence'. To achieve this, it is essential that we 'draw outstanding people into the teaching profession' (ibid.: 109), who understand children, who are able to provide a secure environment, and who provide critical access to knowledge.

There are many studies which demonstrate the parallel rise in mental and emotional disorders among the children and young people who attend (or do not attend) the nation's schools. Around one in five young people in the United States have a current mental, emotional or behavioural disorder (Evans, 2009; National Research Council and Institute of Medicine [NAS-IOM], 2009; *Science Daily*, 2009). In the United Kingdom, according to the results of a large-scale national survey of child mental health by the Office for National Stat-istics, 5 per cent had clinically significant conduct disorders, 4 per cent were assessed as having emotional disorders, and 11 per cent of boys – compared with 8 per cent of girls – had a mental disorder (Office for National Statistics, 2004). Over the last ten years, there has been a growing number of reports of declining pupil motivation to learn, as demonstrated through increasing dis-ruptive behaviour and absenteeism, particularly in areas of social disadvantage. The *A Good Childhood* report shows that the proportion of 15–16-year-olds experiencing significant emotional difficulties in the United Kingdom rose from approximately 8 per cent for boys and 14 per cent for girls in 1974 to close to 15 per cent for boys and over 20 per cent for girls in 1999, since when it has remained roughly stable (Layard and Dunn, 2009). Difficult behaviour also increased significantly between 1974 and 1999, but has changed little since then. In short, the emotional demands on teachers have become more intensive as their work contexts have become more demanding.

Because schools have a key role to play in the socialisation of pupils, teachers need to be concerned with the 'darker side' of pupil relationships. In 2004, expulsions from schools reached almost 10,000, with half accounted for by violence and threats of violence against teachers; 85,000 pupils were also suspended in the same year for assaults, and in total 200,000 pupils were issued with suspensions from school, with secondary schools accounting for 84 per cent of the total. The then secretary of the National Association of Head Teachers (NAHT) commented: 'Inevitably, heads are beginning to have to respond to that [violence] by excluding more pupils until such a time as they understand they have to comply with the school rules' (*The Times*, 2005b: 9).

A survey by the Schools Health Education Unit carried out with more than 40,000 children aged 10–15 found that children were worried about bullying at school. More than one-third of girls aged 10–11 were afraid of going to school, and one-quarter of pupils in primary schools claimed to have been bullied, 'often or daily'. In addition, one-quarter of teenage boys and 18 per cent of girls stated that their friends carried weapons for protection when out of the home. Sixty per cent of respondents claimed to know someone who took drugs:

> For nearly three years Lhamea Lall, 17, a music student … lived in fear of a group of school bullies who every day devised a new form of torture for her. On a good day, the girls who ganged up on Lhamea would restrict themselves to name calling and bitchy comments. On bad days, they would kick, punch and spit.
>
> (*The Times*, 2005a: 17)

Schools, by default, are now more overtly responsible for the emotional and citizenship 'wellbeing' of their pupils than ever before; and many teachers are working in classrooms where significant minorities of pupils are disruptive towards the teacher and the learning of fellow pupils (*TES*, 2009).

2 Uncertain work futures: changes in workforce demands

Schools are not only places within which teachers have responsibilities for mediating values derived from students' world experience. They also exist within dominant socio-economic values and contexts, and contribute to them. Almost 15 years ago, McRae stated that the annual report of the International Labour

Organisation (ILO), a United Nations agency, suggests that part of the problem in Europe, where the unemployment rate is currently 10 per cent, is that international market pressures are forcing rapid changes to the structure of industrial economies. These are now having to move from producing 'low value-added goods and services into high-technology and high-quality service industries'. In America, for example, one effect has been 'to displace low-skill workers and increase the demands for highly skilled ones'. The analysis concluded that if this trend is followed in Europe,

> the only way we can sustain, or even improve, the relatively high living standards that most people in the developed world enjoy is if we are educated, trained and motivated to produce the high quality goods and services that justify such standards.
>
> (McRae, 1995: 4)

Twelve years later, *Skills in England 2007*, a report commissioned by the Learning and Skills Council, again urged employers to raise their game to capture high-value markets and place skills at the heart of their organisations' business plans, to ensure that England can continue to produce high value-added goods for the world economy and retain its competitiveness against the increasing international competition:

> Technology and globalisation will continue to be the main drivers of change in the demand for skills. Innovation and investment in new technologies and skills will be crucial to remaining competitive. Technology offers the potential to offset some labour shortages, but it also creates many new skill demands.
>
> (Learning and Skills Council, 2007: 13)

The need for more highly educated and motivated employees – who are able to use more autonomy and apply skills in combination with flexible technology and work processes to produce more per worker – is recognised in America also. The New Commission on the Skills of the American Workforce, a high-powered, bipartisan assembly of education secretaries, business and policy leaders, released a blueprint in 2006 for 'rethinking American education from pre-K to 12 and beyond to better prepare students to thrive in the global economy':

> We need to bring what we teach and how we teach into the 21st century. Right now we're aiming too low. Competency in reading and math – the focus of so much No Child Left Behind testing – is the meager minimum. Scientific and technical skills are, likewise, utterly necessary but insufficient. Today's economy demands not only a high-level competence in the traditional academic disciplines but also what might be called 21st century skills.
>
> (cited in Wallis and Steptoe, 2006)

It was agreed that the essential skills should include:

1   knowing more about the world;
2   thinking outside the box;
3   becoming smarter about new sources of information; and
4   developing good people skills, as emotional intelligence is as important as IQ for success in today's workplace.

(Ibid.)

According to the National Center on Education and the Economy (NCEE), in response to the unprecedented global economic downturn, the Commission extended their commitment to the 'Tough Choices or Tough Times' reform agenda in March 2009, proposing a major redesign of state education systems in order to dramatically improve the performance of the nation's students and help them succeed both in school and the workplace.

In what was one of the most forward-looking of business books of the late twentieth century, *The Age of Unreason* (1989), Charles Handy predicted that for the job market in this century, companies would be, 'reluctant to guarantee careers for life to everyone.... More contracts will be for fixed periods of years, more appointments will be tied to particular roles or jobs with no guarantee of further promotion' (ibid.: 25).

Indeed:

> It will increasingly be the individual's responsibility to make sure that the opportunities on offer add up to a sensible career path.... Education in those circumstances becomes an investment, wide experience an asset provided that it is wide and not shallow.

(Ibid.: 127)

Before the beginning of this century, in British Columbia, Canada, the Sullivan Commission, in the 'Year 2000 Framework for Learning' report (Ministry of Education, 1991), recognised that society was changing and that the structure of the economy was shifting from being, 'primarily resource-based to becoming a mixed economy', with increasing emphasis on the information and service sections. The report declared:

> In view of the new social and economic realities, *all* students, regardless of their immediate plans following school, will need to develop a flexibility and versatility undreamed of by previous generations. Increasingly, they will need to be able to employ critical and creative thinking skills to solve problems and make decisions, to be technologically literate as well as literate in the traditional sense, and to be good communicators. Equally, they will need to have well developed interpersonal skills and be able

to work cooperatively with others. Finally, they will need to be lifelong learners.

(Ministry of Education, 1991: 6)

This does not sit well with the still-dominant mode of academic knowledge, which is most highly valued in the curriculum of schools in England. It is clear today that the emphasis in schooling must be less narrowly conceived. It is equally clear, also, that teaching and learning will need to be more complex, personalised and differentiated in addressing cognitive, emotional and social development needs of pupils. It follows that the quality of teachers and their teaching will need to be consistently high if they are able to contribute to the endeavour of lifelong learning for the twenty-first century, which is so regularly espoused by government and business as being essential.

Whilst there has never been a guarantee that qualifications gained whilst at school will result in employment, until recently, statistics have shown that those with qualifications tend to do better and are more likely to be secure in employment than those without; and that the more qualifications a person achieves, the greater their income over time is likely to be. According to the Learning and Skills Council (2007) in England, earnings are – on average – increased by between 10 per cent and 15 per cent for each additional year of schooling. In the course of a typical working life, a person with a degree can expect to earn 67 per cent more than those who are without qualifications. Added to this, patterns of employment seem to provide a good – if socially questionable – fit for those with different levels of education. As the manufacturing base in England has declined, service industries have grown. As economic trans-nationalism, in which production is routinely moved from country to country, has superseded economic nationalism, so past certainties of long-term employment in all but the public services have been eroded. One well-publicised consequence of this has been a continuing call by government for a rise in standards of attainment as measured by tests and examinations. Whilst there continues to be much debate about the efficacy, relevance and credibility of these, what cannot be denied is that the increased emphasis upon them has resulted in increased pressures upon teachers in all phases of education, not only to 'produce better results', but also to be more directly accountable for the success or failure of their pupils. The mechanisms put into place by government for quality assurance have been: an independent school inspection system (Ofsted); annual performance management for every teacher; more regular and rigorous internal monitoring; and assessment of pupil progress and achievement. Yet, as we will show later in this book, there is no necessary direct cause-and-effect connection between good teaching and successful learning. Teachers themselves may have increasing difficulties in persuading a sizeable minority of pupils about the value of formal qualifications as they witness for themselves the consequences of economic turbulence.

3 The telecommunications revolution

There is a third strand to be visited briefly if we are to have a clear view of the teaching and learning contexts of the twenty-first century. Both outside and inside school there is a continuing exponential expansion of the use of information technology. We are told that this will provide students – indeed all of us – with more opportunities to learn through 'virtual realities' 'learning platforms' and other mobile and interactive technologies, which will enable people from different parts of the world to talk to each other simultaneously, to 'surf' on the internet, to cruise on the superhighway, to dance to the tune of cyberspace. There can, then, be no doubt that:

> the telecommunications revolution will enlarge the role of the individual with more access to information, greater speed in execution, and greater ability to communicate to anyone or to greater numbers anywhere, anytime. All trends are in the direction of making the smallest player in the global economy more and more powerful.
>
> (Naisbitt, 1994: 357)

Indeed, thanks to the compelling power of the revolution of information technologies, the late twentieth and early twenty-first centuries have witnessed unprecedented change as the volume and speed of global flows of people, information and images, financial capital, policies, knowledge and expertise have increased exponentially (Appadurai, 1996; Friedman, 2005). It is claimed by some that the world has since entered its third phase of globalisation – in which 'people all over the world started waking up and realising that they had more power than ever to go global *as individuals*', and that they have more opportunities to work with, as well as compete against, other individuals all over the planet (ibid.: 10–11). However, whilst Friedman claims that individuals from every corner of the 'flat world' are being empowered by the information revolution, many schools, teachers and parents worry that the new communication technologies have not only opened up wonderful new sources of knowledge, entertainment and friendship for their children, but have also brought them serious dangers (Layard and Dunn, 2009). The challenge of harnessing new technologies into valuable resources for teaching and learning has become paramount for today's schools and teachers.

4 'Every Child Matters'

Born out of the serial neglect that led to the death of a child by all the agencies responsible for her wellbeing, this agenda has caused a sea change in the way education is now conceived and managed at local authority (school district) and school level. Even the names have changed. Whereas schools until 2004 were managed under the auspices of LEAs, these are now LAs, within which are Children's and Young People's Services. Here, psychological, social, health and education are combined, their integration enabling the needs of the whole child to be addressed, at least in theory. Even the national government's arm of school education, formerly known as the Department for Education and Skills (DfES) has become the Department for Children, Schools and Families (DCSF) and the National College for School Leadership (NCSL) renamed the National College for Leadership of Schools and Children's Services. Locally, 'Children's Centres' have been established to work in cooperation with parents, carers, schools and other services.

The development of this new 'inclusive' Every Child Matters agenda (2003) has paved the way for an integration of psychological, social, health and educational services for children and young people of school age. It has, however, also placed additional responsibilities upon teachers, particularly those working in schools in disadvantaged communities. In the social and cultural realities of teaching, teachers' capacities to contribute to pupils' and communities' health, achievement and sustainable development are always moderated by changing national policy, social circumstances, local needs and individuals' commitment. The combinations of these constantly challenge teachers' resilience to sustain their vocation and commitment in the profession.

5 The new demography of teaching

Alongside these measures to increase children's and young people's sense of emotional wellbeing, citizenship, inclusion and their motivation to engage with the attainment agenda, the profile of teachers themselves has begun to change. As Susan Moore Johnson and her colleagues in America discovered in their research, 'the next generation of teachers is ... more diverse in terms of age, prior experience, preparation, expectations regarding the workplace and conceptions of career' (Moore Johnson, 2004: 7).

Recently, all the evidence in this and other Western countries pointed to up to 50 per cent drop-out rates of teachers within five years of qualification (Darling-Hammond, 1997; Kados and Moore Johnson, 2007; see Chapter 4 for details), but then a relatively settled population of teachers who, by their own accounts, have a 'calling' or 'vocation' and are in the job for the whole of their working lives. Whilst there has been some past cynicism about the motivation of married women teachers with a family in primary schools in particular, who, it has been said, entered teaching principally because of the school holidays, these same teachers have consistently spoken of their strong sense of vocation (Ball and Goodson, 1985; Nias, 1989a, 1989b; Troman, 2008). One consequence of this settled population for most pupils has been a sense of continuity of education – though this has not always applied to those in schools serving highly disadvantaged communities, many of which routinely experience high annual staff turnover. A consequence for the system is 'the "graying" of the teaching force' (Grissmer and Kirby, 1997: 49). In England as, for example, in Scotland, America and other OECD countries, the largest cohort of teachers is now those over 40 years old (Aaronson, 2008; Chevalier and Dolton, 2004; Grissmer and Kirby, 1997; Guttman, 2001; Matheson, 2007; OECD, 2005).

This skewed distribution towards older employees means that over the next two decades, on present estimates, three out of every five teachers will become eligible for retirement (Matheson, 2007). Indeed, Aaronson (2008: 2) estimates that in the United States 'the number of teachers retiring over the decade 2010–20 will be the largest in any decade post-World War II'. Given the relatively slower growth in the school-age population in many Western countries and the relatively stable growth in teacher recruitment, the increase in forthcoming retirements may not have a particularly strong impact upon teacher shortages (ibid.). It could, however, have an impact upon the quality of schooling because schools will lose many of their most experienced teachers and be managed and staffed by teachers who are relatively young and inexperienced. We do not argue that experience equals expertise – indeed, earlier research findings suggest that this is not necessarily so (Day *et al.*, 2007). There is, however, a compelling argument for those responsible for raising standards in schools to take measures to ensure, as far as possible, these 'portfolio' teachers' quality retention. In practice, this means that conditions for teaching and learning need to attract rather than repel, stimulate rather than dampen enthusiasm, promote collegiality rather than isolation, provide opportunities for continuing learning and development, promote communities of practice (Lave and Wenger, 1991), and be humane rather than mechanistically driven environments. Certainly in our previous work we found that the quality of leadership and relationships with colleagues, as well as pupils, were key factors in the commitment of many teachers. Such schools were the 'all too rare … finders and keepers' identified in Moore Johnson's (2004) research.

Whilst many teachers in England, as elsewhere, are still first-career entrants, in the last decade government, through the Teacher Development Agency (TDA), has promoted an increased number of routes into teaching for mature and second-career entrants. In addition to the predominantly school/university partnership programmes that are now the norm, and in which students spend two-thirds of their time in schools, two new routes are the Graduate Teaching Programme (GTP) and School Centred Initial Teacher Training (SCITT) programmes. The former is a one-year employment-based route designed for mature people who wish to change career. Trainee teachers are employed by a school in a supernumerary capacity. This route is designed for those with a strong commitment to schools in the local community. The latter is a national programme for would-be primary school teachers, again a school-based course in which trainees are placed within one of a national consortium of 52 schools. In both, universities play support and quality assurance roles. There is also a 'Registered Teacher' programme for people without a degree but with the equivalent of two years of higher education, again school based and carried out over a period of two years. The final, innovative programme is for 'high flying graduates who may not otherwise have considered teaching or aren't quite sure of it as a long term career' (TDA website). In this, graduates work with specifically selected partner schools and businesses over a two-year period, during which they work in, 'challenging secondary schools whilst completing leadership, training and work experience with leading employers' (TDA website).

Together with an increasing number of 'mature' entrants from the mainstream routes (Hobson *et al.*, 2009; Smithers and Robinson, 2004), it is clear that the profession will be more heterogeneous than previously, especially as regards the 'commitment for life' that has characterised teaching in the past.

Conclusions: the new teaching environments

Reforms in schools are different in every country – in their content, direction and pace. However, they have six common factors. They:

1   are happening because governments believe that by intervening to change the conditions under which students learn, they can accelerate improvements, raise standards of achievement and somehow increase economic competitiveness;
2   address implicit worries of governments concerning a perceived fragmentation of personal and social values in society;
3   result in an increased workload for teachers;
4   do not pay attention to teachers' identities – arguably central to motivation, efficacy, commitment, job satisfaction and wellbeing;
5   emanate from a deficit view of teachers; and
6   do not acknowledge the importance of teacher wellbeing and commitment.

There can be no doubts that reforms – particularly those which are poorly managed – at least temporarily disturb the relative stability of teachers' work, the conditions for teaching and learning, their own development and, in some cases, their beliefs, practices and self-efficacy. In general they challenge existing notions of professionalism (Bottery, 2005; Goodson and Hargreaves, 1996; Helsby, 1999; Sachs, 2003). It is important, then, that reformers from outside the school and those who seek to improve from within acknowledge the connection between attending to the wellbeing of the students and attending to the wellbeing of the adults in the school. Teachers' sense of wellbeing is deeply connected with how they define themselves as professionals, and how they see their professionalism being defined by others. Where there are differences, there are likely to be tensions. Thus, understanding variations in the conditions for teachers' professional learning and development that enhance their sense of positive professional identity and wellbeing requires more than a consideration of the functional needs of organisations and needs arising from teachers' personal lives. It requires a consideration of how tensions within and between these interact and how they might be managed by organisations and teachers in ways that build, maintain and enhance, rather than drain the commitment that is essential if teachers are to teach to their best in the new environments in which they work.

Chapter 2

The person in the professional

Learning, identity and emotional wellbeing

Introduction

The changing nature of the contemporary knowledge society, students' needs, policy changes and persistent threats to long-held associations between teacher professionalism and autonomy, as discussed in Chapter 1, pose challenges both to individuals' original 'call to teach' and the continuing relevance and appropriateness of their existing pedagogical and knowledge repertoires. Yet, 'it is through professional and personal development that teachers build character, maturity and other virtues in themselves and others, making their schools into moral communities' (Hargreaves, 2003: 48). This chapter focuses on teacher learning, the cultures that support this, teacher identity (the person in the professional) and the challenges to their wellbeing.

Teacher learning

Wenger (1998: 9) argues: that, 'in a world that is changing and becoming more complexly interconnected at an accelerating pace, concerns about learning are certainly justified'. He proposes that participation in understanding and supporting learning in different contexts should be at three levels:

1   For individuals, it means that learning is an issue of engaging in and contributing to the practices of their communities.
2   For communities, it means that learning is an issue of refining their practice and ensuring new generations of members.
3   For organisations, it means that learning is an issue of sustaining the interconnected communities of practice through which an organisation knows what it knows and thus becomes effective and valuable as an organisation.

(Ibid.: 7–8)

Learning at these three different levels is interconnected and interdependent in terms of supporting individual and collective needs and creating and strengthening learning conditions that support rather than hinder teacher learning and development. Yet these proposals miss the point, since they provide only a first-level analysis of the locations for learning, without examining the nature and efficacy of these. Traditional 'stage theory' conceptualises teachers' professional learning and development as moving through a number of linear skill development stages – from being a 'novice' through to 'advanced beginner', 'competent', 'proficient', and 'expert' (see Benner, 1984; Day, 1999; Dreyfus and Dreyfus, 1986). This linear model of teacher learning and development is underpinned by the belief that 'experience is the adult learner's living textbook' (Lindeman, 1926: 7) and (incorrectly) asserts that teachers' professional learning is grounded in their teaching experiences and that teachers learn from experience and gradually develop their competence within the workplace over time.

Whilst there can be little doubt that, 'from a developmental perspective, individual learning needs will be shaped by factors such as length of experience' (Bolam and McMahon, 2004: 49), the emphases on experience and linearity as defining features of teacher learning paint a too conceptually simple and decontextualised picture of the relationship between, for example, experience, context and expertise, and have been increasingly challenged by research which shows that experience does not necessarily lead to expertise (Bereiter and Scardamalia, 1993; Day et al., 2007). In discussing learning in the context of change, Fullan (1993: 138) has argued that 'reality under conditions of dynamic complexity is fundamentally non-linear', suggesting further that, to be of benefit to organisational improvement, teacher learning must focus upon both inner learning (intrapersonal) and outer learning (interpersonal). From an adult learning perspective, Brookfield (1995) has suggested that an exclusive reliance on accumulated experience as the defining characteristic of adult learning contains two discernible pitfalls:

> First, experience should not be thought of as an objectively neutral phenomenon, a river of thoughts, perceptions and sensations into which we decide, occasionally, to dip our toes. Rather, our experience is culturally framed and shaped. How we experience events and the readings we make of these are problematic; that is, they change according to the language and categories of analysis we use, and according to the cultural, moral and ideological vantage points from which they are viewed. In a very important sense we construct our experience: how we sense and interpret what happens to us and to the world around us is a function of structures of understanding and perceptual filters that are so culturally embedded that we are scarcely aware of their existence or operation. Second, the quantity or length of experience is not necessarily connected to its richness or intensity.
>
> (Brookfield, 1995)

Indeed, adults 'carry their learning in different settings and continue in complex ways' (Evans et al., 2006: 17). In his review of the literature on four major research areas related to adult learning, Brookfield (1995) found that the variables of culture, ethnicity, personality and political ethos assumed far greater significance in explaining how learning had occurred and been experienced than did the variable of chronological age across a life span. This is the case for teachers' learning. Despite their rich experience, not all experienced teachers (as judged by their age and length of experience in teaching) are expert teachers.

To sustain their commitment to learning throughout their careers, teachers must engage in lifelong learning. Haberman (2004: 52) maintains:

> The frequently espoused goal of lifelong learning for our students is hollow rhetoric unless the school is also a learning community in which teachers demonstrate engagement in meaningful learning activities.... In a school learning community, teachers pursue two realms of knowledge: professional development and learning for the sake of learning. The importance for the former is self-evident. As for the latter, inculcating love of learning is the surest way of teaching students to become turned-on learners. Students will model behaviour of teachers they respect – teachers who have strong interests, who love to learn, and who are always reading something of interest.

Ideally, teachers' professional learning will be self-motivated and self-regulated, and will involve both intellectual and emotional processes. It will enrich teachers' knowledge base, improve their teaching practices, enhance their self-efficacy and 'commitment to quality of service' (Hargreaves and Goodson, 1996: 7), and it will contribute to their sense of self as a person and a professional. Love of learning and the 'call' to teach imply that the best teaching involves the head, the hand and the heart (Sergiovanni, 1992); and all good teaching is essentially founded upon both intellectual curiosity and emotional investment.

The reality is, however, that the conditions in which teachers work do not always promote their learning:

> Although attractive salaries are clearly important to improving teachers' appeal ... policy needs to address more than pay. Teachers place a lot of emphasis on the quality of their relations with students and colleagues, on feeling supported by school leaders, on good working conditions, and on opportunities to develop their skills.
>
> (OECD, 2005: 169)

The workplace environments in which teachers work may enhance or diminish their sense of space, time and energy to learn, their sense of identity, efficacy and effectiveness. They will influence teachers' willingness and capacities to sustain or lose their motivation and commitment to teach well in a range of circumstances (Smylie, 1995; Sparks and Loucks-Horsley, 1990).

The nature of this dialogue can, however, vary in different phases of teachers' professional lives, and teachers in the same school may react very differently to the same stimulus, e.g. the introduction of a curriculum innovation or new policy: 'Individuals' dispositions towards work, career and learning [will vary and] influence the ways in which they understand and take advantage of opportunities for learning at work' (TLRP Research Briefing, 2004).

Because classrooms and schools are the most common sites for teacher learning, it is important that the range and quality of learning opportunities relate to their pedagogical and subject learning needs. Whilst training and development of this kind is necessary, however, it will be of limited use if attention is not also focused upon support for their motivation, commitment and self-efficacy.

> The interactionist character of CPD implies that teachers are influenced in their professional development by the particularities of the context, both in time and space. This influence, however, is not a deterministic relationship, but rather a two-way 'dialogue' through which teachers make sense of their experiences and act accordingly, even if this dialogue is partly determined by structural conditions.
>
> (Kelchtermans, 2004: 225)

In a multi-agency project on early career professional learning, Michael Eraut and his colleagues (2007) noted that the following factors affected workplace learning:

- feedback – related to confidence, learning, retention and commitment;
- challenge – the right level;
- appreciation – of the value of their work, by others;
- support – for their personal sense of agency.

However, the extent to which they were able to be effective depended upon other factors:

> The allocation and structuring of work was central to our participants' progress, because it affected (1) the difficulty or challenge of the work, (2) the extent to which it was individual or collaborative, and (3) the opportunities for meeting, observing and working alongside people who had more or different expertise, and for forming *relationships* that might provide feedback and support.
>
> (Eraut *et al.*, 2004: 9)

Although this research was conducted with qualified nurses, graduate engineers and trainee accountants in their first three years of employment, its findings, nevertheless, resonate with much research on the conditions necessary for the continuing professional development of teachers; and Eraut's 'two triangle' model illustrates well the need to develop strategies and cultures which support teachers' confidence, commitment and personal agency needs:

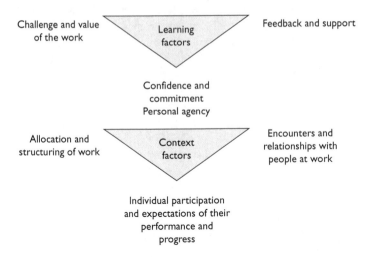

Challenge and value
of the work

Learning
factors

Feedback and support

Confidence and
commitment
Personal agency

Allocation and
structuring of work

Context
factors

Encounters and
relationships with
people at work

Individual participation
and expectations of their
performance and
progress

Figure 2.1 Factors affecting learning at work: the two triangle model.

Learning communities: communities for learning

'The Learning Lives' project (Teaching and Learning Research Programme, 2008) analysed the learning biographies of 120 adults aged between 25 and 85, and combined these with data from the British Household Panel Survey. Its authors (Biesta *et al.*, 2008: 4) investigated 'what learning "means" and "does" in the lives of adults' using a broad conception of learning, i.e. formal education, work settings and everyday life learning. Its findings speak of the different learning contexts that teachers and their pupils may experience and, implicitly, of the need for schools that are communities of learning and achievement for both students and teachers:

> People can engage in learning, yet feel that it is peripheral to what really matters in their lives, or marginal to their sense of who they really see themselves as being. Alternatively, they can value learning as an integral part of their lives, and see it as central to who they are.
>
> (Ibid.: 5)

In such learning and achievement communities, learning will be perceived as central rather than peripheral, integral to the continuing endeavours of teachers to improve teaching, which results in successful learning. The project proposed four broad approaches:

1   Provision of planned courses, workshops, etc. ('formal' education and training).

2   Personal support for the learner, which may be professional (career guid-
     ance, workplace mentoring, tutoring, provision of learning materials, etc.)
     or informed (friends, colleagues, family, local community).
3   Enhancing learning cultures. That is, improving opportunities for learning
     in particular locations (workplace, local community, etc.).
4   Providing opportunities for self-reflection, including talking, writing, think-
     ing about our own life histories and life circumstances.

(Ibid.: 6)

Mitchell and Sackney (2007: 32–34) offer five 'principles' of engagement that
underpin the further development and extension of learning communities:

1   deep initial respect;
2   collective responsibility;
3   appreciation of diversity;
4   problem-solving orientation; and
5   positive role modelling.

Stoll and Louis (2007: 2) assert: 'It is ... generally agreed that effective professional learning communities have the capacity to promote and sustain the
learning capacities of professionals in a school with the collective purpose of
enhancing student learning.'

The characteristics associated with 'knowledge building communities'
(Bereiter and Scardamalia, 1993), 'communities of practice' (Wenger, 1998)
and 'learning communities' (Stoll and Louis, 2007) are: 'sharing knowledge;
progressive discourse; mutual respect; the development of collective expertise
which surpass that of individuals; genuine inquiry; and a determination to
improve communities in which professional learners engage and which they
value' (Aubusson et al., 2007: 134). Yet, building such communities is a
complex, demanding and long-term process (Grossman et al., 2001). In practice, structures, cultures and conditions of work inhibit rather than promote the
sharing of classroom experience and other professional knowledge. As many
researchers have observed, it is not always easy to overcome years of teachers'
experiences of organisational isolation, separation and silence in order to form
collegial, social communities (Grossman et al., 2001; Hargreaves, 2000;
Pomson, 2005).

In a study of nine cases from 82 schools in Australia engaging in school-
based action learning projects, Aubusson and his colleagues found that whilst,
overall, the projects had, 'brought teachers together and supported them in
building some degree of community' (2007: 139), the range and depth of community interaction varied. Although factors that promoted development of
community were common, i.e. dedicated time for professional interaction, focus
upon inquiry, shared dialogue about teaching practices and leadership distribution, it was the presence and development of peer observation for the purpose

of support and transformation rather than evaluation that was the key anteced-
ent of a mature, trusting, professional learning community.

It also assumes the presence of a relatively stable staff who share a common
sense of purpose and values and are committed to working together to achieve
these – a staff who have a strong collective sense of wellbeing, professional identity and self-confidence. Building and sustaining cultures is predicated on the
notion of 'social capital', through which connectedness between all participants
in the school community, among schools and between schools and their communities can improve. This takes time and the building of trust, even for the
most skilled school leaders.

> Social capital flows from the endowment of mutually respecting and trust-
> ing relationships which enable a group to pursue its shared goals more
> effectively than would otherwise be possible.... It can never be reduced to
> the mere possession or attribute of an individual. It results from the com-
> municative capacity of a group.
>
> (Szreter, 2001: 32)

There will be inevitable fluctuations in the development of learning communities, as members of staff come and go, as social intakes of students change
and as new local and national policies place new demands upon schools. The
seven research-informed principles of more sustainable professional learning
communities espoused by Andy Hargreaves combine the particular educational
values and practices that can be witnessed in successful, person-centred schools
of all kinds, in all circumstances and across many countries:

1   Depth: sustainable professional learning communities concentrate on what
    matters. They preserve, protect and promote achievement and success in
    deep and broad learning for all, in relationships and care for others.
2   Breadth: sustainable professional learning communities develop and depend
    on shared learning and leadership for achievement and improvement.
3   Endurance: sustainable professional learning communities last. They pre-
    serve and advance the most valuable aspects of learning and life over time,
    year after year, from one leader or change champion to the next.
4   Justice: sustainable professional learning communities are not luxuries for
    teachers of the privileged, but equal entitlements for all students, teachers
    and schools.
5   Diversity: sustainable professional learning communities promote pedagogical
    diversity with other schools and among themselves and find ways to make
    this diversity work through person-centred leadership, networking and cross-
    pollination of practices, as well as intelligent reference to data and evidence.
6   Resourcefulness: sustainable professional learning communities conserve
    and renew people's energy and resources. They are prudent and resourceful
    communities that waste neither their money nor their people.

7   Conservation: sustaining professional learning communities respect and
     build on the past in their quest to create a better future.

                                                    (Hargreaves, 2007: 185–196)

It is clear, then, that teachers' professional learning will be influenced by their
attitudes to a range of factors, e.g. perceptions of the work environment and the
benefits of participation; support of the senior leadership team; sense of positive
professional identity; self-efficacy; aspirations for career advancement; and events
in their lives outside school (Maurer and Tarulli, 1994). Such factors are important because they affect, positively or negatively, teachers' motivation and commitment to their professional learning and growth and the benefits that they
and the school might derive from this commitment.

Variations in teachers' experiences and competencies to manage the realities of
teaching and work–life tensions, together with the difference in the levels of
support available within the workplace, create particular conditions for their professional learning and development and lead to variations in teachers' concerns
and needs at different critical moments or phases of their professional and personal lives. Effective professional learning requires an understanding, especially by
school leaders, that the conditions that enable its development are dependent
upon the quality of relationships between the professional as an individual and the
school as an organisation. It requires, also, a strong sense of professional identity.

Teacher identity: the person within the professional

Much research literature demonstrates that events and experiences in the personal lives of teachers are intimately linked to the performance of their professional roles (Ball and Goodson, 1985; Goodson and Hargreaves, 1996). In her
research on the realities of teachers' work, Acker (1999) describes the considerable pressures on teaching staff, not just arising in their work, but also from
their personal lives. Complications in personal lives can become bound up with
problems at work. Woods et al. (1997: 152) argue that teaching is a matter of
values. People teach because they believe in something. They have an image of
the 'good society'. If we are to understand the new lives of teachers, then, it is
necessary to take account of the person within the professional. This is essential
because a raft of literature points to teaching as an essentially human endeavour
in which who the teacher is as important as what she teaches (Beijaard, 1995;
Bullough and Knowles, 1991; Hamachek, 1999; Kelchtermans, 2009;
Korthagen, 2004; Nias, 1989a; Palmer, 2007; Russell, 1997): 'Paying attention
to the connection of the personal and the professional in teaching … may contribute to educational goals that go far beyond the development of the individual teacher' (Meijer et al., 2009: 308).

Several researchers (Hargreaves, 1994; Nias, 1989a, 1996; Nias et al., 1992;
Sumsion, 2002) have noted that teacher identities are not only constructed

from the more technical aspects of teaching (i.e. classroom management, subject knowledge and pupil test results), but also 'can be conceptualised as the result of an interaction between the personal experiences of teachers and the social, cultural and institutional environment in which they function on a daily basis' (Sleegers and Kelchtermans, 1999: 579).

Teachers' professional identities – who they are, their self-image, the meanings they attach to themselves and their work and the meanings that are attributed to them by others – are, then, associated with both the subject they teach (this is particularly the case with secondary school teachers), their relationships with the pupils they teach, their roles, and the connections between these, their values and their lives outside school.

Sachs (2003) identifies two contrasting forms of professional identity:

1   Entrepreneurial, which she identifies with efficient, responsible, accountable teachers who demonstrate compliance to externally imposed imperatives with consistently high-quality teaching as measured by externally set performance indicators. This identity may be characterised as being individualistic, competitive, controlling and regulative, externally defined, standards led.
2   Activist, which she sees as driven by a belief in the importance of mobilising teachers in the best interests of student learning and improving the conditions in which this can occur. In this identity teachers will be primarily concerned with creating and putting into place standards and processes that give students democratic experiences.

The former, she argues, is the desired product of performativity, managerialist agendas, while the latter suggests inquiry-oriented, collaborative classrooms and schools in which teaching is related to broad societal ideals and values, and in which the purposes of teaching and learning transcend the narrow instrumentalism of current reform agendas. She identifies five core values that constitute the fundamentals of a proactive and responsible approach to professionalism:

1   teaching, in which teachers are seen to practise learning, individually with their colleagues and students;
2   participation, in which teachers see themselves as active agents in their own professional worlds;
3   collaboration, in which collegiality is exercised within and between internal and external communities;
4   cooperation, through which teachers develop a common language and technology for documenting and discussing practice and the outcome; and
5   activism, in which teachers engage publicly with issues that relate directly or indirectly to education and schooling, as part of their moral purposes.

(Sachs, 2000)

Geert Kelchtermans (1993: 499–500) suggests that the professional self, like the personal self, evolves over time and that it consists of five interrelated parts:

1   Self-image: how teachers describe themselves through their career stories;
2   Self-esteem: the evolution of self as a teacher, how good or otherwise as defined by self or others;
3   Job motivation: what makes teachers choose, remain committed to or leave the job;
4   Task perception: how teachers define their jobs;
5   Future perspective: teachers' expectations for the future development of their jobs.

Added to these are the ways in which they interact with teachers' personal selves. Reporting on research with teachers in the Netherlands, Douwe Beijaard (1995: 288) illustrated the different patterns of change in teacher identities:

> Mary remembers her satisfaction about her own teaching in the beginning because she experienced it as a challenge. This challenge disappeared when she had to teach many subjects to overcrowded classes. The second lowest point in her storyline was caused by her time-consuming study and private circumstances at home. Now she is reasonably satisfied, due to a pupil centred method she has developed together with some of her colleagues. Peter is currently very satisfied about his own teaching; he qualifies his present teaching style as very adequate. In the beginning of his career, however, it was very problematic for him to maintain order. In this period he considered leaving the profession several times. The second lowest point in his storyline refers to private circumstances and to problems in the relationships with colleagues.

Here we see the ways in which personal and professional environments affect teachers' work both positively and negatively. This interplay between the private and public – the personal and professional lives of teachers – is a key factor in their sense of emotional identity and job satisfaction and, by inference, in their capacity to maintain their effectiveness as teachers. In Mary's case, increases in classroom size and role diversification and intensification decreased the challenge of professional satisfaction she had felt on her entry into teaching; in the case of Peter, 'painful beginnings' (Huberman, 1995a) had made it difficult even to survive. Common to both were the times when personal problems in their lives outside the classroom adversely affected their attitudes to teaching.

The challenges of emotional wellbeing

> The self is a crucial element in the way teachers themselves construe the nature of the job.
>
> (Kelchtermans and Vandenberghe, 1994: 47)

Professional identity, then, as people's source of meaning and experience, is different from role, which is the means by which people's functions within institutions and organisations are organised (Castells, 2004). Teachers play a variety of roles within and outside the classroom. However, whilst such roles play an indispensable part in how teachers construct their professional identity, in themselves, they do not define it (Beijaard *et al.*, 2004; Day *et al.*, 2007). For example, in the emotional arena of teaching, pupils' progress and growth constantly fuel teachers' job satisfaction and motivation. Through experiences of positive emotions, teachers are said to be able to transform themselves, 'becoming more creative, knowledgeable, resilient, socially integrated and healthy individuals' (Fredrickson, 2004: 1369). Teachers' emotional capacities to rebound from disappointments and adversity and sustain their commitment to the profession, and with this, grow and sustain their sense of efficacy and wellbeing are, therefore, fundamental to their ability to promote achievement in all aspects of students' lives.

As a result of analysis and critique of different discourses of professionalism and professionalisation which characterise the new lives of teachers, Hargreaves and Goodson (1996: 20–21) proposed seven principles:

1   increased opportunity and responsibility to exercise discretionary judgement over the issues of teaching, curriculum and care that affect one's students;

2   opportunities and expectations to engage with the moral and social purposes and value of what teachers teach, along with major curriculum and assessment matters in which these purposes are embedded;

3   commitment to working with colleagues in collaborative cultures of help and support as a way of using shared expertise to solve ongoing problems of professional practice, rather than engaging in joint work as a motivational device to implement the external mandates of others;

4   occupational heteronomy rather than self-protective autonomy, where teachers work authoritatively yet openly and collaboratively with other partners in the wider community (especially parents and students themselves), who have a significant stake in students' learning;

5   a commitment to active care and not just anodyne service for students – Hargreaves and Goodson suggested that professionalism must in this sense acknowledge and embrace the emotional as well as the cognitive dimensions of teaching, and also recognise the skills and dispositions that are essential to committed and effective caring;

6   a self-directed search and struggle for continuous learning related to one's own expertise and standards of practice, rather than compliance with the

enervating obligations of endless change demanded by others (often under the guise of continuing learning or improvement); and
7   the creation and recognition of high task complexity with levels of status and reward appropriate to such complexity.

Professionals themselves from these perspectives, are said to have various core moral purposes and ethical codes (Day, 2000a; Hansen, 1995; Jackson et al., 1993; Pels, 1999), pursuing teaching as an art, craft (technical) and scientific endeavour (Brown and McIntyre, 1992; Friedson, 1983; Galton et al., 1999). It is claimed that such higher moral purposes of teachers (Sockett, 1993) are threatened by teaching and learning agendas which focus on improving schools and raising student achievement within a restricted, measurable range of subjects, abilities or competencies (e.g. as in England) and by initial (pre-service) teacher education and training programmes that are now primarily apprenticeship models. However, research over the years reveals that whilst professional identities of teachers in schools in England are influenced by personal values, organisational culture, professional life phases, and are challenged by the work and life settings in which they are played out, for the large majority (74 per cent), commitment remains high (Day et al., 2007).

It matters enormously what kind of person the teacher is because 'those of us who are teachers cannot stand before a class without standing for something ... teaching is testimony' (Patterson, 1991: 16). There is also an unavoidable interrelationship between professional and personal identities if only because the overwhelming evidence is that teaching demands significant personal investment:

> The ways in which teachers form their professional identities are influenced by both how they feel about themselves and how they feel about their students. This professional identity helps them to position or situate themselves in relation to their students and to make appropriate and effective adjustments in their practice and their beliefs about and engagement with students.
>
> (James-Wilson, 2001: 29)

Teacher wellbeing is a very broad concept as used in the research literature. Here we define it in terms of two components: teachers' organisational behaviour, including their job satisfaction, intention to leave and absence, and their self-reported health, measured negatively as their experience of symptoms of exhaustion, tension and anxiety and positively through levels of self-efficacy, motivation, commitment and resilience. It is, therefore, both a psychological and social construct: 'A dynamic state, in which the individual is able to develop their potential, work productively and creatively, build strong and positive relationships with others, and contribute to their community' (Foresight Mental Capital and Wellbeing Project, 2008: 10).

To achieve and sustain a healthy state of positive identity and wellbeing, teachers need to manage successfully a range of cognitive and emotional challenges in different – sometimes difficult – scenarios which vary according to life experiences and events, the strength of relationships with pupils and parents, the conviction of educational ideals, sense of efficacy and agency and the support of colleagues and school leadership. As Moore Johnson (2004: 10) reminds us, 'anyone familiar with schools knows that stories about the easy job of teaching are sheer fiction. Good teaching is demanding and exhausting work, even in the best of work places.'

Conclusions: the person in the professional

Experience and research, then, suggest that a dichotomy between promoting technical competence and personal growth in professional learning is false, and that ignoring the contribution of teachers' sense of emotional wellbeing to their capacities to teach to their best is foolish. Rather, teachers at their best combine their professional craft expertise with their personal selves in their work in the knowledge that teaching cannot be devoid of an interest in and engagement with the learner. In other words, it is the extent to which the learner, the teacher and the teaching content are all 'present' which will influence the quality of the process and its results. This journey of the personal and the professional in the here and now of teaching is what Csikszentmihalyi (1990) calls 'flow' and Rodgers and Raider-Roth (2006: 267) term, 'presence': 'Presence from the teacher's point of view is the experience of bringing one's whole self to full attention so as to perceive what is happening in the moment.'

Presence, whilst a necessary condition for successful teaching, is not sufficient to achieve optimal learning. Students themselves must also be willing and able to be 'present'. Many writers on teacher education focus on the role and presence of the teacher in the classroom, emphasising the need for personal strengths or core qualities (Meijer et al., 2009) such as care, courage, fairness, kindness, honesty and perseverance (Frederickson, 2002; Noddings, 2003; Palmer, 2004; Seligman, 2002; Sockett, 1993). Others have combined this with research on the nature, purposes and forms of reflection in, on and about education (Schön, 1983), and developed humanistic pedagogies of teacher education which emphasise the importance to good teaching practice of understanding and interrogating teachers' own belief systems (Loughran, 2004) and the interchange between these teaching contexts and purposes (Korthagen and Vasalos, 2005). Whilst our own research does not dissent from these views, it has identified two key additional and necessary conditions for 'presence'; a positive sense of identity and emotional wellbeing.

Many teachers enter the profession with a sense of vocation and with a passion to give their best to the learning, growth and achievement of their pupils. For some, these become eroded with the passage of time, changing external and internal working conditions and contexts and unanticipated personal events. They lose the sense of purpose and wellbeing that are so intimately connected with their professional identities, self-efficacy and agency, their belief that they can and do make a difference to the progress and achievement of their pupils. Continuing opportunities to learn in environments that enhance a positive sense of identity and emotional wellbeing and achievement are necessary conditions that enable them to manage the inherently unstable, dynamic emotional contexts of teaching in which they teach and in which their pupils learn. In Part II we will, through narrative stories of early, middle and later years teachers, focus upon the critical influences and conditions that promote or act against the commitment, resilience, emotional wellbeing and sense of professional identity of teachers, which are essential to their sense of success and their capacity to teach to their best.

Part II

The professional lives of teachers

Chapter 3

Critical influences on teachers' professional lives

Introduction

> Career development is thereby a process, not a series of events. For some, this process may be linear, but for others there will be plateaus, regressions, dead-ends, spurts, discontinuities. So the identification of phases and sequences must be handled gingerly, as an analytic heuristic, as a descriptive rather than a normative construct.
>
> (Huberman, 1989a: 32)

In this chapter, we will discuss patterns of critical influences on teachers' sense of wellbeing over the course of their professional lives. Understanding the differentiated impact of these on teachers is central to achieving an understanding of what it is in teachers' professional lives that causes variations in their commitment, resilience and capacity to teach to their best.

Professional life phases

Much literature tends to conceptualise a teacher's life in terms of a *career*. This perspective is perceived not only to lend 'focus and boundedness to the study of the human life cycle' in different professions, but also to contain 'both psychological and sociological variables' (Huberman, 1993: 4). However, this conceptualisation is limited, for it fails to provide a nuanced and holistic account of the complexities and variations in the trajectories of teachers over time (Day *et al.*, 2006). We have chosen the notion of teachers' *professional life phase*, rather than *career phase*, because this takes us closer to the meaning of being a teacher and an understanding of the complexities of teachers' lives and work. It enables us to portray a professional landscape which distinguishes teaching from other professions. We share with David Hansen (1995) his proposition of using the language of 'vocation' – rather than 'career' – to explore teachers' inner landscapes and understand what keeps them going or constrains them in their work. Career is too individualistic a concept. It represents lifelong economic support in the job or a sequence of different jobs, but 'can provide little more than that in terms of the meaning a life has had' (ibid.: 7). It takes us away from the every-day personal and professional moral purposes of teaching, which feature core characteristics of many teachers' lives (ibid.). Seligman (2002: 166) extends Hansen's proposition, arguing that a calling is 'the most satisfying form of work because, as a gratification, it is done for its own sake rather than for the material benefits it brings':

> You do a *job* for the paycheck at the end of the week. You do not seek other rewards from it. It is just a means to another end (like leisure, or supporting your family), and when the wage stops, you quit. A *career* entails a deeper personal investment in work. You mark your achievement through money, but also through advancement. Each promotion brings you higher prestige and more power, as well as a raise.... A *calling* (or vocation) is a passionate commitment to work for its own sake. Individuals with a calling see their work as contributing to the greater good, to something larger than they are, and hence the religious connotation is entirely appropriate. The work is ful-filling in its own right, without regard for money or for advancement.
>
> (Ibid.: 168)

Many researchers across the world have reported repeatedly that the large majority of teachers are drawn into teaching in the belief that they have some-thing to offer to the lives of young people (Danielewicz, 2001; Day *et al.*, 2007; OECD, 2005; Sachs, 2003). For those who have such a sense of vocation and who continue to strive to give their best to the growth and achievement of their pupils – despite challenges and setbacks – teaching is more than 'just a job' or a career.

PricewaterhouseCoopers' (PwC) (2001) review of teacher workload in schools in England and Wales suggested that, although on an annual compari-son, teachers work similar hours to other comparable managers and profession-als, the demands of their daily work are more intensive. In addition, PwC reported that teachers in many schools perceived a lack of control and owner-ship over their work because of the counterproductive pace and manner in which government initiatives were implemented, insufficient professional support to meet the changes, increasing pressures caused by rising expectations about what schools can achieve, deteriorating pupil behaviour and insufficient parental support. It is the ongoing and continuing demands on their intellectual and emotional energy, competence and capacity to connect 'self and subject and students in the fabric of life' (Palmer, 1998: 11) that distinguishes the teaching self from the selves of other professionals. Although 'all aware human beings care', not everybody needs to develop the capacity to care for others in the same way as teachers must if they are to engage their pupils in learning:

> When we discuss teaching and teacher–learner relationships in depth, we will see that teachers not only have to create caring relationships in which

they are carers, but that they also have a responsibility to help their students develop the capacity to care.

(Noddings, 2005: 18)

The notion of *professional life phase* – rather than *career phase* – also helps encapsulate not only the impact of psychological and sociological factors on teachers' work and lives (as does the concept of *career*), but also that of personal, emotional and organisational factors. Understanding variations in teachers' professional life progression requires a consideration of policy, organisational and classroom settings, as well as how these interact with events in their personal lives and how they manage (or do not manage) these over time. Thus, the study of teachers' professional life phases provides richer insights into the complex and dynamic nature of the influences on teachers' learning, change and development – and thus their wellbeing, commitment and capacity to teach to their best throughout their professional lives – than accounts which focus upon one or other of the conditions which affect teachers' lives.

Teachers' lives: the research context

Over three decades ago, Huberman conducted a preliminary study (1978–9) with 30 teachers, followed by an extended study (1982–5) with 160 secondary school teachers in Geneva and Vaud, Switzerland. Writing in 1995 about professional careers and professional development, Huberman (1995a: 193) stated:

> The hypothesis is fairly obvious: Teachers have different aims and different dilemmas at various moments in their professional cycle, and their desires to reach out for more information, knowledge, expertise and technical competence will vary accordingly.... A core assumption here is that there will be commonalities among teachers in the sequencing of their professional lives and that one particular form of professional development may be appropriate to these shared sequences.

He suggested that we

> can begin to identify modal profiles of the teaching career and, from these, see what determines more and less 'successful' or 'satisfactory' careers ... identify the conditions under which a particular phase in the career cycle is lived out happily or miserably and, from these, put together an appropriate support structure.

(Huberman, 1995a: 194)

The career development 'process' that Huberman's research with secondary teachers revealed has become the touchstone for researchers in the field worldwide. His work provides an 'in principle' critique of prescribed stage theory.

As discussed in the preceding chapter, linear 'stage' models ignore the complexity and dynamic of organisational life, the discontinuities of learning and the importance of continuing regular opportunities for deliberative reflection 'in', 'on' and 'about' experience (Schön, 1983) as a way of locating and extending understandings of its meaning in broader contexts that research consistently reveals. Teachers' development moves backwards and forwards between phases during their working lives for all kinds of reasons concerning personal history, psychological, social and organisational factors and anticipated and unanticipated current events. Taking on a new role, changing schools, teaching a new age group or a new syllabus will almost inevitably result in disruption to development, at least temporarily, and not all events in personal lives can be anticipated. Professional development over a professional life span, then, is unlikely to proceed in an even, linear sequence, and expertise is unlikely to grow with chronological age and experience. Nor will there be a point at which development needs will end. The path towards expertise is rarely straight (Day *et al.*, 2007).

Teachers' professional life phases: characteristics and trajectories

There are different ways to analyse and define the characteristics of teachers' work and lives. We share with Huberman his criticism of sociological and psychodynamic analysts' interpretations of human development which 'presume that internal or external forces fully determine the substance and the direction of individual conduct' and thus reduce human activity to a *reactive* status (1993: 18):

> Individuals are not passive, are not the puppets of sociological or maturational strings pulled from above. Human development is largely *teleological*; that is, human actors observe, study and plan the sequences they follow and, in doing so, are able to orientate and even to determine the course of events in each succeeding phase.
>
> (Ibid.: 18)

We too have observed that professional journeys are dialectical processes in which many teachers, as activist professionals (Sachs, 2003) rather than victims of their social and educational contexts, manage, sometimes against the odds, to build upon support available in their workplace and at home and draw strength from their vocational commitment, their fascination with their subject and their moral purposes (Nias, 1999).

Our research, however, goes beyond Huberman's conclusion that teachers' 'professional career journeys are not adequately linear' because, in part, 'a large part of development is neither externally programmed nor personally engineered but rather discontinuous' (Huberman, 1993: 195). We identified patterns which were in conflict with Huberman's observation that the development of teachers is 'unpredictable' and 'often, in fact, unexplainable using the tools at our disposal' (ibid.: 264). On the contrary, we found distinctive phases over the course of teachers' professional lives where groups of teachers demonstrated similar professional needs and concerns and characteristics of professional identities. These concerns and characteristics were shown to be associated with their length of service in the profession, rather than chronological age. They revealed not only different levels of psychological, spiritual and emotional strength in the inner landscape of their professional selves (Palmer, 2007), but also the influence of their ability to manage (or not manage) successfully the complex internal and external influences which threatened to impact negatively on their commitment, resilience and capacity to teach to their best.

Thus, in contrast to Huberman, whose identification of characteristics of teachers' career phases focused on central tendencies of change in their *state of mind*, for example, from 'easy beginnings' to 'self doubts', 'renewal', 'disenchantment' and 'psychological serenity' (Gould, 1978), our analyses of characteristics of teachers' professional life phases were grounded in a framework that encompassed teachers' cognitive, emotional, personal and moral engagement in the profession. We found that teachers themselves referred most often to their emotional and intellectual selves and their sense of motivation, commitment and efficacy when describing what it meant to be a teacher and what had kept them going in the changing policy, social, situational and personal realities of teaching. Our interpretations of teachers' professional learning and development trajectories and identification of the nature of their professional lives over time thus were primarily concerned with the impact of these on their commitment and wellbeing in the particularities of the social, political and personal environments in which they lived and worked.

Moreover, our research also extended Huberman's study of secondary school teachers by examining teachers in both primary and secondary schools and by providing additional dimensions of teachers' personal and professional lives which were not included in his work.

Professional life phases and trajectories

'Professional life phase' refers to the number of years that a teacher has been teaching, rather than age or responsibilities. We found that teachers' work and lives spanned six professional life phases: 0–3, 4–7, 8–15, 16–23, 24–30 and 31+ years of teaching. Although years of experience generally relates closely to a teacher's age, some teachers have less experience than might be expected for their age as a result of being late entrants to teaching or through taking a career break. Analyses of these teachers' experiences show that they tended to share similar professional concerns with their younger colleagues in the same professional life phase, but, not surprisingly, that their personal experiences (and tensions) were shown to be closer to those who were in the similar age range but in later professional life phases.

We have reported the detailed features of the six professional life phases elsewhere (Day *et al.*, 2007) and provide detailed illustrations of these in Chapters 4, 5 and 6. A summary of characteristics and trajectories of teachers in different phases follows.

Professional life phase 0–3: commitment – support and challenge

Sub-groups:
1   developing sense of efficacy; or
2   reduced sense of efficacy.

Professional life phase 4–7: identity and efficacy in classroom

Sub-groups:
1   sustaining a strong sense of identity, self-efficacy and effectiveness;
2   sustaining identity, efficacy and effectiveness; or
3   identity, efficacy and effectiveness at risk.

Professional life phase 8–15: managing changes in role and identity – growing tensions and transitions

Sub-groups:
1   sustained engagement; or
2   detachment/loss of motivation.

Professional life phase 16–23: work–life tensions – challenges to motivation and commitment

Sub-groups:
1   further career advancement and good pupil results have led to increased motivation/commitment;
2   sustained motivation, commitment and effectiveness; or
3   workload/managing competing tensions/career stagnation have led to decreased motivation, commitment and effectiveness.

Professional life phase 24–30: challenges to sustaining motivation

Sub-groups:
1   sustained a strong sense of motivation and commitment; or
2   holding on but losing motivation.

Professional life phase 31+: sustaining/declining motivation, ability to cope with change, looking to retire

Sub-groups:
1   maintaining commitment; or
2   tired and trapped.

It is clear from these that teachers' professional life phases are not static, but dynamic in nature. The interaction between a range of critical influences in their work and personal contexts is a sophisticated and continuous process and impacts differentially on teachers' professional selves both within and across different phases of their professional lives according to its intensity and the cognitive and emotional capacities of teachers to manage the interaction.

Understanding variations in teachers' professional lives: from critical incidents to critical influences

In order to explore teachers' perceptions of their sense of commitment and effectiveness and the various factors that they felt had shaped these over the whole course of their professional lives, as well as over the three years of our work with them, we employed a critical incident technique. In narrative interviews, we asked teachers to recall 'turning points' (Strauss, 1959: 67) over their professional and personal life histories which had a significantly positive or negative impact on their commitment and perceived effectiveness. To help visualise these, teachers constructed a timeline on a 'workline' chart indicating these turning points (see the Appendix). This provided us with remembered, historically grounded accounts of experiences which complemented teachers' 'real time' lives over their three-year period of participation.

The critical incident technique

The critical incident technique has its roots in the discipline of psychology and developed out of armed services research during the Second World War. The origin of the technique can be traced back to the studies of Sir Francis Galton in the late nineteenth century, and it was not until 1954 when John Flanagan published his review of the development of the technique that a sound conceptual and methodological foundation for further advancement of the technique was established, particularly in areas of psychology (see Flanagan, 1954).

In his review, Flanagan described the critical incident technique as consisting of 'a set of procedures for collecting direct observations of human behaviour in such a way as to facilitate their potential usefulness in solving practical problems and developing broad psychological principles' (ibid.: 327). To be critical, these observable factual incidents, or human behaviours, must 'occur in a situation where the purpose or intent of the act seems fairly clear to the observer and where its consequences are sufficiently definite to leave little doubt concerning its effects' and 'permit inferences and predications to be made about the person performing the act' (ibid.: 327). Flanagan argued that although the technique itself did not provide solutions, it provided procedures for collecting a record of detailed, specific behaviours from a representative sample, and thus made it possible to identify, determine and formulate the critical requirements of an activity, establish standards, evaluate results and develop recommendations for effective practices.

Given the nature of the discipline out of which the technique has grown, much attention has been paid to the development of procedures which adhere to systematically defined quantitative criteria and ensure 'objectivity and precision in terms of well-defined and general psychological categories' (ibid.: 355). However, in the application of the psychologically informed critical incident technique, the burden of identifying, interpreting and evaluating the nature of a critical incident and its significant contribution to an activity, either positively or negatively, lies primarily in the researcher rather than the researched.

Critical incidents: connecting the self and career

The use of critical incidents in educational research, and research on teachers and teaching in particular, is, however, informed by different conceptual and methodological principles from those outlined by Flanagan.

David Tripp (1993) proposed critical incidents as a means of developing teachers' professional judgements and their own theories of their work. He argued that a critical incident is created and produced by the way we look at a situation and reflects our interpretations of the significance of an event or situation: 'To take something as a critical incident is a value judgement we make and the basis of that judgment is the significance we attach to the meaning of the incident' (ibid.: 8).

Because they are grounded in the realities of teachers' everyday experience, Tripp believed that the interpretation of critical incidents provided a stimulus for professional reflection as to 'who we are' as private people and 'what we are' as trained professional teachers. Viewed through these lenses, the technique offers an effective way to 'involve teachers as both clients and partners in research on the understanding and improvement of their practice' (ibid.: 152).

From critical incidents to critical influences

Strauss (1959) wrote of the striking impact of 'turning points' as a critical, transforming experience that not only points out new directions but also signals some movement in, or transformation of, identity. Drawing upon Strauss' work, Sikes et al. (1985) explored how critical incidents, or 'crises', affected teachers' sense of commitment and career trajectories with a small sample of secondary school teachers in England. In line with Strauss' observation, their study also found a connection between the impact of key events in teachers' lives, the teacher self and their career structures. They reported that critical incidents 'provoke the individual into selecting particular kinds of actions, they in turn lead them in particular directions, and they end up having implications for identity' (Measor, 1985: 61). Sikes et al. (1985: 57) thus described these key events as a flashbulb which helped reveal 'the major choice and change times in people's lives'.

Whilst critical incident research such as that illustrated above may shed light on the major change times in teachers' work and lives, what still appears to be missing in the research literature is a conceptualisation of the nature of the patterns of these significant experiences over the course of teachers' professional lives.

In the existing literature, critical incidents tend to be analysed in a manner in which the researcher's focus rests upon the actions that teachers take (or do not take) as a result of their experience of critical events over a short or longer period. Our analysis of teachers' experiences and professional trajectories revealed that these critical events were perceived by teachers as key influences relating both to their professional worlds and their personal lives. These influences are perceived as critical for two reasons. First, they have radical effects on teachers' commitment and morale, which lead to either a major increase in their sense of efficacy or a decrease and consequently a significant crisis or trough. Whilst some, such as deteriorating pupil behaviour, may have a particularly significant effect on teachers' morale at certain points of their professional lives, others, such as the availability of leadership support and staff collegiality, may have a longer term positive or negative effect on their emotional and intellectual wellbeing in all professional life phases.

Second, the positive or negative effects of these influences on teachers' morale, commitment and wellbeing indicate the extent to which teachers' primary concerns are recognised and differing needs for development are satisfied. According to concerns theory (van den Berg, 2002: 593; see also Richardson and Placier, 2001), 'a concern reflects feelings of lacking the competence needed to conduct new educational activities in a responsible manner'. The difference in individual teachers' cognitive and emotional capacities to manage key influences which concern them at different moments or during particular phases of their professional and personal lives points to the quality of the provision of responsive and appropriate support that they require to meet their primary professional needs and concerns, so that the effects of positive influences on their commitment and wellbeing may be maximised whilst those of negative influences are minimised and controlled.

Our initial analysis, therefore, caused us to shift our focus from examining the significance and meaning of *critical incidents*, or events, to the identification of patterns of *critical influences* that these incidents revealed, their influences on teachers' sense of commitment and resilience and the teachers' ability to manage these.

Patterns of critical influences

By comparing and contrasting the nature of the contexts in which these critical influences had occurred, we were able to further stratify ingredients of the already identified critical influences and integrate them into four distinctive categories:

1   *personal* (related to their lives outside school, such as family support, personal relationships and health-related issues);
2   *pupil* (related to factors associated with pupils, such as pupil intake characteristics, pupil attitudes and motivations, pupil behaviour and teacher–pupil relationships);
3   *practice settings* (related to factors embedded in teachers' workplaces, situated support from management and the staff, teachers' additional roles and responsibilities, promotion, workload and the quality of professional development opportunities); and
4   *policy* (related to external policy agendas, such as educational policies and government initiatives and changes).

Analysis of teachers' remembered experiences of peaks and troughs in their professional lives revealed that the strength of the impacts of practice settings, pupils, policy and personal events on teachers' sense of commitment, wellbeing and capacity to teach to their best varied. In order to gain an overview of the effects of the four categories of critical influences on teachers in different phases of their professional lives, we examined the intensity of their impacts as reported by 179 teachers on their workline charts. Figures 3.1–3.4 illustrate the ratios of the count of peaks (and troughs) caused by each of the four categories of critical influences to the total number of teachers in each professional life phase.

These patterns of critical influences indicate the powerful effects of school contexts on teachers' commitment, resilience and professional identities over time. On the whole, not surprisingly, practice settings have the greatest positive as well as negative effects on teachers' work, particularly for those in their late professional life phases (16+ years of experience).

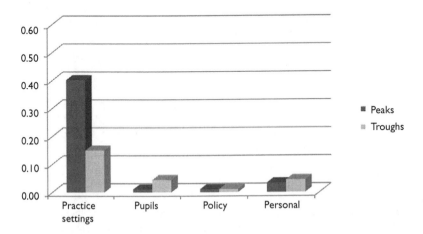

Figure 3.1 Intensity of effects of critical influences: professional life phase 0–3
       (*n* = 179).

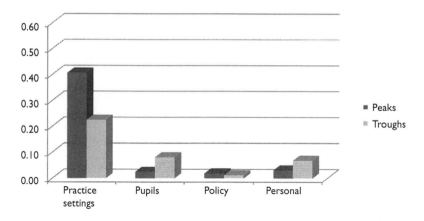

Figure 3.2 Intensity of effects of critical influences: professional life phase 4–7
($n = 160$).

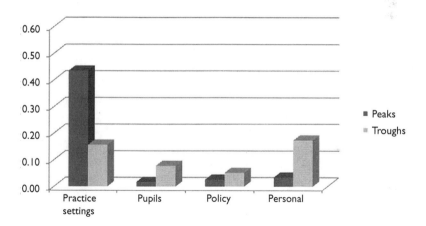

Figure 3.3 Intensity of effects of critical influences: professional life phase 8–15
($n = 115$).

These confirm McLaughlin's (2005: 70) statement:

Context matters in many big and small ways to teachers' work and careers,
and so to policy implementation. The character and quality of schoolteach-
ing found in any classroom on any day signals much more than the
attributes, energy and expertise of an individual schoolteacher. Teachers
carry conditions of their multiple contexts into their classrooms as norm-
ative frameworks, concrete supports, perceived or actual constraints for the
construction of practice.

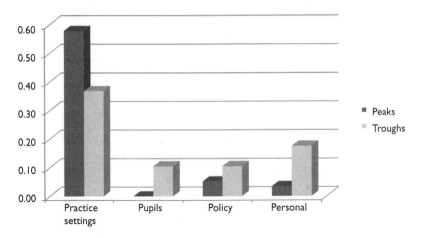

Figure 3.4 Intensity of effects of critical influences: professional life phases 16–23, 24–30 and 31+ (*n* = 57).

A close examination of key critical influences in practice settings suggests also, however, that these situated factors influence teachers' commitment and sense of self differently in different phases of their professional lives and in relation to the contexts in which they work. For example, for teachers in the early and middle phases of their professional lives, promotion and support and recognition within the school context are of crucial importance to help increase their motivation and self-efficacy in the profession. This will be discussed in detail in Chapters 4–6.

Teachers' personal life contexts also played an integral part in sustaining (or constraining) their commitment, sense of efficacy and wellbeing for 'teaching is inextricably linked to teachers' personal lives' (Zembylas, 2001, cited in van den Berg, 2002: 585). Adverse personal events, for example, work against their ability to sustain their sense of effectiveness, and the relative impact of their negative effects may become intensified when teachers enter a later professional life phase (8–15 and then 16+ years of experience). In particular, teachers with 8–15 years of experience often experience growing tensions between their personal and professional commitments. These teachers are often in their thirties and early forties, a time when family and health begin to play an increasingly important part in their lives and when, at the same time, their experience, expertise and confidence make many of them eligible for further career promotion. Thus, in addition to the pressure of prioritising their work and personal commitments and relationships, teachers in this key watershed period not only face the tension of deciding 'where their career is going and what it has brought to them up to now' (Huberman, 1993: 257), but also where their lives are going.

In sum, teachers' ability to manage (or not manage) their commitment and sense of wellbeing is not contingent upon the separate effects of individual critical influences. It is the *relative intensity* of the impact of combinations of these critical influences and their ability to manage these that makes the difference to teachers' capacity to teach to their best in different phases of their professional lives. The clear and unequivocal message for heads – and all those concerned with raising and maintaining standards of teaching and learning and with issues of wellbeing and quality retention of staff – is that responsive, differentiated in-school support is needed for teachers in different professional life phases.

Critical influences that sustain or hinder teachers' commitment: three stories from the classroom

We have selected stories of three teachers in their early (4–7 years of experience), middle (8–15 years of experience) and late professional (24–30 years of experience) life phases. These stories illustrate the nature of the critical influences which help or hinder teachers' commitment, resilience and sense of efficacy. Whilst we do not claim that the experiences of these teachers are representative of all teachers, their profiles are typical of the key personal, professional and situated factors that impact on the work and lives of other teachers within their professional life phases, and of the ways they manage these factors to sustain (or not sustain) their motivation and commitment in the face of adversity.

Story 1: sustaining commitment and career advancement despite professional concerns – an early years teacher (professional life phase 4–7)

> I think I do make a difference. I think that's one of the things that keeps me going in the job.... Every now and again you'll get the odd student that comes up to me and says thanks for all the work you've done and if only one student says it, it still makes me realise I am making a difference.
>
> (Chris)

In this first example, we show how early career promotion may boost a teacher's sense of efficacy in this professional life phase, where there may be personal issues but professional, career-related concerns appear to be more dominant. The example also shows how this teacher's career progression and his motivation and resilience may be challenged by a combination of a lack of collegial support and workload-related tensions, despite his commitment and sense of vocation.

Chris, aged 30, was second in maths in an 11–16, predominately white, rural comprehensive school, with only 6 per cent of pupils eligible for free school meals (FSM2).

Chris liked maths when he was a child. He enjoyed an instructor's course in the Territorial Army and decided to go into teaching as a result. Five years into teaching, he still loved interacting with the children and helping them learn and progress.

Chris' workline indicates that three critical influences within a three-year period had the potential to work against his ability to sustain his commitment – feelings of lethargy because of workload, extra pressure on exam classes caused by staff turnover and an unhappy incident with a colleague. Two of these are related to workload issues and one to in-school support from colleagues. More recently, his promotion to second in the maths department significantly boosted his sense of efficacy, morale and commitment and positively impacted upon his emotional and physical energy to manage the tensions between work and life. His workline provides a poignant illustration of how tensions in staff relationships and workload may, together, test even the most committed teachers' sense of self-efficacy.

Variations in in-school support

Chris described his school as 'a really good school'. School and departmental leadership played 'a big part' in his enjoyment of working in the school.

He greatly appreciated the professional and personal support of the head, who promoted him to second in maths. Support from his head of department

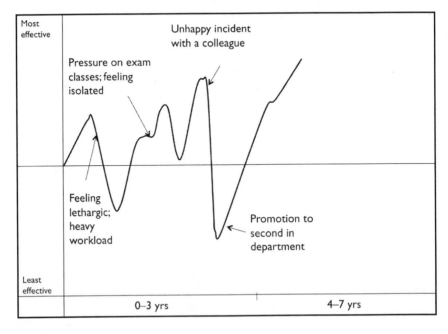

Workline I Chris' workline.

also contributed to his growing sense of commitment and efficacy in the initial five years of his teaching: 'I get massive support from the head of department. He is absolutely fantastic.' The support of colleagues was also very important to him: 'I am really comfortable in the department – mainly males in my age group. Have the same sort of interests.' On the whole, he enjoyed working in his department where he felt that people supported each other.

However, a recent 'altercation with a colleague over an incident during a lesson' led him to reassess his views about staff collegiality. When he noticed that his colleague's class was 'a little noisy', he popped in at the end of the class to discuss it with the children. He only 'wanted to do the right thing' by helping his colleague out but, unfortunately, his offer of help was perceived otherwise and things 'all went very wrong' in the end. Chris felt 'dejected and despondent', and 'angry': 'The reason I teach is to help the children and educate them in all aspects of life. It is a lonely job made more so by the bitching and stabbing in the back by those staff around you.'

It seemed that the detrimental impact of this incident on his sense of self was going to be long term: 'I feel that this incident will haunt me for the rest of my career. As teachers, we all require support but some see this as a weakness. No wonder so many are leaving the profession.'

Career progression

Chris's promotion to second in mathematics significantly boosted his confidence and contributed to his increased commitment and sense of efficacy. Although he had been given more responsibilities in the department and pushed forward to develop as a leader, he felt very positive about these changes. He was pleased with his early career advancement, feeling that he had developed from being someone who only occasionally undertook administrative tasks to someone who was 'at the top of the tree'.

> I think getting the promotion and being more settled than in previous years, I'm starting to realise I am effective as a teacher and I can transfer my enthusiasm to the pupils and I'm doing quite a good job. I'm quite positive actually.

With regard to his role as a teacher, he felt that he was in the best years of his teaching: 'I'm settled in a position where the kids know who I am.' He did not have any issues with his pupils in class and was pleased that this enabled him to concentrate on teaching. He experienced immense satisfaction in seeing improvement in his management of pupils' behaviour and always enjoyed his pupils' good results. Chris appreciated the CPD opportunities organised by his school and felt that they had been of significance in improving his sense of efficacy in behaviour management. He would like to pursue further studies to open up his career options.

Managing workload pressures

For Chris, pupils' academic progress stayed at the heart of his motivation and commitment. However, his motivation varied over the course of an academic year, mainly because of test-related pressures: 'It [motivation] tends to dip at this time of year [end of academic year].... It peaks when exam results come in ... because I'm seeing the fruits of a long term but there are times when it goes quite low.' Chris kept his work and life separate and felt that 'generally' he had a 'really good work–life balance'. He was good at prioritising things and had a stable personal life. He disapproved of the way that government introduced new initiatives but was otherwise 'really happy'.

Story 2: content as a classroom teacher – a mid-years teacher (professional life phase 8–15)

> I feel I'm at the peak of my career. It's a shame I only have eight years left, because I'm probably at my best. I'm in the right job – I'm doing it well ... [but] ... It's only a job at the end of the day. I only do what is particularly relevant. I don't waste time. I decide what I think is a priority.
>
> (Sharon)

This second example shows how government initiatives and the availability of in-school support influenced the commitment and career trajectory of a teacher on her return to teaching after a career break of nine years. Sharon, who was older than her colleagues with similar years of teaching experience, decided to stay in the classroom and be a good teacher in this watershed of her professional life, rather than seek promotion.

Sharon was a Year 6 teacher of 10–11-year-olds at a popular 170-pupil rural primary school, which was in the top group for attainment and had less than 8 per cent free school meals. She was 51 years old and had taught for 15 years, having had a career break of nine years to bring up her children. She had been teaching at her current school for over four years, having previously worked in seven others. She said that she felt 'refreshed' and 'calmer' on her return to teaching, with better knowledge and understanding of the children and of their academic abilities.

Sense of vocation

Sharon had always wanted to teach because it 'suited my personality'. Sharon described herself as 'bossy, organised and not put off by the money'. This still applied. She was a school governor and had additional responsibilities for music, maths and assessment of KS2 pupils aged 7–11. Since being at this school, her motivation and commitment had increased. She rarely felt stressed by her work.

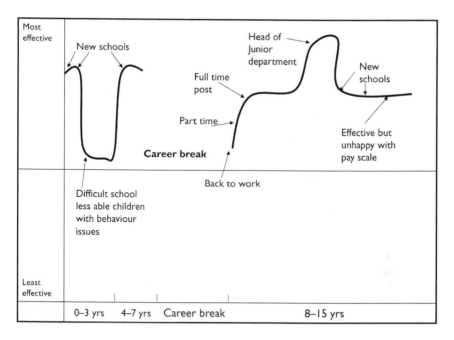

Workline 2 Sharon's workline.

Pupils: source of job satisfaction

Sharon was highly motivated and committed to teaching and enjoyed a very high level of self-efficacy and job satisfaction. She regarded pupils at her current school as being 'outstanding' in every way – 'appearance, behaviour and independence'. However, she found it difficult to handle the parental input and resented middle-class parents' 'fairly arrogant attitude': 'We suffer from a few arrogant children.' She was 'strict' in her teaching to ensure that these arrogant children did not affect her class. She insisted that her pupils understood this and liked her to be strict because they could see the benefit of being able to complete more work in the end.

Her pupils' high test scores had further boosted her personal motivation: 'knowing pupils are performing academically well, knowing you're making a difference to their lives, and knowing that you are sending them out to be good citizens of the society.'

Availability of in-school support

Sharon believed that recent changes in the leadership of the school had a positive influence on the school environment, which she felt had moved from being 'static' to 'more dynamic'. She thought that the changes would also reduce staff turnover. One of the reasons that she liked working in the school was that the head listened to her views.

She received good support from her colleagues. She stressed that the majority of the staff were good, but that there were 'a handful of awkward colleagues' who 'whinge on workload'. She had to take over work from these people and was unhappy that her own workload had increased as a consequence.

Dissatisfaction with government initiatives

She was very dissatisfied with the lack of time she had for responding to new initiatives and, as her workline shows, she was unhappy with the level of remuneration.

Managing work–life tensions

Sharon had positive feelings about being a teacher. She felt settled at school and had a stable home life with no family commitments. Her two children had grown up and this gave her more time to spend on school work. She was pleased that she had 'less personal stress' and more time for a social life.

However, she had recently experienced an extended period of illness which had changed her perspective on teaching. She was now pacing herself. She had eight years to retirement and was determined not to let ill health caused by overwork at school drive her into early retirement. She had no career ambitions beyond being a good classroom teacher: 'I don't have a stressful workload. I'm not going to jeopardise that to go for a deputy headship.'

Sharon wanted to make the most of her time as a teacher before her retirement. She felt that she could make a bigger difference as an experienced class teacher than as a senior manager. She felt 'at the high peak' of her career, enjoying a sense of sustained engagement.

Story 3: increasingly disenchanted, commitment under threat – a late years teacher (professional life phase 24–30)

> I don't think I've got anywhere. I've concentrated on my teaching and that doesn't seem important anymore. I don't know what's going on around me. The older you get, the less you want promotion. I think it is my age.
>
> (Laura)

What this third teacher's story provides is an illustration of the importance of people-sensitive leadership in the initiation and management of change – particularly for some experienced teachers in later life phases, for whom change may mean the destabilisation of long-held values, practices and professional identities.

Laura was a Year 2 teacher of 6–7-year-old pupils in a 450-pupil urban primary school serving a disadvantaged population where 21–35 per cent of pupils benefited from free school meals and 30 per cent had special educational needs. Aged 46, she had been teaching for 25 years, ten of these in her current school where she was acting as KS1 coordinator.

The school itself was described in its inspection report (two years before the project began) as 'providing a good quality of education, pupils attitudes to work, behaviour and relationships'. The overall quality of teaching was good. However, it was also noted that there were, 'an increasing number of pupils coming from homes where there are social problems'.

Although Laura came into teaching because it was 'well paid', 'never boring' and, 'offered job satisfaction', the latter no longer applied.

Laura's workline indicates a number of peaks and troughs. After a series of unsuccessful attempts to seek posts in other schools, she had now 'lost interest in promotion'.

Dissatisfaction with government initiatives

It is worth noting, also, a particular downturn on Laura's return to teaching after a short period of maternity leave when she felt particularly dissatisfied with

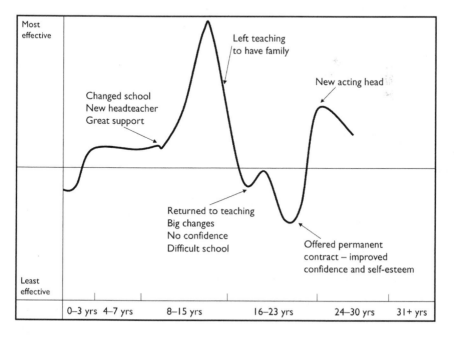

Workline 3   Laura's workline.

centrally initiated government reforms of the curriculum that had resulted in fewer opportunities for her to be creative in the classroom and to 'engage with pupils so that they are excited about their learning'. She experienced a 'high degree' of stress in her work which, she claimed, 'constantly' resulted in adverse effects on her work as a teacher.

Difficult pupil behaviour and a lack of parental support

Laura had returned to teach in a school which drew its pupils from a population which, by and large, was unappreciative of the value of education. She still loved being with children and felt that she could still be effective. However, 'the overall behaviour of pupils has gone downhill and they have become much more difficult to deal with'. She was also 'unhappy' with, 'a lack of support and trust from the parents'.

Variations in in-school support

Because of this and because of being 'side lined' by the school leadership, Laura's confidence in herself dropped. Although she was a KS1 coordinator, it was not a permanent post and she was not involved in decisions, nor in influencing others. She felt that she just passed on others' instructions: 'I didn't want to come to school and to top it all with teaching a SATs (national test) year in the term in which all the work needed to be done. So that made it hard.'

However, although she didn't feel she was being effective as a teacher, in the end her pupils had achieved 'really good' SATs results, and this had restored her belief in herself:

> So I guess I must have performed alright even though I wasn't feeling as though I was at the time. It's made me realise I'm a good teacher still and my performance in the classroom can't be questioned, but as far as gaining promotion in the future, I don't feel I stand much of a chance at the moment.

The head moved to another school and she entered a positive period under the influence of the 'acting' head, who she described as 'excellent': 'Since the change in management, I've been given much more responsibility and feel a lot more valued than before and I think that's made me a lot more effective teacher and more effective leader if you like.'

At the same time, Laura decided to put aside two nights a week when she left school on time to play sport. Establishing a pattern of going home early helped maintain a work–life balance. It coincided with her feeling more positive about work: 'I think the whole school has a completely different feel about it at the moment ... there's much more openness.'

However, the appointment of a new permanent head caused further instability. Laura found it hard to adjust to the way he worked. The new head was, 'desperate to change things', whereas Laura felt that there had been 'too many changes' for teachers already. She became very 'unsettled' and unhappy about proposed changes to her KS1 team. She also lost her position as literacy coordinator in the restructuring. These changes 'cast a shadow' on people because, 'we don't want to change. That's a shame really.' It was perhaps not surprising, therefore, that, for her, the new head 'does have a negative effect on the staff who have been here for a long time'.

Despite all of this, it is worth remembering that she still 'loved being with children' and continued to feel that she could be effective despite the constraints on opportunities to be creative in the classroom.

Conclusions: differentiation and progression in teachers' lives

The accounts of teachers in their early, middle and late professional life phases suggest that understanding teachers' professional life progressions requires not only a consideration of influences within their workplaces, but also of how these interact with and are managed in conjunction with events and experiences in personal lives. Analysis of teachers' professional life phases shows, therefore, that understandings of teachers' work and lives over time require examination of the multiple contexts in which teachers work and live, and the critical influences that affect the character and quality of their personal and professional wellbeing. Implications for the work teachers, school leaders, policy makers and teacher educators are:

- For teachers: helping teachers reflect on their teaching journey, sense of identity and relative effectiveness.
- For school leaders: (1) suggesting the need for close knowledge of their colleagues' concerns; and (2) providing a framework for multi-level capacity building (situated, personal and professional).
- For policy organisations: providing a framework for developing differentiated, concerns-based approaches to the design of teacher development programmes.
- For teacher educators: enabling them to engage in future thinking with pre-service students on factors that influence commitment and effectiveness.

Thus, it is clear that, in addition to individual and work context differences, there are distinctive key influences, tensions, shared professional and personal concerns and commitment pathways or trajectories for most teachers within different phases of their professional lives. Over a professional life span, it is the interaction between different critical influences and the ways in which tensions between these and personal/professional identities are played out and managed that produce relatively positive or negative outcomes in terms of teachers' sense of commitment, resilience, wellbeing and, ultimately, capacity to teach to their best. Knowledge of the impact of such interaction is central to achieving an understanding of what causes variations in teachers' professional lives and the quality of their teaching.

Chapter 4

Portraits of beginning teachers

Schools matter

Introduction

> Schools that support teachers over time succeed not only in hiring new
> teachers, but also in retaining and developing them. These schools are
> finders *and* keepers. They leave little to chance and do not assume that
> good teaching inevitably flows from innate talent, best nurtured in privacy
> and isolation. Rather, they purposefully engage new teachers in the culture
> and practices of the school, beginning with their first encounter.... Efforts
> to address the teacher shortage must take note of these findings and pay
> careful attention to the school conditions that new teachers find upon
> entry.
>
> (Moore Johnson, 2004: 255–256)

Sustaining the commitment and wellbeing of new teachers has been an area of
considerable interest to policy makers and researchers for over three decades.
One of the major and sustained challenges has been to balance the disparity
between theory and practice in teacher education programmes so that new
teachers can be better prepared to cope with the 'reality shock' in the physically
and emotionally demanding realities of classroom teaching (Allen, 2009;
Johnson and Down, 2009; Kyriacou and Kunc, 2007; Neville *et al.*, 2005;
Shulman, 1987). However, since the mid-1990s the startling 30–50 per cent
drop-out rates of teachers within the first 3–5 years of teaching and the rapidly
ageing teaching population in many developed countries have led to a growing
attention to the role of school-level factors in determining beginning teachers'
decision to leave schools (turnover) or the profession (attrition) (Darling-
Hammond, 1997; Gallo-Fox, 2009; Ingersoll, 2001, 2002; Kardos and Moore
Johnson, 2007; Kelchtermans, 1996; Moore Johnson, 2004; OECD, 2005;
Smithers and Robinson, 2003, 2005; Ulvik *et al.*, 2009; Wassell and LaVan,
2009). This is because, at least in part, of the disruptive and detrimental impact
of teacher attrition and turnover on pupils' learning and achievement. Over time
the literature has provided consistent empirical evidence suggesting that lack of
in-school support, poor pupil behaviour and excessive workload are key negative

influences on new teachers' decisions to remain in teaching (Achinstein, 2006; Betoret, 2006; Chan, 2007; Dorman, 2003; Egyed and Short, 2006; Goddard and O'Brien, 2003; Hobson *et al.*, 2009; Kyriacou, 1987; Maslach *et al.*, 2001; Schaufeli and Enzmann, 1998; Webb *et al.*, 2004).

Research perspectives

On entry, most teachers have a strong sense of vocation (Day *et al.*, 2007; Hansen, 1995; OECD, 2005), and at the beginning of their professional lives their work is underpinned by their intrinsic motivation and emotional commitment to provide the best service for their students. The 'profit' which they gain from their work can be seen in the extent to which their pupils grow; and they measure growth in terms of their ability to enhance their cognitive, social and personal knowledge, qualities and competencies. Like those in other human services professions, teachers' emotional commitment is an important element of their ability to teach to their best and is associated with an ethic of care for the wellbeing of their students. However, to continue to exercise care over a professional life span demands considerable intellectual and emotional commitment. For new teachers especially, support in managing the emotional unpredictability of classroom teaching and learning is as important as support in developing their pedagogical and classroom management skills; and the availability, extent and appropriateness of such support in the workplace are likely to be key influencing factors in retaining their commitment to the school and to their decisions about remaining in the profession over the long term.

Compared with their more experienced colleagues, beginning teachers' challenges primarily stem from two distinct but interrelated realities: one is to develop a sense of professional self in their interactions with their colleagues, pupils and parents; and the other is to develop a sense of belonging during their socialisation into the school community and the profession (Allen, 2009; Cherubini, 2009; Lortie, 1975; McGowen and Hart, 1990). As a result, many new teachers often find themselves immersed in complex social relations and sophisticated professional roles inherent within established school communities (Lee *et al.*, 1993), whilst at the same time fighting to make sense of their own experiences and understand what it means to be a teacher. In his extensive review of the literature from 1969 to 2005 on pre-service teachers' transition from student teacher to professional educator, Cherubini (2009: 93) concluded that belonging to a school's culture can be precarious to the beginning teacher's notion of self:

> Established school cultures seem to have an embedded self recognition as an elitist membership not easily earned by newcomers into the profession. Belonging to this exclusive membership is contingent upon the cultural gatekeepers of the school who model what is acceptable to that culture.... New teachers are situated as passively active subjects of a much more

aggressive conceptual force that drives their enculturation to the profession. How the novice first sinks or swims and second adapts to the respective culture, and it to them, significantly influences their professional and social stability.

In such challenging processes of professional socialisation, Blumer (1969), writing 40 years ago, emphasised that beginning teachers negotiate the varying perceptions of self:

> There are however, multiple selves, an inner or core self, and a situational self; much of what constitutes our selves is situational, varying with context, [but] we also have a well defended, relatively inflexible substantial self into which we incorporate the most highly prized aspects of our self-concept and the attitudes and values that are most salient to it.
>
> (Cited in Cherubini, 2009: 85)

In the same vein, Hargreaves (2003: 48) argues that 'it is through professional and personal development that teachers build character, maturity and other virtues in themselves and others, making their schools into moral communities' (see also Mitchell *et al.*, 2009). In their study on the effects of workplace conditions on teachers' commitment to their profession, Rosenholtz and Simpson (1990) found that school organisations that help new teachers focus on tasks that improve their performance efficacy tend to produce greater commitment in them. Almost a decade later, Linda Darling-Hammond (1999) reported that beginning teachers develop their teaching competence more quickly and thus are more likely to stay in teaching if they have access to intensive mentoring and professional learning opportunities in their schools. More recently, Flores and Day (2006) emphasised the importance of school collaborative cultures in (re)shaping new teachers' understanding of teaching, (re)constructing their professional self and facilitating their professional learning and development, particularly when the meanings, values, images and ideals of what it means to be a teacher, with which they enter teaching, are challenged. In addressing the critical challenge of supporting new teachers and enhancing their enthusiasm in the profession, Kardos and Moore Johnson (2007) urged policy makers and school leaders to create an 'integrated professional culture' in schools – a culture of professional support and commitment that 'promotes frequent and reciprocal interaction among faculty members across experience levels; recognizes new teachers' needs as beginners; and develops shared responsibility among teachers for the school' (ibid.: 2083).

The quality of professional cultures in schools is, therefore, central in supporting and retaining able, enthusiastic and committed new teachers, and plays a key mediating role in influencing their decision to leave or stay in the school or the profession.

Factors that sustain or hinder beginning teachers' commitment: portraits of four teachers

> It is during this period that one makes a durable commitment to teaching, with a corollary sense of liberation from strict supervision. One also enjoys a sense of belonging to a professional peer group, and begins to consolidate a basic repertoire of pedagogical skills and materials at the classroom level.
>
> (Huberman, 1993: 244)

Huberman described two contrasting experiences of entering teaching: 'easy beginnings' and 'painful beginnings'. Good rapport with pupils could bring about a sense of discovery and enthusiasm in new teachers, and thus easy beginnings of their professional lives; constant struggles to cope with challenging pupil behaviour would often result in feelings of exhaustion and thus painful beginnings. However, we found in our research that although disruptive pupil behaviour may have a detrimental effect upon new teachers' abilities and willingness to sustain their commitment, where there were strong leadership support and responsive professional development opportunities, many were able to build upon their initial sense of vocation and resilience.

In the VITAE project (Day *et al.*, 2007), the large majority (75 per cent) of teachers in the first seven years of their professional lives remained highly committed and motivated. However, one in four ($n=25$) found it difficult to cope with the social and cultural realities of teaching and were at risk of being lost to the profession. In addition, more teachers in the first three years of teaching showed a negative commitment trajectory than their peers in the 4–7 years range (Table 4.1). This, and much other research internationally, identifies provision of in-school support as being of particular importance in helping those with less than three years of experience, 'probably the most stressful times in their teaching careers' (Martin *et al.*, 2001: 55), survive and thrive (see also Flores, 2006; Kardos and Moore Johnson, 2007; Moore Johnson, 2004; Roehrig *et al.*, 2002).

Table 4.1 Professional commitment trajectories of teachers in early professional life phases (0–7 years of experience)

	Professional life phase 0–3 (n = 26)	Professional life phase 4–7 (n = 75)
Positive trajectories	15 (60 per cent)	59 (80 per cent)
Negative trajectories	10 (40 per cent)	15 (20 per cent)

Professional life phase 0–3: commitment – support and challenge

In the VITAE research, the large majority of teachers in this professional life phase entered teaching with an initial energy and passion for teaching. Over half (61 per cent) indicated that they had been primarily attracted to teaching because of their teaching family backgrounds and/or their expectation of a rewarding opportunity to work with children and contribute to their progress.

Two sub-groups were identified within this professional life phase:

1   Sub-group *a*: one with a developing sense of efficacy (+15) (six primary = 67 per cent, nine secondary = 53 per cent);
2   Sub-group *b*: one with a reducing sense of efficacy (−10) (three primary = 33 per cent; seven secondary = 41 per cent).

Teachers in sub-group *a* were most likely to enjoy career advancement and a strong sense of efficacy, whilst those in sub-group *b* were likely to head for a different school, or leave teaching for other occupations.

Figures 4.1 and 4.2 illustrate the weighting of key critical influences on the work and life of these two groups of teachers. Support from school leadership and colleagues, in conjunction with good rapport with pupils and the provision of appropriate CPD, were perceived as critical to their cognitive and emotional management of the challenges they faced and, also, to their decision to stay in teaching. In contrast, a combination of disappointment with pupils' disciplinary

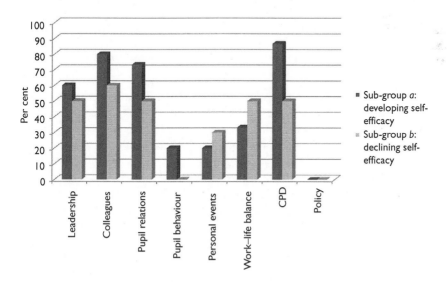

Figure 4.1 Positive critical influences reported by sub-group *a* (*n* = 15) and sub-group *b* teachers (*n* = 10).

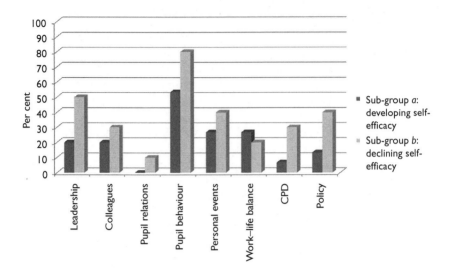

Figure 4.2 Negative critical influences reported by sub-group *a* (*n* = 15) and sub-group *b* teachers (*n* = 10).

problems, a lack of leadership and collegial support, the struggle to balance demands from both personal and professional lives, and dissatisfaction with educational policies and professional development opportunities were the major reasons for new teachers' diminishing efficacy and commitment.

Professional life phase 4–7 – identity and efficacy in classroom

Teachers in this professional life phase demonstrated a primary concern about their confidence, sense of efficacy and feelings in being an effective teacher. However, promotion and additional responsibilities had already begun to play a significant role in their sense of wellbeing, commitment and self-efficacy. Fifty-eight teachers (78 per cent) had additional responsibilities, and among them, 23 (31 per cent) particularly emphasised the importance of promotion to their growing sense of efficacy (six primary and 17 secondary).

The differences in teachers' career development trajectories observed in different studies may be consequences of the differing educational contexts and dates when these studies were carried out. In England, there have been changes in the way that teaching posts have been structured, resulting in a greater differentiated pay scale to reward successful teachers for high performance, in addition to the increase in positions of responsibility (DfES, 2003). Thus, for many teachers in the twenty-first century, this professional life phase is a period in which teachers, whilst consolidating their professional selves in the classroom, also have challenges beyond these.

In the VITAE research, three sub-groups were identified on the basis of teachers' levels of motivation in the profession and commitment to the school:

1 Sub-group *a*: growing – teachers who had a strong sense of self-efficacy and whose expected trajectories were continuing to develop strong agency, commitment and achievement (14 primary (39 per cent); 22 secondary, (56 per cent));

2 Sub-group *b*: coping and managing – teachers who had sustained a relatively moderate level of efficacy and commitment and who were most likely to continue to cope with or manage their work in their next professional life phase (16 primary (44 per cent); seven secondary (18 per cent));

3 Sub-group *c*: vulnerable/declining – teachers who felt that their efficacy and commitment were at risk because of workload and difficult life events, and as a result, might find their professional life trajectories vulnerable and see their efficacy and commitment decline (six primary (17 per cent); nine secondary (23 per cent)). Few teachers in this sub-group had promotion opportunities.

As Figures 4.3 and 4.4 show, support from the school and/or departmental leadership, staff collegiality and good rapport with pupils continued to be important critical influences on teachers' work in this professional life phase. However, in contrast with new teachers, they tended to make more frequent

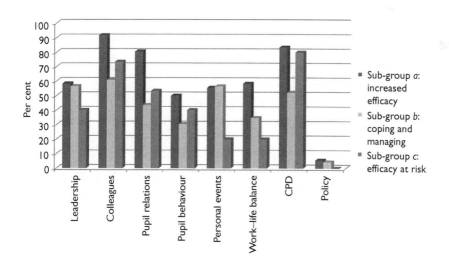

Figure 4.3 Positive critical influences reported by sub-groups *a* (*n* = 36), *b* (*n* = 23) and *c* teachers (*n* = 15).

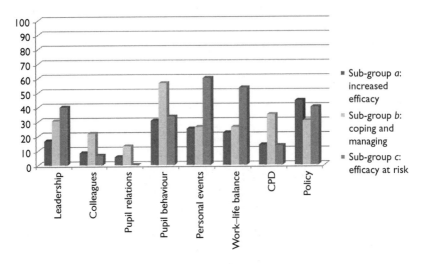

Figure 4.4 Negative critical influences reported by sub-groups *a* (*n* = 36), *b* (*n* = 23) and *c* teachers (*n* = 15).

references to the detrimental effect of heavy workload on their commitment, self-efficacy and capacity to teach to their best. Those in sub-group *c*, in particular, struggled with the management of their heavy workload and work–life tensions. This, together with a lack of leadership support and adverse personal events, put a strain on their already-at-risk wellbeing and commitment.

In sum, teachers in the two early professional phases, like their veteran colleagues (Chapter 5), face challenges of combinations of a range of personal and professional critical influences. As the following four portraits of teachers will show, during the period when they are primarily concerned with establishing a sense of professional self in the classroom, the availability of support matters most to their decision to leave or stay in the school or the profession. All schools are *finders* of new teachers (Moore Johnson, 2004), but good schools are those which nurture and keep them. In order to sustain their inner enthusiasm and energy, they provide them with opportunities to collaborate with colleagues in what has been described as an 'integrated professional culture' (Kardos and Moore Johnson, 2007: 2083). Schools that help new teachers achieve success in the classroom and also provide them with opportunities to advance in the profession become *keepers* of their enthusiasm, commitment and motivation.

The four portraits will also show that, in contrast to observations of the mainstream literature on beginning teachers, which tend to be conceptualised within a negative framework of teacher burnout, stress and vulnerability (Cherubini, 2009; Kelchtermans, 2009; Terry, 1997), despite 'bumpy moments' (Romano, 2006), many are able to draw strength from their personal values and altruistic beliefs, build upon support and positive intellectual and emotional experiences in their workplaces, and ultimately manage fluctuations and setbacks and continue to enjoy satisfaction and success in the school and the profession (see Chapter 9 for a discussion of teacher resilience).

Story I: improved self-efficacy – the leadership effect

> Absolutely exhausted! I just love it, just to see the smallest sign of progression, moving a child on, even just a little bit, motivation, building confidence and independence is a big part of how I make a difference in their lives.
>
> (Pat)

In this first example we show how the professional development and growth of beginning teachers may benefit from the support of strong school leadership and the collaborative school cultures which good leaders create, shape and transform. It is within such positive working environments that this beginning teacher was able to regain her efficacy and commitment and continue to enjoy the achievement of her pupils and the advancement of her professional life.

Pat was 36 years old, a classroom teacher and science coordinator at her first school, where she has taught for three years. Prior to this she had run a 'parent and toddler' (small child) group.

The school was an urban, moderate socio-economic status (FSM2), primary school of 220 pupils. It served an ethnically diverse community. The proportion of pupils who were of an ethnic heritage other than white British was 75 per cent, the largest groups being from eastern European, Pakistani and Chinese backgrounds. The proportion of the pupils with special educational needs was 27.8 per cent, above the national average. Pat's own class of about 24 pupils contained 15 pupils with one language in common and three with complex learning support needs. After two years of teaching in her current school, Pat was promoted to become a member of the senior leadership team. She described herself as having reached 'the point in my life where I wanted a promotion'.

Pat had always enjoyed teaching and working with the children, who she described as, 'delightful'. She gained immense pleasure and satisfaction from her pupils' good results, progress and achievements. Her confidence and sense of efficacy had greatly increased as a consequence of their good results. The general improvement of children across the school had also greatly impacted on Pat's relationships with the pupils in her class. Although their socio-economic background had some impact on her teaching, she felt that the overall behaviour of children in the school was generally quite good: 'There are a handful of "low level disruptive" children, but discipline is helped by the fact that everyone deals with problem behaviour, rather than any one teacher. Discipline has improved, and this is mainly due to raised expectations.'

Very shortly after Pat first joined the school, it was placed in 'special measures' (under threat of closure because it was failing to meet basic educational standards). However, one year later, under the leadership of a new head and deputy head, it had emerged from this. This had an important influence on refocusing the teaching, with more freedom to develop the children's skills 'without sticking to too rigid a timetable'. Thus, over her time the school had improved, and after two very difficult years, in Pat's words, 'the school is now "getting somewhere" '. Her upward trajectory, as shown in her workline, parallels this.

> It just gives you a buzz to keep going, even when a lesson that has been terrifically planned goes pear shaped. It's enjoyable, but it is also exhausting. It's not having enough hours in the day, but you want it to be right.

Pat's workline shows that support and recognition from strong leadership and the transformation of negative cultures in her school had consolidated her long-term commitment to teaching. Not surprisingly, she had highly positive views on the school leadership: 'Everything seems to filter down really well, and everything seems to be discussed openly, and decisions then made as a whole

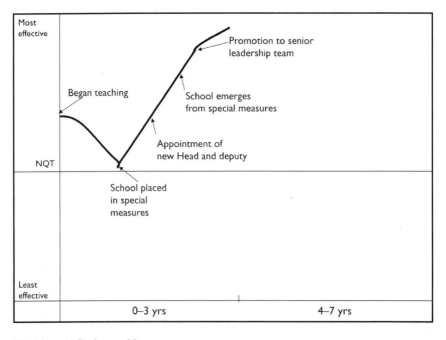

Workline 4 Pat's workline.

staff. Everyone is allowed to develop.' She described the new head as 'exceptional':

> With our new head there is a lot more support for your own development in the sense of your position in the school. It's the encouragement or making decisions for the school, also the literacy adviser from the LA [school district] is wonderful; team teaching, observations together, very good. She's exceptional.

Pat consistently described the staff at her school as extremely supportive of one another, both professionally and socially. Her teaching colleagues helped to keep her commitment strong. As part of her growing self-efficacy, she had become more aware of not letting herself slip behind because 'If you let something slip, it builds up and builds up – so you don't feel good about yourself anyway.' As such, she set herself targets and was getting more organised.

Although she was still 'juggling' her family life, as she gained in teaching experience she was able to spend less time in detailed planning of lessons, and could look to meeting pupils' needs instead of 'racing through the curriculum'. Positive external and internal professional feedback, and good professional and personal support from school management and staff spurred her on even more: 'OK, I can make it even better.'

Her passion for teaching continued to grow, and she saw her professional life developing further over the next period:

> I would like to be in charge of a particular area which I feel passionate about ... Physical Education, Religious Education or Art. I think the children often miss out on these because of the emphasis on literacy and numeracy. Personally ... I would like to learn to play the piano or some sort of musical instrument, not purely for myself, but also so that my students can enjoy it in the classroom.

Story 2: high and growing commitment – sense of belonging

> I think commitment to the job and doing things outside the classroom has a lot to do with the support that you get. If I didn't have people to support me I would have been quite reluctant to do it. My head of department and second of department are always supportive.
>
> (Kim)

This second example illustrates that, in addition to leadership support, a sense of belonging and feelings of being able to learn from and make contributions to a collegial staff community also have a critical effect upon the intellectual development and emotional wellbeing of beginning teachers, particularly for those who strive to survive and succeed in schools serving highly deprived communities.

Kim was in the fourth year of her teaching career and enjoyed working in her current school of nearly 700 pupils aged 11–16. More than 70 per cent spoke English as an additional language, well above the national average, and were of Asian heritage. The school itself was situated in a highly deprived urban area.

The school was described by national school inspectors as being one that was 'dynamic in which the many and increasing strengths outweigh weaknesses', with 'a strong support from its local community' and 'a good learning ethos in which each individual is important'. Overall behaviour and relationships were good and the leadership and management of the school were described as 'very strong with clear purpose, strong teamwork and excellence tracking of pupils' performance'.

Kim came from a teaching family, loved maths when she was at school and always wanted to be a good teacher and 'change pupils' negative opinions about Maths'. Unlike her previous school, which she left after one year, here she had established herself as an effective teacher. She was also involved in extra curricula activities, had a clear sense of professional, individual and organisational identity and was aiming for further career advancement:

> I do more for the children now. I'm willing to get more involved in different aspects. I feel more relaxed with the children. In your first year you tend to be quite strict but I feel more comfortable with the relationship.

The quality of leadership from the head and senior leadership team and colleagues had played 'a big part' in her positive work experiences, providing advice and support for her as a classroom teacher, and in her responsibilities for managing the 'gifted and talented' development in the school and as deputy head of the maths department: 'I definitely feel a part of a team in the department and we do a lot of things together ... [therefore] ... the school ethos is that we are one big family.'

Teaching at what Kim described as a 'tough' school required, in her view, high commitment to the job and close and harmonious working relationships with colleagues. 'Doing things together' outside the classroom played, 'a big part in the support you get inside the classroom.'

Pupils were the main source of her job satisfaction. Although this fluctuated according to the level of class behaviour that needed to be managed, Kim believed that she made a difference through her teaching: 'I try to be effective but I find it hard with children who are not willing to cooperate with what you want to do with them.'

Her greatest challenges were pupils who were either 'lazy' or 'over-confident'.

Administrative support from the faculty clerk, new government imposed initiatives and a happy personal life had the most impact on her wellbeing and self-

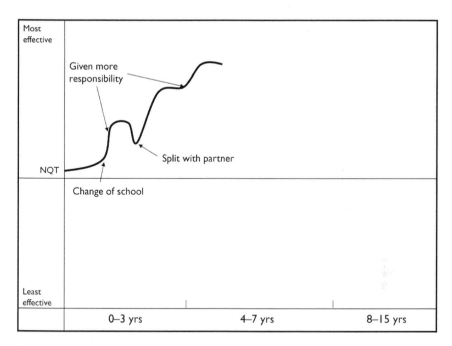

Workline 5 Kim's workline.

efficacy over the last three years. Although she generally felt quite positive about new initiatives, she wished that they could come through at a slower pace so that she could concentrate on one thing at a time and do it properly.

Kim's workline traces her relatively short journey as a teacher. So far she had shown herself to be maintaining her sense of vocation. Due to this, the high level of colleague and leadership support, the externally acknowledged success of the school itself, the social bonds with colleagues that extended beyond the school, her knowledge of the locality in which she lived and went to school, and her belief that she was making a difference, Kim was clearly following an upward trajectory, with her sights firmly fixed on further promotion to head of department in order to make changes at the school level and consequently make a 'bigger difference' to the pupils.

Story 3: continuing to cope in challenging circumstances – connecting with students and colleagues

> There is too much work. The workload is horrendous and it just means that I have little time for other activities and people. It doesn't help your relationships outside. It narrows your life really.
>
> (Hayley)

In the third example we show how positive emotions derived from students' learning, progress and achievement, together with feelings of belonging to a supportive staff community, may contribute to a beginning teacher's ongoing commitment, despite a lack of leadership support, heavy workload and the detrimental effects of government's performativity agendas.

Hayley was in her mid-forties. She had been teaching for only five years, all of them in an urban Catholic primary school situated in an area of high socio-economic deprivation. She was also art coordinator for the school. Its 250+ pupils included 35 per cent from ethnic minority backgrounds and 26 per cent with special educational needs. According to an independent inspection report, the school was 'underperforming':

> Although there are some commendable strengths in the school, there are nevertheless, some areas of its work that have serious weaknesses. The leadership and management are unsatisfactory and this impacts on the work in the school.... The school, though providing an acceptable standard of education for its pupils, nevertheless has serious weaknesses in some areas of its work.

Hayley entered teaching because she wanted a change in career and felt that teaching would meet her needs. Her elder sister was also a teacher.

She enjoyed the Catholic culture, which 'permeates into all that we do' and 'does bring with it supportive relationships'. She suggested that the support of other colleagues and the sharing of ideas and experience impacted positively on her self-efficacy, commitment and sense of efficacy in teaching:

> If you're unsupported then you're not going to feel as good about yourself, so then your motivation is lower. It is hard to be motivated if you don't have any support or encouragement or feedback. So yes, I think this [effectiveness] does increase as we have a very supportive team.

However, what she described as the 'deprived backgrounds' of the pupils did have negative effects on her teaching. Because of poor parental support, some pupils did not complete their homework and had 'behavioural problems'. Her class of 25 pupils contained nine who had special learning needs. She felt that the support she received from the support staff for children with severe learning difficulties helped her teaching in the classroom. This enabled her to concentrate on her teaching and 'continue the flow of the lesson with minimal disruption':

> If you're unsupported then you're not going to feel as good about yourself so then your motivation is lower. It is hard to be motivated if you don't have any support or encouragement, or feedback, so yes I think this does increase as we have a very supportive team.

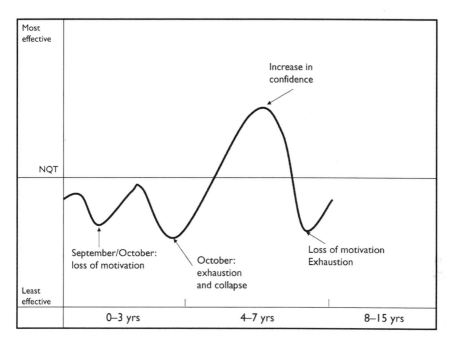

Workline 6 Hayley's workline.

In the initial two years of her teaching. Hayley felt that poor whole-school leadership had been a negative influence on her work as a teacher. As a consequence of this and the unsatisfactory external school inspection, which had stated the school had 'serious weaknesses', she felt that her stress had dramatically intensified and that she suffered from exhaustion and a loss of motivation. She was negative about the 'target driven culture' following the first external inspection. She had experienced a dip in her motivation and enthusiasm for her work during the two years of 'hard work' in preparing for the second external inspection. She criticised 'outsiders', including the government, for imposing a vast amount of paperwork on teachers. Because of this heavy workload, her work–life balance had suffered. She resented the high level of stress caused by Ofsted inspections, although she had derived immense satisfaction and confidence from her good Ofsted results. The two low points in her workline illustrate the dramatic negative impact.

Hayley continued to feel angry about the impact of external demands on her workload and the way that, despite the support of her husband and church, this impinged on her personal life. Nonetheless, in the classroom Hayley was highly confident of her ability to inspire pupils and make a difference to their learning and achievement:

> It is a mix really, but we have a high ethnic minority and of course there are
> cultural differences there, and also there is a mixture of how much parental

support you get as well. So that impacts on their reading and literacy skills, stimulation at home. You have to take account of that when you're planning, obviously, because they won't have the skills or they haven't got the knowledge, or experience.

Hayley was not sure that she wanted to seek promotion to deputy headship, but wanted to remain in teaching and was considering specialising in working with pupils with special educational needs.

Story 4: decline and growth – changing roles

I used to be a real racehorse. I was working every hour, but now I don't feel it's worth it anymore. It is more of a duty to come into school. I used to really love the job and a lot of this has worn off over the last year. It's been getting less fun and I've been less inclined to try new things and push myself that little bit extra as I used to do as a teacher.... I'm sure the pupils must be picking up on it now.

(Len)

The fourth example illustrates well how change in beginning teachers' professional roles may reboost their sense of efficacy and commitment, reshape their perceptions of self within the school and, ultimately, enable them to exericse their resilience and capacities to teach to their best.

Len was in his thirties, in his seventh year of teaching and had been at this, his second school – an 11–16 years, 750+ pupil urban school set in a highly deprived area in which there was long-term unemployment – for four years.

Len had 'always wanted to work with children' and still liked coming into school every day. He was pleased with his pupils' progress, and a school inspection by Ofsted during his second year had been positive: 'I had never been through Ofsted. The department and I came through quite well and that was pleasing.'

However, following the inspection, into which everyone had put a huge amount of effort, morale decreased:

I think it's a general feeling. I think mine has dropped with everyone else.... There's no sort of support and no sort of reward. Often people are just waiting so you can trip up and they can catch you out, so I just want to keep my head down and do the best job I can without being noticed.

He had been second in the English department at the time, and his commitment continued to decline, largely because of the change in the professional ethos in the school and, more particularly, the behaviour of the senior leadership team:

> I don't think it's anyone's fault. I don't think they are doing it on purpose. Certainly on a department level and higher up everyone's playing their own game and making sure their bases are covered. No one is playing the team game anymore, so the support is not there because everyone's watching their own back. I think it's an atmosphere that's been manufactured in the school. I think it's been created here through managerial decisions.... There's a feeling that rather than checking up on your work to make sure you're doing the right thing so they can guide you, it's people checking up on your work to see where they can put you down.

Not surprisingly, Len had experienced 'a lack of self esteem' in his teaching:

> I would like to say that my teaching's not suffered. I've always been a 'bouncy' teacher and I still am, but my lesson plans aren't as varied or exciting as they once were and the children are going to notice that.

This malaise had caused Len's enthusiasm for the job to wane. He experienced a 'lack of goodwill' which stifled initiative. He gave, as an example, a school outing which he had planned:

> If you come up with something you want to do yourself, like you decide you want to run your own trip, people will give you the go-ahead, just to see you come crashing down. Sometimes you'll have some good ideas and you'll get stonewalled straight away. It takes away your confidence and you don't want to do it anymore.... I don't feel valued or supported anymore. I came here as a very open person and I just realise you can't be like that. I'm just simply not as trusting anymore.

He described the changes in his commitment as moving from a 'desire to contribute' to 'performing a duty'. At this point, his experience of school had caused him to start smoking again, two years after he had stopped, and this had adversely affected his relationship with his parents, one of whom was suffering from smoking-related cancer.

However, within another year, as a result of a change of role and promotion from second in the English department to coordinator of special educational needs (SEN) in the school, Len recovered his sense of commitment. He described himself as having 'got my verve back'. He had again stopped smoking and begun to take 'a lot more exercise, trying to keep myself fit'.

Len's workline provides a good illustration of the fluctuations in the life of a young teacher as he struggles to find his professional identity in a national policy climate that affects the life of a school already in highly challenging

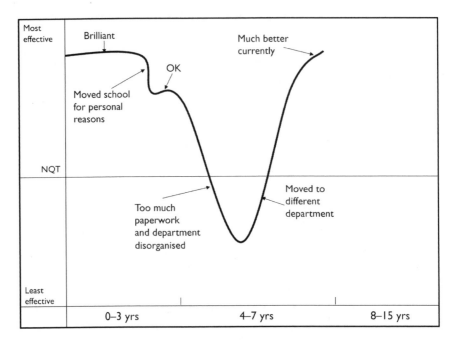

Workline 7 Len's workline.

circumstances and, in particular, the way in which senior leaders may interact with other staff in the school. It also indicates that qualifying as a teacher is only the first step in developing a professional self and that, for some teachers, early commitment may be strongly tested by the circumstances and school cultures in which they work.

Conclusions: schools matter

> Schools are complex, demanding institutions.... The challenge and opportunity for school leaders is to nourish the know-how of staff and students in their work, their thinking, and their daily actions. Through competence, expertise, and knowledge comes achievement.
>
> (Peterson and Deal, 2009: 250)

The way schools are matters enormously to early career teachers. This is because, at least in part, school sites are immediate venues of opportunity, as well as challenge. Some serve as oases of learning and development, where new teachers are engaged in close collaborations with their more experienced colleagues, enjoy professional and personal support, derive joy and satisfaction from good rapport with their pupils and continue to grow their sense of professional self. Others, in contrast, can be minefields of hostile challenges and problems where the joy and optimism of learning and development is replaced with negativity and 'toxic cultures' (ibid.). Thus, understanding the nature of critical influences embedded in the conditions of schools provides a useful lens through which we can understand how and why some new teachers survive and thrive in teaching whilst others leave the profession or hesitate to stay.

Stories of our four new teachers show how those who had an 'easy beginning' (Huberman, 1993) as in the case of Kim, benefited from a combination of influences that were more positive than those for teachers with a 'painful beginning' (ibid.) as in the case of Hayley and Len. Whilst the important role of school conditions or contexts in supporting the professional learning and development of beginning teachers is well documented in the literature, relatively little attention has been paid to the significant contribution of school leaders, and school principals in particular, in creating such positive working environments for them (see Chapter 8 for a discussion of leadership effects). For Pat and Kim, recognition and support of strong school leadership played a central role in facilitating their professional socialisation into the school communities, developing their sense of professional self and sustaining their commitment and positive trajectories in the profession. Writing more than three decades ago, Barth (1976) asserted that,

> It is not the teachers, or the central office people, or the university people who are really causing schools to be the way they are or changing the way they might be. It is whoever lives in the principal's office.
>
> (cited in Lieberman and Miller, 1992: 61)

Critical influences – such as support and recognition from school leaders, staff collegiality and collaborative school cultures, relationships with pupils and parents and the quality of professional development – combine to impact teachers' professional trajectories. In particular, for teachers who are struggling to survive the challenges of a new professional life in the reality of the classroom, the impact of combined support from the school (and/or departmental) leadership and colleagues may have a more influential and significant effect on their commitment and self-efficacy than that of other combinations of influences, because such school-based support is crucial to their learning about how to behave, how to belong, how to teach well and how to be as professionals.

Chapter 5

Managing tensions and transitions in the middle years of teaching

Teachers at the crossroads

Introduction

> People ask serious questions of meaning and purpose at different moments
> in their lives. Teachers are no exception. They raise personal questions
> regarding their choice of career, school, grade level or educational district.
> As other studies have shown, several teachers even ask the fundamental
> question: do I stay in this profession or do I leave.
>
> (Huberman, 1993: 138)

There is relatively little research on teachers in the middle years of their professional lives. The search for fine-grained accounts of their commitment, resilience
and wellbeing during this phase is further complicated by a lack of consensus on
the definition of where exactly are the middle points. In their work on teacher
commitment, for example, Rosenholtz and Simpson (1990) described those with
6–10 years of experience as 'mid-career teachers' and those with 11 or more years
of experience as veterans (see Chapter 6 for a discussion about veteran teachers).
In her research into primary teachers' lives and life histories, Nias' (1989b) 'mid-
career' teachers were between the ages of 32 and 42, having 12–20 years of
experience. Almost a decade later, Grissmer and Kirby (1997) described teachers
aged between 30 and 50 as 'mid-career' teachers. More recently, in his study on
teachers' emotional responses to educational change, Hargreaves (2005) categorised teachers with 6–19 years of experience as being in 'mid-career'.

Research perspectives

The discrepancies in the categorisation of 'mid-career' may have, to a greater or
lesser extent, contributed to two different researcher perspectives on teachers in
this phase. One tends to suggest that they are experiencing a relatively stable
period in their professional lives, with the lowest attrition rates, growing competence and enhanced confidence, resilience and efficacy. Grissmer and Kirby
(1997: 49) found that teacher attrition rates follow a U-shaped curve, 'high for
teachers early in their career, very low during mid-career, and high again for

retirement-eligible teachers'. The attrition level for teachers with 10–19 years of experience was the lowest, at a rate of less than 3 per cent, followed by under 4 per cent of those with 20–24 years of experience. A similar distribution of teacher attrition was also reported by Bobbitt *et al.* (1991), Boe *et al.* (1997), Dworkin (1980) and Rinke (2008). Hargreaves' analysis of teachers in mid-career demonstrates that, 'experience and experiences' make them more confident, more able to cope with change and more resilient to change demands: 'Mid-career teachers were typically more relaxed, experienced and comfortable about their job and themselves than they had once been, but still enthusiastic and flexible enough to respond to change in a broadly positive way' (Hargreaves, 2005: 979).

Other studies, however, have characterised teachers in mid-career as being at a transitional phase in which they experience new challenges and tensions (Hamon and Rotman, 1984; Huberman, 1993; Prick, 1986; Sikes *et al.*, 1985). They point to indications that teachers experience 'mid-life crises' during these years as they review their lives and careers, contemplating alternatives with a certain sense of urgency, 'while it's still possible' (Huberman, 1989b: 253). Huberman (1993) found that teachers with 11–19 years of experience in particular tended to have a latent fear of stagnating. In her follow-up study of 47 mid-career primary teachers, Nias (1989b) reported their pursuit of 'a form of parallel career' in order to offset boredom or frustration during the middle years of their career, 'treating home and school as separate but equally fruitful areas of personal development and switching between them at different times of their lives in response to the dictates of felt-need' (ibid.: 400). In a similar vein, Rosenholtz and Simpson (1990) and Cinamon and Rich (2005) argue that, as we found also with beginning teachers, positive organisational conditions and appropriate professional support are also critical for mid-career teachers experiencing a 'crisis of independence' – in terms of either helping them make the transition to committed veterans or causing them to 'reduce their commitment and perhaps leave the field' (Rosenholtz and Simpson, 1990: 253).

> Administrators must find means to create appropriate professional climates to enable good teachers to realise their career and family goals whether they attribute primary importance to their career or to their family or to both. Otherwise, the teachers will suffer from stress and frustration and may leave the profession or function at sub-optimal levels (Kossek & Ozeki, 1998).
> (Cinamon and Rich, 2005: 374)

Our research found, also, that greater support which focused on maintaining and increasing their morale and capacities to manage work–life tensions and sustain their commitment and sense of efficacy, from knowledgeable heads and colleagues in whom teachers could trust, was important (Day and Gu, 2007). We identified two distinct phases in the middle years of teachers' professional lives: a key watershed between eight and 15 years of experience, followed by the next phase of 16–23 years of experience in which – despite intensified work–life tensions – almost all teachers had additional administrative responsibilities and in which most sustained their commitment, resilience and capacity to teach to their best (Day *et al.*, 2007).

Factors that sustain or hinder teachers' commitment in the middle years of their professional lives: portraits of four teachers

Many of these teachers reported moments of reassessment or 'crisis' and attributed these to changes within the school system, poor workplace environments, family events, difficult classes and heavy investments in curriculum and pedagogical changes that had little or no beneficial effects: 'While mid-career may well be a period of increased vulnerability, of increased reflectiveness, there is no strong evidence in empirical studies of teaching that it brings on necessarily the perception of a "crisis"' (Huberman, 1989b: 353).

Whilst mid-career may not be a distinctive phase of self-questioning or 'crisis' for all teachers, for many it is an important watershed in their professional lives, which presents, on the one hand, greater career progression opportunities, but on the other, greater challenges to manage the tensions between two equally important teaching and personal lives. This led Huberman and other scholars internationally to argue that '[W]hile difficult moments can crop up at any phase of the career, there are periods of greater vulnerability' (ibid., 1993: 255; see also Nias, 1989b; Prick, 1986; Sikes *et al.*, 1985).

The large majority of our mid-years teachers managed to remain highly committed and motivated (Table 5.1). Indeed, they do not appear to be any more 'vulnerable' than their less or more experienced colleagues (see Chapters 4 and 6). Like their peers in the first seven years of teaching, almost one in four with 8–15 years of experience were struggling to maintain their commitment and capacity to teach to their best; and it was during this phase that teachers were more likely to experience a greater decline in commitment than those with 16–23 years of experience (Table 5.1). Our research found that it is in this 8–15-year phase of their professional lives when work–life tensions are most likely to test their sense of resilience. However, it also suggested that where there is appropriate personal and professional support from school leaders and

Table 5.1 Professional commitment trajectories of teachers in the middle phases of their professional lives (8–23 years of experience)

	Professional life phase 8–15 (n = 86)	Professional life phase 16–23 (n = 46)
Positive trajectories	62 (76 per cent)	38 (86 per cent)
Negative trajectories	20 (24 per cent)	6 (14 per cent)

colleagues, many teachers are able to build upon their experience, energy and enthusiasm, respond positively to their internal 'quest for stimulation, for new ideas, challenges and engagement' (Huberman, 1989b: 352) and continue to pursue a professional life path in which they develop and deepen their capacity to teach to their best.

Professional life phase 8–15: managing changes in role and identity – tensions and transitions

With growing commitments at home and more professional demands at work (most had taken on administrative responsibilities (79 per cent, $n = 68$) in their workplaces), many teachers in this phase had begun to face additional challenges in managing both. Trying to do well both as a manager and as a teacher had, however, created, for some, difficult dilemmas.

Huberman (1993) also identified this 8–15-years phase as a notable moment in teachers' 'career cycle': 'when teachers begin asking themselves where their career is going and what it has brought to them up to now' (ibid.: 255). In this phase, they are 'at the crossroads' of their personal and professional lives, experiencing a period of radical self-questioning, reviewing the meaning of their work and life, and asking serious questions about whether to continue or leave teaching (Huberman, 1989a, 1989b, 1993). Almost two decades later and in a different country context, our research identified additional questions regarding the intersections and interactions between their professional life paths – whether to pursue further promotion and career advancement or to remain in the classroom fulfilling the original call to teach – and their personal life paths.

Two sub-groups were identified on the basis of their levels of motivation and commitment:

1 Sub-group *a*: sustained engagement – teachers who enjoyed a strong sense of efficacy and whose expected trajectories were career advancement with increased commitment (+62) (40 primary (78 per cent); 22 secondary (63 per cent)).

2 Sub-group *b*: detachment/loss of motivation – teachers who felt a sense of detachment and diminishing motivation and who were most likely to experience declining self-efficacy in their next professional life phase or even career shift (−20) (seven primary (14 per cent); 13 secondary (37 per cent)).

Approximately 67 per cent ($n = 42$) of teachers in sub-group *a* had additional managerial responsibilities. For them, leadership roles comprised an important part of their professional selves. Some were looking into further promotion, aiming at head of department, deputy headship and/or headship roles, whilst others who were settling into their current leadership roles were learning to manage the changes. In contrast, a small group of teachers within this sub-group reported that they were 'content' and 'happy' with their current work–life balance and that they had no intention of taking up any further additional leadership or managerial roles. Some wanted to focus upon improving their capacities to teach to their best in the next phase of their professional lives, whilst others, particularly those late entrants who had entered teaching from other professions and who were nearing retirement age, experienced immense job satisfaction from their ability to make a difference to the learning and growth of their pupils.

Our observation of these late entrants' strong sense of vocation and commitment supports findings of other research on 'career changers' which shows that '[I]n the move to teaching, career switchers often bring an articulated sense of mission and agency, a strong sense of commitment, maturity and professionalism' (Mayotte, 2003: 681; see also Arthur *et al.*, 1999; Chambers, 2002; Freidus, 1994; Grier and Johnston, 2009). Notwithstanding this, as Sam's and Jodie's portraits will tell us later in this chapter, they were as much in need of personal and professional support as their younger colleagues, although the nature of these differed greatly because of differences in needs which were determined by their age (Madfes, 1989, 1990; Mayotte, 2003).

Figures 5.1 and 5.2 illustrate the key positive and negative critical influences on teachers in the two sub-groups. Like their colleagues in the initial seven years of teaching, they reported that personal and professional support from school and/or departmental leadership, staff collegiality, good rapport with the pupils and appropriate CPD opportunities were the most important contributing

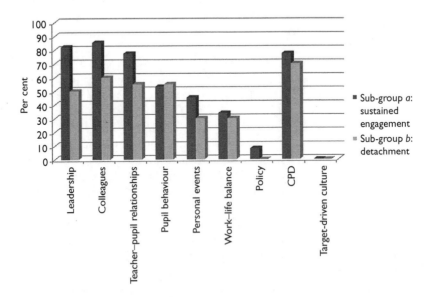

Figure 5.1 Positive critical influences reported by sub-group *a* (*n* = 15) and sub-group *b* teachers (*n* = 10).

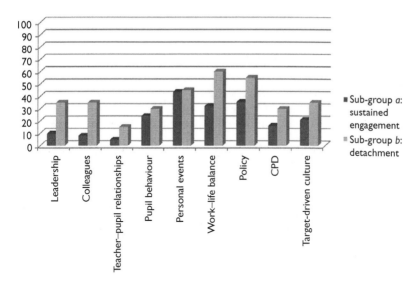

Figure 5.2 Negative critical influences reported by sub-group *a* (*n* = 15) and sub-group *b* teachers (*n* = 10).

factors in sustaining their sense of resilience, commitment and their capacity to teach to their best. However, compared with their less experienced peers, more teachers in this professional life phase struggled with work–life tensions. Slightly over 40 per cent of teachers in both sub-groups reported the detrimental effect of adverse personal events on their commitment and close to 60 per cent of teachers in sub-group *b* reported the negative influence of work–life tensions on their sense of resilience and wellbeing (Figure 5.2).

Professional life phase 16–23 years: work–life tensions – challenges to motivation and commitment

Within the broader middle years span of teachers' professional lives, this phase had a greater proportion of teachers who reported high levels of commitment and motivation and positive professional trajectories. Compared with both their more experienced and less experienced colleagues, fewer teachers in this phase struggled with diminishing self-efficacy or commitment, although almost all (89 per cent (41 out of 46)) had additional leadership responsibilities. This is in contrast to the findings of other studies. For example, Prick (1986) observed a period of 'crisis' in men between 36 and 55 and in women between 39 and 45 in terms of questioning whether to remain in teaching. In their review of the state of the art on teachers' professional lives, Floden and Huberman (1989) also found 'suggestive evidence' indicating that teachers with 12–20 years of experience, or who were between 35 and 50 years of age, felt that they were experiencing a problematic 'stock-taking' phase, 'during which one projects oneself to the end of the career cycle, an end one can now concretely construe, looks around at older peers – and thinks seriously about leaving the profession' (ibid.: 462). Although most of the middle year teachers in our research were experiencing a period of stock taking, there were no strong signs that suggested they were considering leaving the profession.

Three sub-groups were identified on the basis of their levels of commitment and motivation:

1   Sub-group *a*: growing motivation and commitment – teachers who had seen their motivation and commitment increase as a result of their further career advancement and good pupil results/relationships and who were most likely to see their motivation and commitment continue to grow (+23) (17 primary (63 per cent); six secondary (32 per cent));

2   Sub-group *b*: continuing to cope with work–life tensions – teachers who maintained their motivation, commitment and sense of efficacy as a consequence of their agency and determination to improve time management and who were most likely to cope with work–life tensions in their next professional life phase (+15) (eight primary (30 per cent); seven secondary (37 per cent));

3   Sub-group *c*: declining motivation and commitment – teachers whose workload, management of competing tensions and career stagnation had led to decreased motivation, commitment and self-efficacy and whose career trajectories were expected to be coupled with declining motivation and commitment (−6) (one primary (4 per cent); five secondary (27 per cent)).

Figures 5.3 and 5.4 illustrate key critical influences on the work and lives of the three sub-groups. As Figure 5.3 shows, the combinations of leadership and collegial support, good rapport with pupils, positive pupil behaviour and opportunities for CPD continued to play an important role in helping teachers manage the tensions between work and life and boost and sustain their commitment, wellbeing and motivation, particularly for those in sub-groups *a* and *b*. In contrast, for the small number of teachers whose commitment and sense of efficacy had declined after having worked with 16 or more yearly cohorts of pupils (sub-group *c*), the combined effects of adverse personal events, negatively received educational policies, a lack of leadership and collegial support and few professional development opportunities were believed by them to have strongly contributed to their decreased motivation and sense of career stagnation (Figure 5.4). In particular, for those teachers whose wellbeing and commitment were already at risk of declining, disruptive pupil behaviour and work–life tensions appeared to have had significantly detrimental effects.

Thus, having survived and, for the most part succeeded, in the early phases of their professional lives, most teachers in these two mid-career professional life

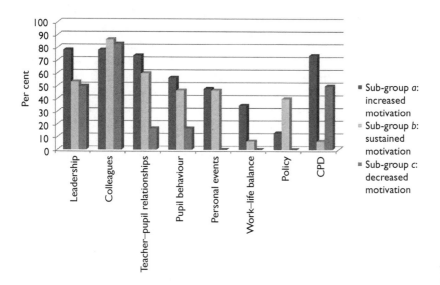

Figure 5.3 Positive critical influences reported by sub-group *a* (*n* = 46), sub-group *b* (*n* = 23) and sub-group *c* teachers (*n* = 36).

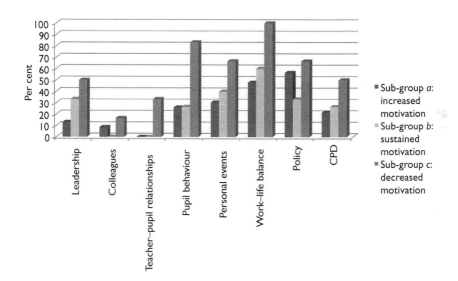

Figure 5.4 Negative critical influences reported by sub-group *a* (*n* = 36), sub-group *b* (*n* = 23) and sub-group *c* teachers (*n* = 15).

phases were more confident, efficacious and enthusiastic. The vast majority had taken on additional leadership responsibilities but many, also, had begun to face challenges to their capacities to maintain a 'working equilibrium' (Floden and Huberman, 1989: 462) between additional domestic commitments and professional demands. Nonetheless, as portraits of the following four teachers which follow will show, where there is professional as well as personal support from school leaders and colleagues, together with harmonious teacher–pupil relationships and opportunities for professional development and progression in the school, despite growing work–life tensions, most teachers are able to sustain their commitment, sense of efficacy and wellbeing and continue to teach to their best.

Story 1: moving onwards and upwards – personal and professional challenges

> I have always loved the idea of working with children – never wanted to be anything else. I get up every day and I come into school and I do a job that I love – not everyone can say that.... I am at an important juncture of my career.
>
> (Alison)

In this first example we show how leadership support and recognition and the provision of promotion opportunities may help to boost the self-efficacy, self-esteem, commitment and activism of teachers in this key transitional phase of their professional lives.

Alison was 30 years old and had taught for 11 years. She had been teaching in her current primary school for nine years, having previously worked in one other as a temporary 'supply' teacher. The school had 550 pupils, was situated in an urban area and drew its pupils from a relatively advantaged population (FSM2). She had taught Year 6 classes of 10–11-year-old pupils for the last four years. She also had additional school-wide responsibilities (literacy coordinator, year group coordinator (Year 6), responsibility for gifted and talented children).

Becoming a teacher had been one of Alison's early ambitions. She had worked first as a nursery nurse and later entered teaching because of a 'big push' from a previous head who had faith in her ability to be a teacher.

The quality of school leadership played a strong role in Alison's happiness at the school. The three members of the Senior Leadership Team (SLT) complemented each other in their skills. She found them approachable about both school and personal issues: 'Any of the three in the SLT will support you 100 per cent, which is fantastic.' The SLT encouraged her professional development and she appreciated, also, the personal support that she received from her school when she was undergoing a divorce. Moreover, she felt that the head and the senior managers valued her ideas and allowed her to be innovative and to have a 'free rein' to experiment in her leadership roles: 'The leadership is so good so no matter what comes from outside, we work with it, discuss it, make it our own.'

Alison also liked 'the wonderful working environment of enthusiastic and committed staff [on the whole]' in her current school. Relationships with colleagues remained good and played a very large part in her job satisfaction. She especially enjoyed working in partnership with the three colleagues in the year group she led: 'They all pull their weight and no one moans.'

She saw the presence of a classroom assistant for the special needs child in her class as a bonus because 'it's an extra pair of hands in the class at all times who can be asked to work with individual children', and so she could spread her workload.

Alison felt that the pupil behaviour at her school was 'not as good as it could be: children have little care for each other and are inclined to break school rules', but she was optimistic that when the school behaviour policy was fully updated, the general behaviour would change. She could indeed already see signs of improvements in the school. It was the lack of parental support that she was most concerned about: 'There are some parents who don't support the teachers when they take a disciplinary role.'

She did not think that the general increase in problematic pupil behaviour in the school had affected the good rapport that she had established with her pupils. She was a firm believer that 'You have to have a special relationship [with the pupils] – the children have to feel secure in their friendship with you and trust in you to know that they can tell you things and you'll deal with it appropriately.' Because Alison was a year group coordinator, she was always given the most challenging class of the three. But she was used to this and worked hard every year to develop a good relationship with her group. In some years pupils were more challenging than others and, because of this, within an overall sense of self-efficacy and commitment, her motivation fluctuated – as her workline demonstrates.

Her workline indicates that her two promotions over a three-year period positively impacted on her work life as a teacher. However, because of a challenging class, coupled with her failure to obtain an internal promotion and her stressful experience with an Ofsted inspection, Alison experienced a dip in her motivation and job satisfaction. A year later, her success in gaining further promotion in the school and her new 'lovely' class re-ignited her motivation and self-esteem and ultimately made a significant contribution to the rise in her sense of efficacy and commitment. Reflecting on her recent divorce, Alison felt that she had grown stronger as a person – because being a single parent meant that she had to push herself to become more organised in her personal life.

Alison felt that it was difficult to see the divide between work and life: 'So much of personal time is taken up with teaching matters, so much of teaching is

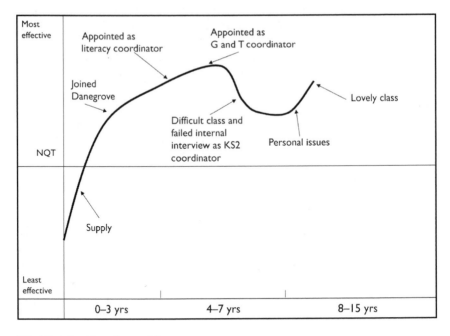

Workline 8   Alison's workline.

about me as a person. The standards and boundaries I have in my personal life are those I bring to the classroom.'

Not surprisingly, although 'workload increases and social life diminishes', she was still full of enthusiasm for the job. She had reclaimed her personal and social life. However, whilst she loved being a member of the teaching profession, when in social situations, she found herself constantly defending teachers and the education system. Non-teachers and parents appeared to prefer to focus on negative press rather than on teachers' achievements: 'Sometimes when you say you are a teacher, it's a conversation killer.'

Alison felt that the current phase of her professional life was notably different from the previous ones. Then, she had enjoyed the professional recognition that her early promotions had brought about and gained immense satisfaction from her rapidly growing sense of efficacy. However, at the beginning of this phase, she felt unsettled and 'dithery' and could not help wondering what steps she ought to take to advance her career path: 'Should I go or should I stay at this school?'; 'Is it time for me to be looking for deputy headships?'. She went through an unsuccessful period of seeking promotion. She now felt more 'settled' and content and was no longer looking for further promotion within the school. She enjoyed leading a 'big and exciting push' on literacy and knew that she would be teaching a new year group the following year – another, different challenge ahead!

After 11 years of teaching, then, Alison continued to feel 'engaged' and 'committed'. She felt that she had a 'new lease of life', but understood that, if she wanted to become a deputy head, she would have to leave her current school when the right opportunity arose.

Story 2: conflicting values

I cannot regurgitate the same stuff every year particularly when you have a very prescribed curriculum in terms of the objectives of the literacy and numeracy strategy. You really have to begin to own it and that's what I have tried to do.

(Philip)

This second example shows how the challenge of implementing national policies with which the teacher disagreed and the conflict of his educational values with those of the school leadership served to destabilise his commitment and motivation – despite the positive support of colleagues.

Philip was 49 years old and had been teaching 6–7-year-old pupils for 21 years at his current urban primary school of 325 pupils. It was his first school. Philip was also the KS1 coordinator and maths coordinator in this low socio-economic status (FSM4), low-achieving school. The proportion of pupils with English as an additional language at this school was very high (37 per cent) and there were 43 languages spoken. Around 35 per cent of the pupils on the school roll were on the SEN register, which was well above the national average.

Philip had originally trained to be an accountant, but felt that he was more of a 'people person'. It was suggested to him by a friend who was already a teacher that he was well suited for teaching in a primary school and, in his own words, decided to 'give it a go'. He began teaching, 'wanting to make a contribution towards developing pupils as independent, critical thinkers', but now his belief that he could do so was, 'far less'. Rather, he found himself spending 'innumerable hours on non-productive paperwork, which would be more usefully devoted to teaching'. He described the national Ofsted school inspection system as having the greatest negative impact on his work as a teacher and was 'very dissatisfied' with the time he had to reflect and work with colleagues.

Philip believed that the socio-economic background of his pupils 'probably' had an impact on his work as a teacher. Because of the high mobility rate and the high level of deprivation of the catchment area (e.g. many in temporary accommodation, poor area, racially very mixed), teachers had to 'work a lot harder to get the motivation of parents': 'Many are in temporary accommodation and there are problems with punctuality, attendance and pupils' motivation to learn.'

Nonetheless, he remained highly committed to teaching, mainly because, 'I've got a lovely class ... their behaviour is excellent and their motivation is good.' He took advantage of 'the outdoor curriculum' and had organised creative out-of-school visits with his class. This had made a big positive impact and, as a result, he felt more motivated at work. Philip was more confident of his ability to make a difference to his pupils' achievements, and derived great pleasure from positive feedback from the parents and from his pupils' academic progress. Although he saw his self-efficacy temporarily dip because of the poor national tests results of his pupils, his job satisfaction had remained high. Opportunities to participate in CPD had the greatest positive impact on his work as a teacher. He had completed an MA, which broadened his academic views on teaching. As a result, he felt more autonomous, more in control and more committed.

Philip's workline indicates that formal planning and Ofsted special measures had worked against his morale and sense of efficacy. He believed, however, that he had always been given support on professional and personal issues. When the school was in 'special measures', the deputy head became head and worked with the staff to find out, 'where we were going a bit wrong'. Philip felt, also, that the commitment and self-efficacy of other teachers were highly important to him. He enjoyed good cooperation and professional support from his colleagues and thought that his achievements had benefited from good teamwork amongst

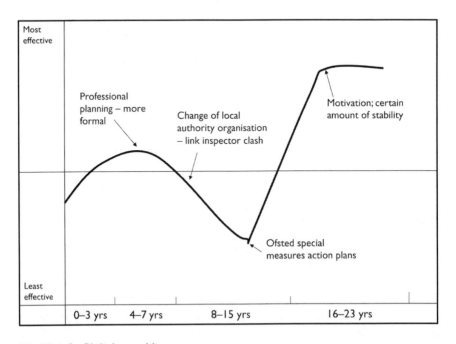

Workline 9 Philip's workline.

the staff who shared the belief that 'We're all in the same boat and you've got to pull together, otherwise, the boat is going to sink.'

Philip's commitment to teaching, then, had varied over time and there was a relationship between this and the variations and changes in educational policies. In the late 1980s he felt his 'values were being eroded' because of the introduction of the national curriculum, which was more prescriptive than he was used to. He approved of current moves to more whole-class teaching and felt more confident with the national strategies. However, he regretted what he experienced as fewer opportunities to be creative in the classroom and resented following what he described as a 'prescriptive' curriculum. He believed that he was a good teacher and that narrowly defined test results had little to do with his teaching because they depended largely on the quality of the individual cohort of pupils. He no longer worried about meeting targets because 'They are unrealistic and if they're unrealistic, then you can't attain them and that's an end to it.'

One of Philip's strong beliefs that teaching and learning should be fun and creative was also in conflict with the school ethos, and this had a detrimental effect on his sense of efficacy. The conflict had begun with the appointment of a new head, for whom 'results are the be all and end all': 'She seemed obsessed with tracking children's achievement and measuring things rather than creative learning.'

Philip described the new head as 'autocratic'. He no longer enjoyed working in the school as he had 'lost the autonomy given by the last head'. Instead, he felt increasingly constrained by the target-driven culture of the school. Also, he felt 'shattered as the school has gone back to a system of overwhelming paperwork'. The constant demands for paperwork were stifling his creativity. Moreover, he realised that his professional role had begun to encroach on his personal life. He felt frustrated and undervalued, and even considered resigning from the school.

Story 3: tired and trapped but not yet losing commitment – a late entrant

This third example illustrates how a lack of leadership support and recognition of late entrants' particular personal and professional needs, compounded by pupils' challenging behaviour and the government's relentless reforms, may contribute to their decreased career ambitions. As a result, although still feeling committed to making a difference, this teacher had started to look forward to the end of his professional life.

Sam worked in the same school and same department as Philip. He was of similar age but with much less experience of teaching, nine years, all but one spent in his present school. The contrast was pronounced. Unlike Philip, Sam was a late entrant to the teaching profession, after spending 20 years in industry. Anticipating redundancy, he had retrained as a teacher of maths and ICT. His only responsibility outside the classroom was 'lockers coordinator'.

He had been attracted to teaching, in his own words, by the 'interaction with young people and the opportunity to help them achieve what they are capable of'. Nine years later, this was still true. The idea of sharing knowledge and 'helping people develop in the best way they can' still motivated him in his teaching and the current level of his commitment, job satisfaction and self-efficacy was 'quite high', though 'slightly less than three years ago', because of the 'interference' from the government and the school's senior leadership team. The school had become 'the victim of its own success', and teachers were 'having to run to stand still'.

He described the pupils at his current school as 'fantastic' and his relationships with them as 'generally good'. Individuals' achievements mattered greatly to him and he enjoyed sharing in their success. Although he felt very unhappy about the deteriorating pupil behaviour in his school, he did not think that it was 'as bad as that in other schools in the same area'. Nonetheless, it seemed to be 'getting worse year by year', and was having negative effects on his teaching.

Sam's view was that he had a job to do and that he would do it to the best of his ability – but without it becoming all-consuming. For example, he resented taking his marking home. He enjoyed working at his school 'most of the time' and felt very positive about the professional support from his colleagues. He felt, however, that although the school was supportive, there was a lack of communication between the school and the department. The lack of support from the SLT also worked against his self-efficacy and commitment as a teacher.

Recent losses of his father and a friend, together with his wife's involvement in an accident, had caused him to question his priorities. Because he believed 'there's a lot more to life than work', he had decided to reduce his school workload at certain times of the week so that he could use that as quality time for himself and his wife.

Like Philip, he was disenchanted at the negative influence of external initiatives and strategies, 'most of which have not been well thought through or properly tested'. He felt that his commitment was still there, but that, 'sometimes motivation can be a question'. He was considering taking early retirement.

Story 4: sustaining commitment but declining self-efficacy and potential disengagement

> It's a job but you've got to get your balance right. It's a job when all's said and done.... I don't see myself staying in teaching until 65. I don't think I can survive beyond another six years.
>
> (Jodie)

In the 8–15-year phase, professional recognition and personal support from school leadership continue to work as an important booster to teachers' self-efficacy and commitment. Jodie's portrait, however, illustrates how the detrimental effects of nation-wide and school-wide reforms, together with age-related family concerns, may lead teachers to reconsider their continued commitment to teaching – despite their sustained commitment to serving the learning and achievement needs of the children.

> Jodie's current school catered for 1,000+, 11–16-year-old pupils, had high socio-economic status (FSM1) and was situated in a semi-rural area, with less than 1 per cent of the pupils having English as an additional language. This was her third school and she had been in this school for five years.

Aged 42, and a late entrant to the profession, Jodie had been teaching for eight years. Teaching was a second career, her first having been in the police service. She had entered teaching because of the challenge and intellectual stimulation that she saw it as offering and because of her enjoyment of her subject. In this respect she followed the path taken by her brothers and sisters, all of whom had begun their working lives in other professions before becoming teachers.

> In policing you are dealing with people but with very small numbers in comparison with the numbers of kids' lives you are actually dealing with in school. You are responsible for each and every one of those, whereas in policing you can only do so much in an 8-hour shift.

On her switch to teaching from the police, she had a poor initial assessment in her first school and had needed considerable support from her head of department.

During the five years in her current school, she had been promoted to deputy head of the English department. Initially, this had given an added boost to her self-efficacy and motivation, though she was not interested in further promotion because of family issues. She claimed to work between 51 and 60 hours each week and to take work home. She described work as 'always on top of you no matter what you do', and 'frequently' suffered a high level of stress, often feeling 'guilty' because she felt that there was always more to do. As with most other teachers in our research, she found that she did not have enough planning time or time to reflect upon her teaching.

Support from the senior leadership team had the greatest positive impact on her commitment and wellbeing. She valued, also, the support of the staff around her ('department ... quite close, have a good whinge together') and a 'sense of community with the staff'. She was 'at my happiest in the classroom'. However, her pupils had not performed as well as expected in recent national tests and this had been 'a big kick in the teeth' for her.

Jodie's workline shows her increased sense of confidence in her sense of efficacy in the school, with a more recent plateauing.

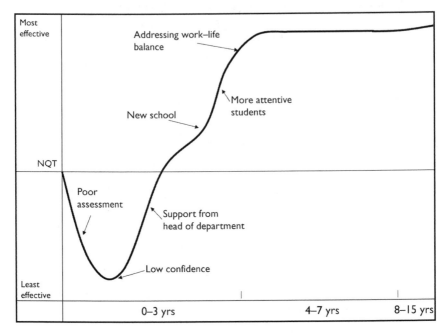

Workline 10   Jodie's workline.

She cited pupils as the main source of her happiness and enjoyment, describing them as 'nice kids' with whom she had formed good relationships. The overall behaviour of the pupils in her school was 'generally very good'.

In common with Sam, Jodie also felt strongly about what she experienced as the negative influences of 'endless' external initiatives and changes that had been imposed on teachers. She was particularly unhappy with the 'target-driven culture' and the changes in the assessment systems. She saw her philosophy for teaching English as having been 'drained' and was reluctant to change the way she taught. She was also stressed about the constant changes within the school, some of those being 'on a daily basis'. Her school was to become a 'specialist' science college and Jodie was unhappy that English might become a 'second-class subject'. As a result, she felt 'a lot of resentment' and her motivation had decreased over the last three years. Her husband planned to retire in six years, when she too would consider 'a total lifestyle change'.

Conclusions: teachers at the crossroads

By this time in their career, a number of teachers had experienced different systems, different roles. Beyond the open-eyed enthusiasms of youth but before the later career phase, many teachers in mid-career drew on their range of life and career experiences in ways that left them still open to and interested in change as well as healthily sceptical about it.

(Hargreaves, 2005: 980)

Whilst most teachers in the middle years of their professional lives do not leave teaching, they are, nonetheless, experiencing a critical transitional phase in terms of their level of commitment. As some 'mid-career teachers' in Hargreaves' study noted, they had 'a double empathy' with beginning teachers as well as their older veteran colleagues and indeed felt themselves to be 'in the middle' (ibid.: 981). Portraits of the four teachers in this chapter reveal, however, an even more nuanced, complex picture of teachers' lives than that portrayed by Hargreaves. Although most remained committed, tensions caused by growing demands of bureaucracy, deteriorating pupil behaviour, increasing emphasis on meeting imposed attainment targets at work and changes in their personal life circumstances placed them at a crossroads of commitment.

Thus, the extent to which their new challenges, frustrations and differentiated personal and professional development needs are recognised and supported by heads and others concerned with raising standards in schools and classrooms is crucial, for it is this phase in their professional and personal lives, more than any other, which is likely to influence their commitment and their capacities to teach to their best in the next 10–20 years of their work in schools.

Chapter 6

Veteran teachers

Sustaining commitment, exercising resilience

Introduction

> Older teachers do not always continue to grow and learn and may grow tired of their jobs. Furthermore, the benefit of experience may interact with educational opportunities. Veteran teachers in settings that emphasise continual learning and collaboration continue to improve their performance.
>
> (Rosenholtz, 1984: n.p.)

Whilst Rosenholtz's work rightly points to the importance of school leadership and culture in supporting teachers' learning and performance, it also runs the risk of oversimplifying the conditions which affect these. This chapter examines the effects of a wider range of critical influences in order to extend understandings of the work and lives of this important and large group of highly experienced 'veteran' teachers. It will use narrative accounts of four teachers – two primary and two secondary – as springboards for a discussion of research that seeks to uncover and understand how and why veteran teachers sustain or do not sustain their motivation, commitment and sense of resilience in their third and fourth decades of teaching.

Research perspectives

Much research on teachers has focused on the early phases of their work and lives, because of the particularly pressing and continuing problem of attrition amongst these teachers (Ingersoll, 2003). In contrast, relatively less is known about the nature of the tensions and challenges facing those who have had a substantial amount of experience in teaching (i.e. so-called 'veteran' teachers) and how and why they have managed (or not managed) to continue to fulfil their original calling to teach (Hansen, 1995). Throughout their professional lives these teachers will have been confronted by professional, workplace and personal pressures and tensions which, at times, at the very least are likely to have challenged and perhaps ultimately eroded their values, beliefs and practices: for some, their willingness to remain in the job, and for others, their capacity to continue to teach to their best in the classroom as commitment becomes eroded.

In Chapter 2, we discussed how, in many countries, notions of professionalism have changed as national priorities have focused more closely on teachers' accountability for student achievement as defined by national tests and examinations; how the emergence and growth of these priorities have been accompanied by the development and use of national standards and systems of inspection and evaluation. The effects of these have been claimed by some to diminish teacher autonomy and challenge traditional identities (Friedson, 2001; Ozga, 1995; Sachs, 2003). In many industrialised nations, also, the teaching workforce is ageing (OECD, 2005), and whilst governments are aware of this and the need to plan increases in cohorts of less experienced and/or younger recruits, other consequences concerning the effect on quality of teachers who have served in excess of 24 years in schools seem not to have been addressed. Our VITAE research (Day *et al.*, 2007) found, for example, that more experienced, 'veteran' teachers, particularly those who teach in secondary schools, are at greater risk of diminishing commitment and effectiveness (both in terms of their perceived effectiveness in the classroom and effectiveness as measured by their pupils' progress and attainment). In addition, there are issues of mobility and retention which apply particularly to teachers in schools that serve disadvantaged communities and those who teach 'special needs' students. These replicate research findings in the United Kingdom, Australia and Europe that state:

> Organisational influences were the major factors in teachers' decisions to stay, or leave. Most teachers enter the profession with an early commitment to teaching and to students, but find that factors in the structure and organisation of schools work against their sense of professionalism.
>
> (Certo and Engelbright Fox, 2002: 69)

Many research studies of teacher retention focus too narrowly upon 'attrition', the externally assessable result of loss of commitment, rather than upon the ways in which wellbeing and commitment may become eroded. Others place an emphasis upon teacher stress, again an outcome of pressures which lead to loss of commitment. Most of these studies tend to be based on self-reports by teachers and focus upon finding solutions for their physical retention. Dinham and Scott (1996, 2000), for example, provided detailed accounts of teachers' personal characteristics in their work and identified working conditions in schools as key factors in teacher attrition. These include class size, teaching resources, bureaucracy, sense of autonomy, engagement in school and classroom decision-making processes, personal status and salary. What is clear in the most recent authoritative research is that the long-held traditional theory of hygiene factors (Herzberg *et al.*, 1959) does not now hold true. Simply adding to those extrinsic factors which attract teachers to stay (e.g. salary) without at the same time reducing the dissatisfiers (e.g. increases in bureaucracy and decreases in classroom autonomy) will not retain teachers' commitment (Dinham and Scott, 1996, 2000; Nias, 1989a).

A further limitation is that these studies do not focus on relationships between the positive or negative effects of ageing, social and policy changes and the working environment and teachers' effectiveness. Yet it is these matters that are crucial for all those concerned with raising and maintaining standards of teaching, learning and student achievement. There is a real sense, then, that physical retention, whilst important, is no more so than the retention of teacher quality. At a time when the age profile of teachers in many countries is skewed towards those with more than 20 years of experience, and in which most of these would be unlikely to feel able to change career for financial and domestic reasons, we believe that it is important, also, to investigate whether the demands and challenges over time have dimmed these teachers' sense of wellbeing and commitment and thus their capacity to teach to their best. We see retention, therefore, as a process rather than a result. We know that these teachers have survived to become veterans, but we know relatively little about the conditions which have added to or diminished their sense of commitment and wellbeing, and the relationship of these to their felt capacities to teach to their best.

As teachers grow older, so do the challenges of maintaining energy increase in the complex and persistently challenging work of teaching children and young people, whose attitudes, motivations and behaviours may differ widely from those with whom veteran teachers began their careers. Moreover, teachers' own professional agendas may have changed in response to their experiences of many policy and social reforms, school leaders, and cohorts of students, as well as the ageing process and unanticipated personal circumstances. The persistence of such combinations of challenges, which are part of the experience of most of those who work for prolonged periods of their lives in one occupation, may have begun to take its toll on the motivation, commitment and resilience which are essential to the willingness and capacity of veteran teachers to maintain teaching at its best.

The need to understand the challenges of teaching to their best over a long career span on veteran teachers' work and lives in these contexts is thus especially important. It is important, also, because they form the majority of teachers in schools in many Western countries (OECD, 2005). For every teacher who leaves the school, there are many others who stay. What it is that keeps them believing and demonstrating daily that they can and do continue to 'make a difference' in the lives of the children they teach is, therefore, hugely important to heads, colleagues and, more importantly, their pupils. Burnout and attrition, about which there is so much concern, may be the tip of an enormous iceberg. What lies beneath the surface? What factors help or hinder the capacity of those who are more experienced to teach to their best? Who are these so called 'veterans'?

Defining 'veteran' teachers: a tangled web

According to the *Oxford English Dictionary* (2006), 'veteran' originates from the Latin word *veteranus,* meaning 'old'. A veteran is 'a person who has had long experience in a particular field' (ibid.: 853). Based on this definition, veteran teachers are those who have served in the teaching profession for a lengthy period of time. However, what is missing in the literature is a consensus on the length of experience that qualifies a teacher to be identified as a 'veteran'. In some studies, teachers with only seven or eight years of experience are already seen as 'veterans' (e.g. Rich and Almozlino, 1999; Teitelbaum, 2008); by contrast, others regard those with as many as 15 or even 35 years of experience as 'veterans' (e.g. Brundage, 1996; Cohen, 1988). This lack of clarity, particularly the interchangeable use of 'experienced' and 'veteran' in the literature (Feiman-Nemser, 2003; Kauffman *et al.*, 2002; Moore Johnson and Kardos, 2002; Snoeyink and Ertmer, 2002), tends to imply the professional homogeneity of this group of teachers, and thus fails to contribute to knowledge and understanding of the differentiated nature of teachers' work and lives in different phases of their careers. For example, veteran teachers with six or seven years of experience are very likely to have distinctively different professional identities and characteristics from those who have served in teaching for over 30 years. Thus, current notions of veteran teachers do not enable detailed examination of the characteristics and effectiveness of those ageing, experienced teachers who form the majority in many countries.

It is also important to note, as Margolis' (2008) study on teachers' career cycles reports, that a veteran teacher is not necessarily an expert teacher. This observation is in line with Huberman's (1993) and other scholars' criticism of traditional 'stage theory', which conceptualises teachers' professional learning and development as moving through a number of linear skills-development stages (see Chapter 2). Thus, in relation to debates on experience and expertise, the single most important conclusion from recent research is that, although veteran teachers may have experienced many years of teaching and become proficient in routines in their classrooms and schools, they will not necessarily have become expert teachers.

Taking into account the original meaning of *veteran,* i.e. *veteranus* ('old') and the classification of older workers in organisational psychology (i.e. aged 45 and above), and building upon the identification of teachers' six distinctive professional life phases in the VITAE research, we propose veteran teachers as those who have served in the teaching profession for 24 years or more – i.e. teachers who are in the final two phases of their professional lives.

Factors that sustain or hinder veteran teachers' commitment and resilience: portraits of four teachers

Huberman's (1993) research on secondary and middle school teachers' lives in Switzerland found that teachers in the later stages[2] of their career became either 'disenchanted' or 'serene' as they approached retirement. The VITAE research provided broad confirmation of this picture, but also more nuanced portraits of teachers' lives and work, finding that a distinctive sub-group of the teachers in the final two phases of their professional lives (24–30 years and 31+ years) demonstrated, alongside 'serenity' and 'positive focusing', a high level of motivation and commitment and a strong sense of 'active' engagement in the profession. However, it showed, also, differences in the relative proportions of teachers in each group who were sustaining their commitment, motivation and sense of efficacy. Whereas overall, the positive and negative trajectories of veteran teachers were 57 per cent ($n = 42$) and 43 per cent ($n = 32$) respectively, when their professional life phases were analysed more closely, there was a marked difference between those with 24–30 years of experience and those with 31+ years of experience. Table 6.1 shows that there were a relatively larger proportion of teachers in the 24–30 range who were in a negative trajectory than in the 31+ range. Although the numbers of teachers in each phase were relatively small, this might suggest a particular support need for teachers who have, likely, up to 15 more years of service before retirement.

Professional life phase 24–30 years: challenges to sustaining motivation

Teachers in this professional life phase began to face more intensive challenges to sustain their motivation in the profession, compared with their early and mid-years colleagues. Forty-six out of 52 teachers (88 per cent) (31 primary (97 per cent); 15 secondary, (75 per cent)) had additional leadership responsibilities. In contrast to teachers in the previous four professional life phases (i.e. early and mid-years teachers), where a clear majority reported positive professional outlooks, close to half in this professional life phase found that it had become a struggle to continue to give their best to the profession. Resentment at being forced to jump through hoops by a constant stream of new initiatives, taking stock of their careers (and

Table 6.1 Professional commitment trajectories of teachers in late professional life phases (24+ years of experience)

	Professional life phase 24–30 (n = 52)	Professional life phase 31+ (n = 22)
Positive trajectories	54 per cent	64 per cent
Negative trajectories	46 per cent	36 per cent

lives) and length of service in the school exercised strong negative impacts on the perceived effectiveness of teachers in this professional life phase.

On the basis of their levels of motivation and commitment, two sub-groups were identified:

1   Sub-group *a*: teachers who had sustained a strong sense of motivation and commitment (+28) (19 primary (59 per cent); nine secondary (45 per cent)) and who were most likely to continue to enjoy an increase in their self-efficacy, motivation and commitment.
2   Sub-group *b*: teachers holding on but losing motivation, which was most likely, without intervention, to lead to a sense of detachment and early retirement (−24) (13 primary (41 per cent); 11 secondary (55 per cent)).

Figures 6.1 and 6.2 illustrate the weighting of key critical influences on teachers' work (see also Chapter 3). In common with findings for early and middle professional life phases, support from school leadership and colleagues were shown to continue to exert an important impact on teachers' ability to manage (or not manage) their sense of commitment and motivation. A lack of support was reported as having worked against the moral of these teachers. In addition, good-quality professional development opportunities, also a key critical influence in the category of practice settings, were perceived to be consistently positive factors in boosting teachers' morale, commitment and motivation. Moreover, in line with findings for their younger peers, teacher–pupil relationships continued

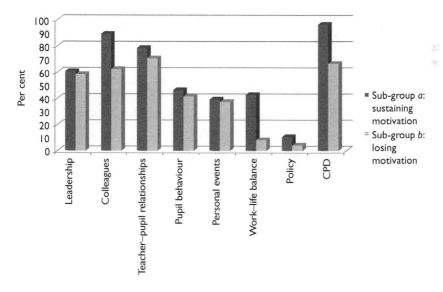

Figure 6.1 Positive critical influences reported by sub-group *a* (*n* = 28) and sub-group *b* teachers (*n* = 24).

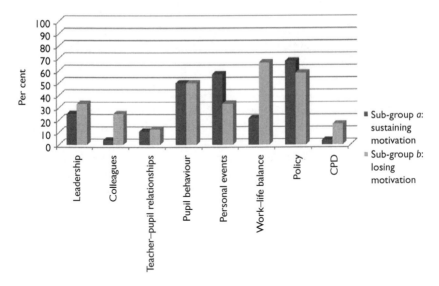

Figure 6.2 Negative critical influences reported by sub-group *a* (*n* = 28) and sub-group *b* teachers (*n* = 24).

to contribute to the positive professional identities of teachers in the final phases of their professional lives.

In contrast, critical influences – such as external policies and initiatives, work–life tensions and deteriorating pupil behaviour – imposed particularly strong challenges to the motivation and commitment of sub-group *b* teachers, who reported that they would consider early retirement or part-time teaching if their financial situation permitted.

Professional life phase 31+: sustaining/declining motivation, ability to cope with change, looking to retire

Two sub-groups were identified based on teachers' levels of commitment and motivation:

1   Sub-group *a*: teachers whose motivation and commitment remained high despite or because of changing personal, professional and organisational contexts and whose expected trajectories were continuing to develop strong agency, efficacy and achievement (+14) (seven primary (64 per cent); seven secondary (64 per cent)).
2   Sub-group *b*: teachers whose motivation was declining or had declined, and whose expected trajectories were increased fatigue, disillusionment and exit (–8) (four primary (37 per cent); four secondary (37 per cent)).

In contrast to Huberman's (1993) observation that there is a 'distinct phase of "disengagement" (serene or bitter)' towards the end of teachers' careers, a clear majority of the teachers in the final phase of their professional lives in the VITAE study had maintained a strong sense of purpose and agency (belief that they can make a difference in the lives and achievements of their pupils) to fulfil their enduring commitment to teaching – a meaningful profession which they believed shapes the lives of future generations.

Patterns of the effects of critical influences were very similar to those found for teachers in the professional life phase 24–30 years (Figures 6.3 and 6.4). On the one hand, support from leadership, colleagues and the home environment were shown to have played a critical part in helping most teachers sustain their commitment, and pupils' progress and positive teacher–pupil relationships were at the heart of their job satisfaction. On the other hand, a lack of work–life balance and national policy initiatives were perceived by 19 out of the 22 veteran teachers as having worked against their morale and ability to maintain their high level of commitment in the profession.

In sum, for most teachers with over 24 years of experience, the immense value and self-worth that they derived from their pupils' growth served to reinforce and fulfil their original calling to teach, enhanced their morale and built their psychological, intellectual, social and professional resources, which charged them with emotional strengths necessary to manage the negative influences they might experience. Key negative influences which were identified included

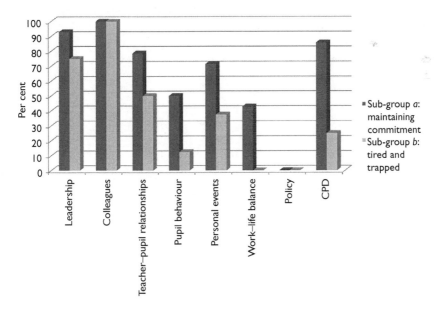

Figure 6.3 Positive critical influences reported by sub-group *a* (*n* = 14) and sub-group *b* teachers (*n* = 8).

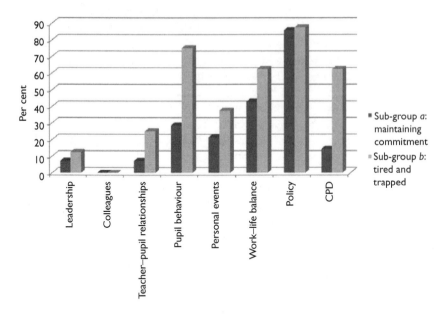

Figure 6.4 Negative critical influences reported by sub-group *a* (*n* = 14) and sub-group *b* teachers (*n* = 8).

national policies, excessively bureaucratic results-driven systems, disruptive pupil behaviour, poor health, heavy workloads and the consequent long working hours. They had negatively impacted upon the motivation and self-efficacy of teachers in this professional life phase. For these teachers, in-school support played a major part in their continued commitment to improving their knowledge within the classroom, and professional identity was crucial to their sense of professionalism. As the following four portraits of veteran teachers will show, it is teachers' ability to manage the interactions between their internal values, sense of professional competence and agency and the external environments in which they work and live that determine the extent to which they are able to draw upon positive emotional and professional resources, and exercise their resilient qualities, rebounding from disappointments and adversity, sustaining their commitment to the profession, and with this, their effectiveness.

Story 1: restoring lost commitment – the key role of leadership

> You hope to make them enjoy learning, you hope to make them feel that they want to come to school. And if they are happy, they will learn. I still love coming into work each day.
>
> (Andrew)

In the first portrait, we illustrate the influence of school leadership upon a veteran teacher's ambition to remain in teaching and, in doing so, to continue to strive for improvement.

> Andrew was 53 years old and had taught for 33 years, 16 of them in his current primary school of 200+ pupils. He was a member of the school leadership team, responsible for maths, design and technology and physical education. The school was in an urban area with moderate socio-economic status, with 13 per cent of pupils eligible for free school meals (FSM2), close to the national average. The proportion of pupils who were of an ethnic heritage other than white British was 75 per cent, the largest groups being from Eastern European, Pakistani and Chinese backgrounds. Sixty per cent spoke English as an additional language. The proportion of pupils who had special educational needs was 27.8 per cent, which was above the national average.
>
> Recently, the school had been put in special measures, but came out of special measures a year later under a new head's leadership. An independent inspection report found that standards of attainment were rising and revealed 'significant improvement'. The leadership and management of the new head were judged to be good:
>
> > Her commitment and determination to improve the school are clear. The senior leadership team has been re-established and is making sound progress ... the staff have shown considerable commitment to her ... [and] ... the parents appreciate her open and communicative style.

Andrew came into teaching because he had 'hated' school and thought that he could do better. He was still enjoying teaching in the school. Each day he arrived at 7.30 a.m. and left at 5.30 p.m. He lived about one hour's travel time away. His only negative was that sometimes the paperwork became 'a bit much': 'I don't know whether or not now, with all the paperwork, it would be something I would do if I was just starting.'

The school leadership was very supportive and 'quite open about what is happening'. His colleagues were 'always very helpful and supportive', if he needed any assistance. The staff worked as a team and people were not left to do things on their own.

> I just think we're a very close staff. We're a small staff, which does make things easier, but we do try whenever there's any stressful situation to get out of an evening all together, so we can sit and talk away from the environment, which is a big help.

Andrew talked about his resentment of the excessive paperwork and saw it as having negatively impacted on his morale: 'It's absolutely ridiculous. Why do you always have to write down what you are doing?' He thought that the heavy workload had resulted in high mobility of staff at his school. He complained about the cost of living in the area in relation to teacher salaries. He felt demotivated when reflecting on the 'value' placed on teachers by society. He disapproved of the target-driven culture and felt that SATs were a 'demoralising event' for both himself and his students.

Andrew had good relationships with the children and parents, but found it 'distressing and unfair' that some parents targeted new teachers and were destructive towards them. He saw the culturally diverse backgrounds of the pupils as a strength of his school.

> You do what you think is best for the children in this school and this school is different from other schools. The number of nationalities we have in this school, we have from all over the place, which is wonderful. I love it but you've got to be careful the way you do things.

Andrew had moved to teach a different year group recently. He was enjoying teaching and 'getting his head' around teaching different aspects of the curriculum to younger children, without the pressure of end-of-year national testing that he had with his previous class. He had always been highly motivated and committed to teaching. Pupils were always the main source of his job satisfaction and he continued to gain immense pleasure and enjoyment from seeing them blossom: 'When you see how the children move on you definitely have great job satisfaction.' He was confident that he made a difference in the lives and learning of his pupils.

> They turn up. They are always there, normally smiling, knowing that if I am having a go at them, it is not at them personally. It is because I feel they can do more and that I want them to achieve, which I think they know.

Andrew's workline shows his sense of effectiveness over time following an initial entry period in which he built his classroom management and teaching skills and established his sense of professional identity. It shows, also, that in the mid-career, 'watershed' phase, he sought new professional challenges through promotion to a different school. His renewed enthusiasm, commitment and strong sense of self-efficacy were maintained until an adverse external inspection report placed his school in 'special measures'. However, within a year the school had recovered under the leadership of a new head: 'There have been quite big changes in the school. Management have got an awful lot sorted out and have worked hard. Everything is working well at the moment.'

This had resulted in a change of teaching group for Andrew, significant in that he no longer taught the year group that was subject to national testing. This had a positive effect on his work life. As the workline was 'unpacked' during further conversations, it became clear that Andrew continued to be devoted to his pupils, despite his distaste for the effects of reforms upon his work.

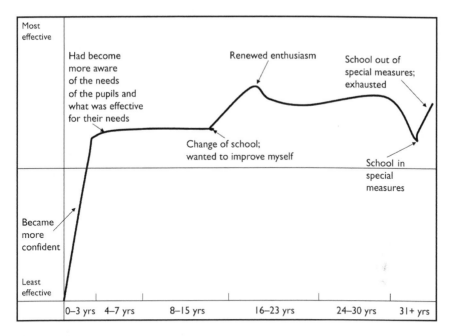

Workline 11   Andrew's workline.

Story 2: continuing to grow in a stable environment

> I always wanted to teach – teachers are in my family. I wouldn't want
> another job.
>
> (Helen)

In this second example, we show how positive in-school support can revitalise a
teacher's commitment and motivation and enable her to manage work–life tensions and continue to fulfil her original calling to teach in the final phases of her
professional life.

Helen was 47 years old and had worked previously at five other schools. She
had taught Year 6 (10–11-year-old) pupils in her current village primary
school of 100+ pupils for nine years. The school had a close-knit, stable staff
and Helen was the literacy and assessment coordinator. According to the
external school inspection report, almost all pupils lived in private housing
where levels of prosperity were high relative to the national average. No pupils
were eligible for free school meals and all spoke English as their first language.
Parents were not always satisfied with the amount of homework set or the
amount of information about their child's progress. The school was embedded in the local community and Helen knew many of the families. Her pupils

> visited 'elderly friends' at harvest festival time, and there was a whole-school play at Christmas time, with a special afternoon performance for these friends. For Helen, parental and community support had positively impacted on her level of commitment: 'When that's all working really well together, it's great. I wouldn't want another job.'

Helen had always wanted to teach and still enjoyed her work. She found planning her lessons very time consuming, but emphasised that her school's policies on curriculum, pupil behaviour, target setting, learning support and CPD were highly important and that they 'make me more focused on the pupils'. On the negative side, she stated that there was 'not enough time to digest and work on new initiatives'. She worked between 55–60 hours each week, experienced a high level of stress and took work home in the evenings and weekends. However, this only occasionally adversely affected her teaching and she was satisfied that she was able to make a real difference in the learning and achievement of her pupils. In the last two years Helen had classroom help for one hour per day from the SEN coordinator to help with literacy, and was provided with three extra hours per week to help with science. Alongside this, Helen also had a classroom teaching assistant (TA) for an hour each day. The classroom support required extra planning work on Helen's part, but they had all worked together for some time and knew each other's ways. Without this help she believed that she would be struggling.

She was confident in her ability to make a difference to her pupils' learning, though 'it depends on the cohort, and the group as well'. She described her self-efficacy as going 'up and down quite a lot'. Helen derived immense job satisfaction from her pupils' good SATs results and progress. She believed that she had a positive impact on her pupils.

> On the whole the self-esteem of the children has improved and they're ready to move on, so I feel I've got there.... I am very direct with them and they know exactly where they stand with me. I try to be fair but also depending on specific children's needs, I think I must be doing something right because this particular difficult child is a lot calmer. The strange behaviour he was showing last year has gone and he merged in with the whole crowd.

Like Andrew, Helen 'disapproved' of the target-driven culture. She was now less concerned about the 'imposition' of external standards because she believed them to be misleading and inaccurate and not focused on pupils' individual contexts. She thought that these standards ignored the individual context and had a negative effect on pupils due to having to take so many tests. Because of changes in the curriculum tests, Helen had found it stressful trying to keep on top of things. Nevertheless, she remained highly motivated within the classroom.

The challenge of balancing home and work life had been a barrier to her taking on further responsibility at school: 'My family would complain that I spend all my time with school and then when I am at home it is all school work.' Her eldest son had recently left home for university and this had changed the dynamics at home. Her life now revolved increasingly around school.

Helen's workline shows that she spent her early years of teaching in a challenging urban school, where she was provided with no targeted support. Initially, her second school had provided her with opportunities to improve her teaching and take on more leadership and management responsibilities. However, she had little support when she was covering another teacher's maternity leave and felt inadequate. Her morale rose again when she changed year group and became part of a supportive team. Recognition of her work from the school inspection and the head, coupled with her promotion to head of Year 5, had resulted in a dramatic increase in her morale and feelings of effectiveness as a teacher.

Three years later, Helen had moved to another school for a higher salary. She saw her sense of efficacy decrease during this period, which coincided with her marriage breakdown. This sense of low morale lasted for two years until she moved to a different area with her two children. She started teaching again as a supply teacher, but had to give up in the end because her journey to school was

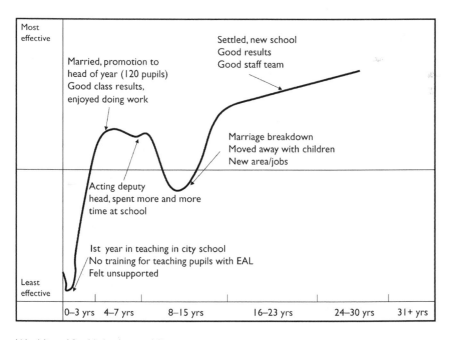

Workline 12   Helen's workline.

too long and she had less time for her own children. She found work in her current school, where she felt more settled, and enjoyed her pupils' good exam results and staff support. As a consequence, Helen saw her sense of efficacy and morale rise again.

The school encouraged supportive relationships between the staff. The support 'is just there': 'It is difficult to put your finger on it, but it is there for the children, for colleagues, and the staff.'

> I'm in a very happy environment in this school. We get on really well as a team in this school and we support each other, whether we're going through a good time, a bad time or whatever. I don't think the children would realise because everyone moves in and covers. It's a nice environment here. It's a lovely school. A good leader leads from the top and you know exactly where you are. The head will support us and advise. I think that underpins everything.

Helen identified 'very supportive leadership' as a key feature of her school experience. She greatly appreciated that the head (a teaching head) understood the challenges of the classroom teachers as part of her own regular experience. The school was 'good' on support on personal issues. During the project, the current head retired and a new head was appointed. The new head had been readily accepted and Helen described her as having, 'new ideas but there is a good two way communication'.

It was the combination of her own vocation, colleagues, good leadership, supportive parents and the intimacy of the small 'village like' environment of the school itself that enabled her to sustain her strong commitment.

Story 3: still committed but about to disengage – managing work–life tensions

> I can't imagine why a young person would want to come into teaching quite frankly. That's why they're leaving – they come and they see and they try. It's not me ... It's the attitude of children and things you have to do. No child of mine would ever teach. Over my dead body.
>
> (Faith)

In Faith, we see an example of how the effects of changes – in this case, changes in the nature of 'accountability' and 'trust' environments and the attitudes and behaviours of pupils – may test the capacity of teachers to sustain their commitment over a lifetime of teaching. Despite this, the teacher continued to gain her satisfaction from her classroom teaching – why she came into teaching in the first place – and the support of close colleagues.

Faith had taught for 31 years in a Roman Catholic school with 1,000+ pupils, set in a semi-rural area in the North of England. She described herself as working in 'a very caring school and environment' where she could turn to any member of staff and be supported. She enjoyed working in her department, in which people worked together well – 'there is a lot of work and expectation of high standards, but you're supported as well'. Her head of department was 'fantastic', 'very supportive' and 'efficient' and this was 'very encouraging' and 'motivating' for her. Although Faith had maintained her commitment, she had become tired and frequently stressed.

Originally, Faith described herself as 'falling' into teaching: 'In those days teaching was seen as a good job for women. It fitted in well with family and children.'

Ironically, it was personal contexts which continued to affect her. Despite the fact that her family were now grown up, she felt that stress at work made it impossible for her to establish a 'work–life balance' and that it had caused deterioration in her home relationships. The recent, unexpected death of a close colleague had also caused her to reflect upon the amount of work she did.

Like many teachers, she began work at 8.15 a.m., arrived home late and continued to work at home. This had led to a decline in self-efficacy (her belief in

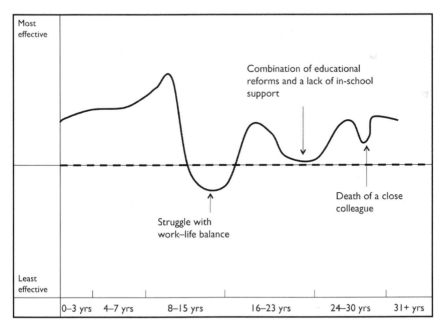

Workline 13 Faith's workline.

her ability to make a difference) and, over the years, her resilience had been eroded. She attributed this to a raft of externally imposed initiatives which had resulted, in her view, in unnecessary additional workload. Chief among these were the national standard attainment tests (SATs) which had 'steadily chipped away at my confidence' and left her with 'absolutely no self belief'. This had led to sleepless nights. The deterioration of pupil behaviour and pupils' declining respect for teachers had also affected her motivation. She criticised the 'general movement' in which pupils were now expected to talk and speak out for their rights without equal attention to teachers' rights.

In common with Andrew and Helen, Faith had become increasingly resentful of externally imposed changes. The lack of support from the school senior leadership team put a greater strain on her work. In her own words, 'we are pushed to succeed' and 'this has created real pressures for teachers'. She blamed the SLT for the heavy workloads teachers had:

> They [SLT] are more interested in becoming a leading edge college and the people who are teaching in the classroom are forgotten. Teachers have 220 pieces of work to mark a week but only six half-hour free lessons a week which leaves a lot of work to be done at home. There seems to be no thought about this on the part of SLT – and half of free lessons are lost each week filling in for absent colleagues – the classroom teachers are hit very hard as far as time goes.

In addition to these challenges, she expressed concerns over the deterioration of pupil behaviour and believed that it was a general trend through society: 'children are more challenging'. Nevertheless, she described the overall behaviour of the pupils in her school as 'generally good', and this enabled her to focus on teaching and learning without fear of disruption by pupils.

Faith felt that her motivation had decreased over the last three years because of the external changes and initiatives that had been imposed on teachers. She did not agree that teachers 'should be made to teach in the same way' because they all had different strengths. She thought that there should be 'scope for the individuality of teachers' and a period for the consolidation of new initiatives and changes. As a consequence of these negative influences, Faith had come to feel less 'enthusiastic' and 'inspirational'.

She had, however, tried to overcome these issues. Whilst they had not affected her motivation to teach to the best of her ability and enjoy the 'fun' with the children, they had affected the satisfaction she obtained from teaching. Her commitment remained high because of a sense of professional pride. Although wanting the pupils to exceed expectations was still 'an ideal to which I am committed', she was only five years away from retirement and planned to move into part-time teaching in the school.

Story 4: holding on but losing motivation – the school effect

> Personally I love working down here. It's the best place I've ever worked for the team spirit, keenness and motivation that I have and the rest of the department has.
>
> (Michael)

This final example illustrates how a lack of in-school support, compounded with adverse personal events, can serve to challenge the commitment and motivation of the most dedicated teachers – despite the positive support of colleagues.

> Michael had taught English in this 11–16 age group school of almost 800 pupils for four years, having been in nine other schools over a 22-year period. He was also the school's literacy coordinator. The school drew its (mainly white) pupils from public housing areas of a town which suffered from severe socio-economic deprivation and associated drug/alcohol-related problems. Approximately 43 per cent were entitled to free school meals and the majority were well below the national average in attainment levels in English, maths and science on entry. Both authorised and unauthorised pupil absences were well above national comparative data. Many were from single-parent homes, with high levels of unemployment. Whilst he described his relationships with pupils as being positive, he also identified the behaviour in a significant minority as 'challenging'.

Michael had always wanted to teach and the satisfaction he gained from this and working closely with his colleagues was still at the centre of his professional life. In this sense, his motivation and commitment had not dimmed. He achieved good examination results with his pupils and had been assessed as 'excellent' in an Ofsted report on the quality of his teaching. This had boosted his sense of self-efficacy.

> Over here [department] I'm happy, I'm enjoying things, I'm with people that I rate and value and I feel value me, and I'm working in an environment I'm happy with and I've created with pupils I get on with.

Michael's workline indicates that his sense of effectiveness had experienced sharp dips during his career. After 16 years of teaching, he found a new job as head of year. But he had soon seen his morale and self-efficacy decrease because of tiredness (he was commuting three hours per day), difficult pupils, excessive paperwork and politics.

His job at this school as social inclusion manager had initially boosted his morale. His main responsibility involved improving social inclusion for those students who were experiencing either short-term or long-term social, emotional or behavioural difficulties in order to enhance their educational performance and

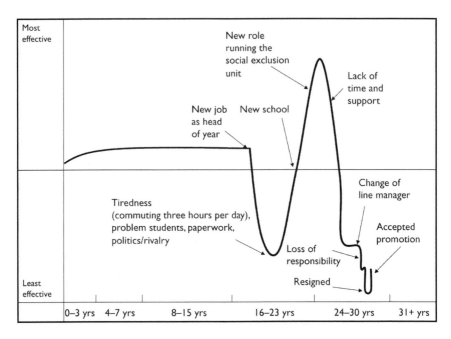

Workline 14   Michael's workline.

social interaction. However, the increase in his sense of effectiveness had only lasted for a year or two. Three critical incidents negatively affected his work life – a lack of time, support and the change of his line manager. As a consequence, his morale and self-efficacy diminished so much that he submitted his resignation. He was persuaded to retract this, was promoted to his present position of school literacy coordinator, and felt that his sense of self-efficacy had increased as a result. During this period he had separated from his wife of more than 20 years and had growing financial concerns, although he felt personally 'much happier now' and had recently found a new partner. However, he continued to experience a decline in his job satisfaction and sense of wellbeing. He had no support from the head and, despite promotion to school literacy coordinator, was actively seeking another job.

He felt that there was no future for him at his current school. He saw the senior management team as having a lack of focus and initiative, and believed that this was the consequence of the head's poor management.

> I've worked with nine different headteachers and she is the worst without a shadow of a doubt. No consistency, no communication, no logical progression. It's all knee jerk. With someone like that you can't see it changing until the head leaves.

The climate in the school was dominated by accountability and fear of not getting the required level of results. Michael, then, whilst still getting 'a buzz' from his classroom teaching, described himself as 'holding on but losing motivation'. He attributed this to the lack of positive support from the head and the senior management team.

Discussion

Variations in the professional experiences of these four veteran teachers suggest that the provision of appropriate and responsive support in their work contexts is key to ensuring and promoting the quality and wellbeing of their professional lives in teaching. When such support is available, veteran teachers are more likely to sustain their commitment, motivation, resilience, self-efficacy and capacity to teach to their best, despite possible health problems and other negative influences in their work and lives. Their experiences, their educational values and their sense of vocation also serve as important sources of wisdom and strength which enable them to bounce back from adverse circumstances and continue to fulfil their original calling to teach.

Andrew, Helen and Michael all became teachers with an 'inner urge' (Hansen, 1995: 9) to make a difference in the learning and achievement of their pupils. Such an inner urge, or sense of vocation, had a decisive impact upon their perceptions of their role with students, and upon their willingness to exercise their agency and resilience in difficult conditions to sustain and improve the quality of their work (ibid.). For all three, at an earlier point in their professional lives, a positive belief in their capacity to help each child reach their full potential in learning had enhanced their sense of efficacy and 'optimism' in the profession (Hoy et al., 2008). However, lack of support or recognition of worth in the work environments, as in the case of Helen, can lead to diminishing commitment, decreasing job fulfilment and enthusiasm and a sense of detachment. Long ago, Eliot (1871–2 [1985]: 896) reminded us that 'there is no creature whose inward being is so strong, that it is not greatly determined by what lies outside it' (cited from Hansen, 1995: 90). For Andrew and Helen, professional trust and support from their current heads revived their sense of vocation and gave them the motivation and strength to devote themselves whole-heartedly to the progress and growth of their pupils – to the last day and last minute of their professional lives in teaching.

Teachers with 24–30 years of experience form a significant proportion of the total teaching force. They have ahead of them at least another decade in the profession. Understanding factors that help or hinder them in their management of their work and lives is important for schools and policy makers if these teachers are to continue to maintain educational standards and fulfil their moral responsibility and obligation for the growth and quality of future generations.

There is a growing recognition of the value to organisations of older workers, indicating that they perform as well as younger, less experienced workers, and that they demonstrate more positive work values (Griffiths, 2007a, 2007b; Rhodes, 1983; Warr, 1994). Griffiths (2007b: 124) asserts that 'many common myths and stereotypes about older workers' decreased performance and availability for work are not accurate' (see also Benjamin and Wilson, 2005; Waldman and Avolio, 1986). Capitalising upon experience is clearly a good investment strategy:

> On a more positive front, employers could focus on older workers' strengths; they could capitalise on their job knowledge, encourage them to take on mentoring and coaching roles, and encourage horizontal as well as vertical mobility. By exploring what older workers want from the latter stages of their working lives, it may be possible to maximise their job satisfaction and performance.
>
> (Griffiths, 2007a: 55)

In this respect, it is important to note the differentiated roles that 'outside' support plays in different phases of teachers' professional lives. For early years teachers, in-school support plays a central role in helping them establish their professional selves within the classroom and the profession (Chapter 2), whilst for mid-years teachers, support is crucial in enabling them to manage professional and personal tensions in the key watershed or crossroads phase of their professional lives, when they face the decisions about whether to stay in the classroom, apply for senior leadership and management roles or leave teaching (Chapter 5).

Veteran teachers, who will have been recipients of, and respondents to, generations of changes in educational policies and societal values over the two or three decades of their teaching lives will continue to need support in adapting, adjusting and learning new ways of working, because reform is often synonymous with the need to change existing (and in the case of veteran teachers, long-held) attitudes, values and practices.

Veteran teachers, more than any others, to a greater or lesser extent, may well regard reforms, however well intentioned and efficacious, as a challenge to the values, status, experience and expertise which they have nurtured and honed throughout their professional lives. In their study on the sustainability of reform through the lens of teachers' nostalgia, Goodson *et al.* (2006: 42) claimed that

> As teachers age, their responses to change are influenced not only by processes of degeneration (loss of commitment, energy, enthusiasm, etc.) but also by the agendas of the generation – historically situated missions formed decades ago that teachers have carried with them throughout their careers.

Whilst this is likely to be the case generally, it assumes a world without the possibility of change for individuals whose responses may be affected by other, more contemporary interventions. Despite the experience for some teachers in their later years of declining energy, 'embittered' experiences of the present (Lasch, 1991) and nostalgia for the past, many continue to demonstrate a strong sense of commitment to their work – particularly within workplaces where there is sympathetic and supportive management, as shown in Faith's story. Indeed, the positive professional outlooks of the majority of those with 31+ years of experience would seem to challenge over-generalised notions of degeneration.

Teachers with 24–30 years of experience are also more likely to face extreme professional life phase scenarios in addition to processes and agendas of degeneration. Pupil behaviour, adverse personal events, resentment at 'being forced to jump through hoops by a constant stream of new initiatives', and career stagnation were key negative influences on the morale, professional identity, commitment and effectiveness of teachers in our study. These teachers, mostly aged 45+, were also undergoing a life transition and a change in identity where they began to face increasingly frequent occurrences of age-related deficits and work–life tensions. In other words, their journeys into 'veteranhood' and the ultimate 'third age' were accompanied by constant demands for workplace adjustments. Almost half of the teachers in this professional life phase demonstrated a negative professional outlook – holding on but losing motivation – as in the case of Michael, and struggled to manage extreme fluctuations caused by combined negative influences from outside and within the workplace and their professional and personal lives. In-school support that focused on mediating the effects of unsolicited and undesired external policy initiatives, and assisted them in adjusting successfully to these, had a significant role to play in sustaining their motivation and commitment and enabled them to teach to their best (Day and Gu, 2007). Helen's renewed enjoyment of teaching towards the final phase of her professional life provides strong testimony of the importance of such support.

Conclusions: sustaining commitment

This chapter has shown how, in the emotional contexts of life in schools and classrooms, pupils' progress and positive teacher–pupil relationships provides the main source of job satisfaction, motivation and sense of achievement for teachers in the later phases of their professional lives. These positive emotions are able to be 'banked' or 'stored'. They function as reserves in times of challenge, which fuel and promote teachers' sense of resilience and commitment (Fredrickson, 2004). Key to this is the in-school support of heads and colleagues.

As we have illustrated in the preceding chapters, however, it is the management of combinations of personal, situated and policy-related circumstances over time which affect teachers' resilience. It is unlikely, also, that enthusiasm and motivation will be able to be sustained without the active support of significant others. In this respect, research into teachers' work and lives has noted consistently the importance of the influence of the school head and close colleagues. Thus, as well as being concerned with recruitment, it may be that policy makers should also focus on retaining the commitment of the existing majority of their more experienced colleagues.

Sustaining veteran teachers' sense of commitment, belief in their capacity to teach to their best, resilience and wellbeing is an important part of what we called in our earlier work 'quality retention' (Day et al., 2007). It has profound implications for the standards agenda because, as we have noted earlier, the current teaching reality is that the population of teachers in most Western countries is ageing (OECD, 2004, 2005). In most OECD countries, the majority of primary and secondary school teachers are above 40 years of age. In the United States, two-thirds of its teaching force has to be renewed in the next decade (Guttman, 2001). In England, 40 per cent of all teachers are aged 45–55, and those aged over 55 account for another 6 per cent of the workforce (Chevalier and Dolton, 2004). Thus, while it is necessary for most governments to recruit and retain capable and committed younger teachers, it is equally important for them to promote veteran teachers' willingness, abilities and capacities to teach to their best in the classroom and school (Gu and Day, 2007).

The illustrations of four veteran teachers in this chapter provide three important messages for researchers, school leaders and policy makers interested in understanding teachers' work, lives and effectiveness, and raising and maintaining standards.

The first message is that there are associations between teachers' wellbeing, commitment and their capacity to teach to their best. It follows that researchers need to examine what supports and builds and, on the other hand, what adversely affects veteran teachers' commitment. These four stories show that there are likely to be a combination of factors (poor leadership, changes in the social dynamic of classroom teaching, working conditions, challenges to long-held notions of professional identity, and wellbeing – as well as generational and ageing factors) which may erode teacher commitment, causing either early burnout – as in the case of Faith – or gradually feeling tired and trapped – as in the case of Michael.

The second message, for school leaders and those who recruit and provide training programmes for teachers, is that attending to the broader personal wellbeing of staff – through building trust via genuine regard and sustained interaction – must go alongside the raising of expectations and relentless pursuit of standards.

The third message, for policy makers, is that to ignore the specific commitment and resilience needs of this large group of veteran teachers is to fail to realise the long-term investment that they and their employers have made to teaching. It is this group that – at least in theory – should be at the peak of their expertise and teaching wisdom. It is this group that should be providing a model for their less experienced colleagues. Rather than fighting off difficult challenges, they should and could be beacons of hope and optimism for all.

Part III

Conditions for success

Chapter 7

Teacher commitment

A necessary condition for success?

Introduction

> The teaching pool keeps losing water because no-one is paying attention to the leak. That is, we're misdiagnosing the problem as 'recruitment' when it's really retention.
>
> (Merrow, 1999: 64)

This chapter focuses on issues of teacher commitment as a factor in what we have elsewhere termed 'quality retention' (Day *et al.*, 2007). We use this phrase as a means of focusing on the importance not only of retaining teachers in classrooms, but ensuring, as far as possible, that their commitment to making a difference in the learning lives and achievement of their pupils is sustained and, where appropriate, revisited, reviewed and renewed. Little attention has been paid to this in the past and, as a consequence, most resources have been invested in recruitment and pre-service training and development programmes. Yet, for those concerned with standards of teaching, learning and achievement, it is vital, also, to ensure that teachers are supported in ways that ensure they do more than survive and maintain a minimum level of basic professional and pedagogical competence over their 30+ years in schools.

Research perspectives

Teacher commitment has been identified as one of the most critical factors in the progress and achievement of students (Day *et al.*, 2007; Huberman, 1993; Nias, 1981). If you talk with any teacher, teacher educator, schools inspector, headteacher, teacher or parent about reform in raising standards or the quality of education, it will not be very long before the word 'commitment' enters into the conversation. They 'know', also, that without commitment, change efforts – those within and especially those which are initiated from outside the school or other organisation – will be limited in their success.

Commitment to the workplace is understood as 'a hallmark of organisational success' (Rosenholtz and Simpson, 1990: 241). In their research, Rosenholtz and Simpson (ibid.) found that the commitment of teachers to their profession and to the schools in which they work varied across different phases of their professional lives. Their research supports our observations regarding the impact of critical influences on teachers' work and lives (Chapter 3), which points to the importance of various qualities of organisational contexts in promoting or hindering teachers' ability to sustain their professional beliefs and emotional commitment. For example, to avoid teacher stress and burnout, Rosenholtz and Simpson (ibid.) argue that teachers' felt commitment and performance will be enhanced most by different kinds of organisational support that are fit for the purpose and are context sensitive over the course of their professional lives.

Like other more experienced teachers, Peter had experienced many changes of policy and practice during his 21 years of teaching. Not all were to his liking, and he expressed considerable frustration with many of the broad policy changes from relative teacher classroom autonomy to increased results and target-driven teaching, more prescriptive curricula and the external school inspection regime that had resulted in the school being placed on 'special measures', the failing category. He saw all of these as detracting from his capacity to add value to pupil learning and achievement rather than improving it as they were intended to do, and felt that they and those who advocated them, contributed to the erosion of his long-held values of autonomy and creativity in the classroom because the school itself had been placed on 'special measures' for a period.

> I don't feel able to relax now that my teaching is being rigorously monitored by local authority and national school inspectors.
>
> (Peter)
>
> Peter felt that, until recently, 'a disproportionate' part of the day was given over to literacy and numeracy teaching, that there were fewer opportunities for cross-curricular activities and that curricula guidelines acted as a 'straightjacket'. He believed that many had left teaching 'because they no longer have the opportunity to explore with children what they [the teachers] know they can do well'. For Peter, teaching had become 'more tiring with more pressures and less satisfaction'. He spoke of fluctuations in his belief that he was able to make a difference:
>
> I'm always OK until it comes to the SATs and then there is a bit of a down.

The following illustration from Faith shows the extent to which changes in assessment procedures and the challenges to her self-belief over the years have eroded her confidence in her belief that her work can make a difference:

Since these SATS I've got absolutely no self-belief. I think as teachers, we're our own worst critics. We're very, very critical, we do evaluate almost every lesson ... and we're always striving, even after 30-odd years I'm still looking to learn and therefore you never feel satisfied, you never feel as being as efficient as you could be. I mean people tell you you've done well, you've made a difference, but I don't know. I don't believe it as much as I used to.

(Faith)

Faith criticised the high levels of external target setting which, far from improving standards, in her view just made things unnecessarily harder for the teacher:

I get so cross about their intervention, because they're not altering my commitment – I teach the way I've always taught; you want to achieve the very best you can like you always have and they're not altering that one iota, it's just making it more difficult and making you feel deflated when you want to do well and want to be committed and do what you've always done ... setting stupid targets doesn't make you more hard working, you can't be.

At my age, I tend to think, 'Is it me, am I becoming disenchanted with it?' But I don't think so. I still want to do a really good job but I think sometimes ... the children are becoming more challenging and more difficult and they just don't treat you with the same respect they used to. I don't know whether we are old-fashioned in our approach at my age ... that is affecting my motivation.

Commitment is also, often, associated with quality. It has been defined as a predictor of teachers' performance, burnout and attrition, as well as having an important influence on students' cognitive, social, behavioural and affective outcomes (Day *et al.*, 2005; Firestone, 1996; Louis, 1998). It is a term often used by teachers to describe themselves and each other (Nias, 1981, 1989a). It is a part of their professional identity (Elliott and Crosswell, 2001), and may be enhanced or diminished by factors such as student behaviour, collegial and administrative support, parental demands, and national educational policies (Day, 2000b; Louis, 1998; Riehl and Sipple, 1996; Tsui and Cheng, 1999). Teachers who are committed have an enduring belief that they can make a difference to the learning lives and achievements of students (efficacy and agency) through *who* they are (their identity), *what* they know (knowledge, strategies, skills) and *how* they teach (their beliefs, attitudes, personal and professional values embedded in and expressed through their context-sensitive behaviours in practice settings).

Ebmeier and Nicklaus (1999) connected the concepts of commitment and emotion, defining commitment as part of a teacher's affective or emotional reaction to their experience in a school setting and part of the process which determines the level of personal investment they make to a particular school or group of students. (We will focus particularly on the emotional dimension in Chapter 9, because this connection is central to understanding teachers' perceptions of their work, colleagues, school leadership, and the interaction between these and their personal lives.)

In a report of empirical research on teachers' commitment in Australia, Crosswell (2006: 109) suggests that there are six dimensions of commitment:

> Commitment as passion
> Commitment as investment of extra time
> Commitment as a focus on the wellbeing and achievement of the student
> Commitment as a responsibility to maintain professional knowledge
> Commitment as transmitting knowledge and/or values
> Commitment as engagement with the school community

Research into retention issues in order to understand the dissatisfaction in teaching in England, Australia and the United States has highlighted consistently the factors of pay, morale and increased workload resulting in lack of time to teach and plan (Bingham, 1991; Day, 2004; Dinham and Scott, 2000; Gold, 1996; *Guardian*, 2003; Ingersoll, 2003; Johnson *et al.*, 2005; PricewaterhouseCoopers, 2001; Smithers and Robinson, 2003). In their major survey of teachers in England that investigated reasons for attrition, Smithers and Robinson (ibid.: 5) reported key reasons for leaving the profession: 'Among secondary teachers the most frequently given reason for going was workload (58% of leavers) followed this time by pupil behaviour (45%). But in 2001 the new category of "government initiatives" had to be added (37%).'

A report by Britain's leading mental health charity (MIND) in 2005 (*Independent*, 2005) found that teachers were among the five most stressed workers – the others being social workers, call centre workers, prison officers and the police. It is not so much the extreme negative acts (e.g. bullying and

> I'm one of those people who would never take anything on unless I can commit to it fully. I've looked at me personally to see if I could manage to take on board all the extra areas, issues and workload that is involved.
>
> (Alison)

Alison provides a good illustration of how personal events and experiences may, at least temporarily, threaten teachers' sense of professional commitment and test their resilience.

She had some 'awful and terrible times' when she was going through a divorce. But she felt that this made her a stronger person. She returned to the gym after an injury. Health and fitness were 'in the forefront' of her life outside of school and as a consequence she felt healthier and more motivated at work.

She is now a single parent and her children study at her current school. Although she has to spend a lot of time on school-related work at home, she does not feel it is a major hindrance to her personal life because teaching is 'so much a part of me that it just fits into my life style'. With both her children now in secondary schools, she was looking forward to 'getting my career back on track'.

other forms of abuse) that some teachers in some schools face on a daily basis, but, as Munn (1999) reported in her analysis of three surveys, the 'drip, drip' effect of seemingly trivial behaviour – such as students talking out of turn, avoiding work and hindering other pupils – which seem to be the most wearisome for teachers (ibid.: 116). It is these, most of all, which without supportive organisational structures, cultures, colleagues and leadership, sap the commitment over time of all but the most resilient teachers.

Commitment is felt by many teachers as part of their professional values and sense of moral purposes. Such commitment is not an option, but a necessity, since it is an essential condition for teachers' success.

Nurturing good teaching that results in successful learning is not something that can be left only to the accumulation of experience by teachers, reflective or otherwise. It must be nurtured by deliberate acts of care by leaders whose job it is to establish and develop conditions for the growth of expertise which provide sustained attention to the four ingredients identified by Fenstermacher and Richardson (2005) as being essential to quality teaching:

1 the teachers' content, task and person knowledge (including self knowledge);
2 the desire to learn and the effort of the learner;
3 the social contexts of family, peers and community, which will exert positive and/or negative influences;
4 the facilities, time and resources necessary to accomplish learning.

It is through an acknowledgement and understanding of the dynamic mix of these ingredients, through acts of care, challenge and support that leaders will promote teaching that is both good and successful. Yet such teaching expertise does not appear overnight in most schools. Whilst it may be present in some, or even many teachers, it takes time to build. It also needs regular attention for, as we see from the examples in this book, there are many challenges posed to teachers which may hinder the individual and collective growth of good and successful teaching. As Michael Huberman observed in his classic study of the lives of teachers, the career development process is filled with 'plateaux, discontinuities, regressions, spurts and dead ends' (Huberman, 1995a: 196).

Although many teachers begin their professional lives 'with a sense that their work is socially meaningful and will yield great satisfactions', this can be lost as

> the inevitable difficulties of teaching ... interact with personal issues and vulnerabilities, as well as social pressure and values, to engender a sense of frustration and force a reassessment of the possibilities of the job and investment one wants to make in it.
>
> (Farber, 1991: 36)

- Career development is often accompanied by 'a sense of inconsequentiality' (ibid.).
- Many teachers in mid-to-late career become disenchanted or marginalise themselves from learning, no longer holding the good of their pupils as a high priority.
- Low self-esteem and shame (at not achieving desired results) are directly correlated with less variety of teaching approaches and thus less connection with students' learning needs.

The expression of commitment is based upon teachers' inner sense of vocation and care (Day, 2004; Fletcher-Campbell, 1995a, 1995b; Hansen, 1995; Nias, 1989a, 1989b; Noddings, 2005, 2007; Palmer, 2007) and, as with the 18 teachers featured in this book, these may fluctuate, increasing or diminishing according to their ability and capacity to manage different work and life circumstances. We have seen, for example, how external policy initiatives may increase workload and how increased accountabilities may impact negatively upon some teachers' sense of self-efficacy, commitment and capacity to teach to their best. We have also seen how these may be mediated by school cultures that promote teachers' professional development and, through this, their sense of belonging, wellbeing and achievement.

Huberman's (1993: 194–195) work demonstrated that teachers who are 'playing out their careers in periods of social turbulence ... or in moments of structural reform within their school system are likely to have different trajectories from peers working in different social environments'. He wrote:

> The quality of the relationship between teacher and pupils can be one of the most rewarding aspects of the teaching profession, but it can also be the source of emotionally draining and discouraging experiences. Because burnout has considerable implications for teachers' performance relative to pupils and colleagues – not to speak of teachers' own well being – it is a problem with serious consequences both for the teaching career and, more fundamentally, for the learning outcomes of pupils themselves.
>
> (Huberman and Vandenberghe, 1999: 3)

Burnout is not a new phenomenon and, over the years, several studies have identified its effects. We know, for example, that:

1   In New York secondary schools, only 50 per cent of the teachers looked forward to each working day in school (Rivera-Batiz and Marti, 1995).
2   Burnout teachers give less information and praise to students, and interact less frequently with them (Mancini *et al.*, 1984).
3   In the United Kingdom, 23 per cent of a sample surveyed indicated having significant illness over the last year (Travers and Cooper, 1996).

I don't think you can become a teacher and not have it impact on home life.

(Claire)

Although aged 36 years, Claire has been teaching for only three years. During this relatively short period, in addition to the initial 'failure' of the school which had affected her professional life, her niece had died unexpectedly and she herself had experienced a major health problem. These unanticipated events had caused her to, 'prioritise differently'. Previously, she had worked at home in the evenings and all day Sunday:

Last year I got so bogged down in everything. I've made an effort to make time for myself. I go to the gym. I've got a cleaner. When I go home with my own children I'm not saying to myself, 'You've got to clean up'. I feel a lot calmer ... I try to keep my work and life very separate. I discipline myself and say, 'No'. I've done enough, the rest of the time belongs to home. I try to do as much as I can in the school, without bringing it home.

Working long hours was a feature of the lives of many teachers in the larger project and this was particularly so for those in their early years and those with additional school-wide responsibilities in the middle phase of their professional lives. Attempting to prioritise between time and effort in work and home environments was not always easy, as Claire's case demonstrates.

Claire had two children of school age. She reported that because of her high commitment to her job, the time she was able to devote to her home life was curtailed. This was a source of tension, also, with her partner. She tried to keep her personal life and work life separate. As she progressed in her teaching career, she was finding more success in achieving this.

As ever, Huberman pointed the way forward:

This is not to say that burnout is endemic to the teaching career but rather that there are sources at the individual, institutional, and societal levels that can compromise career satisfaction: meaningfulness, successful execution, enduring commitment, professional growth through increased experience and the learning of new skills, caring relations with peers and pupils, and the balance between work and family life.

(Huberman and Vandenberghe, 1999: 3–4)

Teaching in the complex and unpredictable psychological and social conditions that classrooms present has always been challenging for teachers – indeed, their accounts show that this is often a source of great satisfaction for them (Danielewicz, 2001; Day *et al.*, 2007; Evans, 1998; Floden and Huberman, 1989; Nias, 1989b; Huberman, 1995b; OECD, 2005). Yet, in the fast-moving worlds of twenty-first-century schools in England and many other countries across the world, in which changes in curricula, conditions of service and new technologies have become the norm, what Romano (2006) calls 'bumpy moments' when teachers are 'required to make critical decisions about how to respond to a particular problem in practice' (ibid.: 973) are likely to increase in frequency and intensity. Being a reflective teacher, then, is not only desirable, but essential to building and sustaining the range of personal and interpersonal qualities and content and pedagogical competencies that are necessary components of expertise in teaching. Whilst expertise itself has been identified by some as the single most important factor in determining student achievement (Berliner, 1994; Darling-Hammond, 2000), its close and inseparable companion is commitment. Both are necessary components in effective teaching.

There seems to be little doubt, therefore, that commitment (or lack of it) is a key influencing factor in the performance effectiveness levels of teachers (Bryk *et al.*, 1993; Kushman, 1992). As we have seen in the illustrations of teachers in this book, initial commitment, however, rises, is sustained or declines depending on teachers' life and work experiences and their management of different scenarios. Commitment for teachers in the earlier VITAE study (Day *et al.*, 2007) was both a condition for teaching and an outcome of their experience. The research revealed, also, a clear association between teacher commitment, their sense of vocation, wellbeing and the support they received from colleagues.

Individual and collective efficacy

A powerful indicator of commitment that has been the subject of much research over the last four decades is self-efficacy (Bandura, 1997; Pajares, 1996, 1997), the belief by teachers that they are 'making a positive difference in the lives of students' (Darling-Hammond, 1990: 9). It is generally agreed to play an important part in their motivation, continuing commitment (resilience) and achievement. More recently, research has been conducted into 'collective' efficacy (defined as the belief of group members about 'the performance capacity of the social system as a whole' (Bandura, 1997: 469), the 'aggregate of individual members' perceptions of group capability' (Goddard *et al.*, 2004).

A collective sense of efficacy is also a consequence of the level of teacher influence over decisions about school improvement and is expressed in their willingness to help colleagues beyond the formal job requirements (Goddard, 2002; Somech and Drach-Zohavy, 2000) on behalf of the school, and, importantly, a commitment to remain in the school. High levels of self-efficacy are also associated with teachers' willingness to work collaboratively with others within and without the school, especially parents.

There is an important reciprocal connection between an individual's sense of self-efficacy and collective self-efficacy. Whilst it is quite possible for individual self-efficacy to survive in organisational contexts in which others do not have the same efficacy beliefs, the reverse is not the case. So, for schools to build perceived collective efficacy beliefs among staff, they must first attend to those of the individuals who work within them. Moreover, as Bandura (1997: 35) notes: 'A capability is only as good as its execution. The self-assurance with which people approach and manage difficult tasks determines whether they make good or poor use of their capabilities.'

Both individual and collective self-efficacy, then, are necessary conditions for good teaching and successful learning. As with research on children where it has been found that the relative strength of their efficacy beliefs influence their problem-solving success (Bouffard-Bouchard et al., 1991), so it is with teachers: 'The higher teachers' sense of efficacy, the more likely they are to tenaciously overcome obstacles and persist in the face of failure. Such resiliency, in turn, tends to foster innovative teaching and student learning' (Goddard et al., 2004: 3)

The same is true of collective efficacy:

> Organisations with strong beliefs in group capability can tolerate pressure and crisis and continue to function without debilitating consequences; indeed, such organisations learn to rise to the challenge when confronted with disruptive forces. Less efficacious organisations, however, are more likely to react dysfunctionally, which, in turn, increases the likelihood of failure. Thus, affective states may influence how organisations interpret and react to the myriad challenges they face.
>
> (Ibid.: 6)

It is clear, then, that whilst an individual sense of self-efficacy plays an important part in sustaining teachers' commitment to building and sustaining the quality of their work, and in their resilience over time, a collective sense of efficacy is likely to promote good teaching and successful learning even more. It is also clear that this will result from particular organisational purposes, cultures and structures promoted by school leaders who possess particular transformational qualities and enact these through context-sensitive strategies and relationships:

> Evidence suggests that teachers' sense of efficacy is positively related to aspects of organisational context such as positive school climate, lack of

> impediments to effective instruction, and teacher empowerment ... as well as principal influence with supervisors and the academic press of a school ... when group influence is staged, people are more likely to see the events around them as outside their control.
>
> (Ibid.: 8–10)

It is easy to see the relationship between these findings and, for example, Fielding's (2004) review of 'person-centred' schools as being morally and instrumentally successful; such schools are professional learning communities in which high levels of individual, relational and organisational trust and resilience are present (Gu and Day, forthcoming).

Organisational commitment

Schools in the twenty-first century must now rely more than ever on teachers who are willing to provide considerable effort and expertise beyond the traditional job requirements of classroom teaching. Even though most gain additional remuneration, schools have become more dependent upon teachers' individual and collective organisational commitment and, alongside this, their organisational citizenship behaviours (OCB), for their success. These behaviours, it has been claimed, are important to the success of the organisation because, 'through formal job descriptions, organisations cannot anticipate the whole range of behaviours needed for the achievement of organisational goals (Bogler and Somech, 2004: 280). Examples of dimensions of OCBs are altruism, conscientiousness, loyalty, participation in decision making, volunteering and providing innovative ideas. In a survey that focused on the relationship between teacher empowerment and teachers' organisational commitment, individual professional commitment and OCB, Bogler and Somech (ibid.) found that self-efficacy, professional growth opportunities and valuing (by status) were significant predictors of professional and organisational commitment, whilst self-efficacy, status and participation in decision making were significant predictors of OCB. In passing, the authors note:

> Without applying discretionary behaviors that go beyond the existing role expectations, and that are directed to the students, the teachers and the school organisation as a unit, it would be almost impossible for a community of teachers to become a professional learning community.
>
> (Ibid.: 285)

OCBs do, by definition, also require *trust*. The implications of this and a range of other studies for school leaders are clear. They need to:

1   establish conditions that will enable teachers to perceive themselves to be individually and collectively efficacious with a high level of competency;
2   provide significant, wide-ranging and sustained opportunities for professional

growth in the knowledge that teachers will feel that, through these, they can commit themselves even more to the organisation;

3 engage in joint decision-making processes in the knowledge that this will increase a sense of ownership, belonging and shared success, as well as valuing the status of all those who are in leadership roles.

Again, there are close associations between these, the characteristics of professional learning communities, the ingredients of good teaching–successful learning relationships. However, to achieve these requires that heads and other key leaders possess particular qualities, skills, dispositions and strategies. One key quality is the ability to trust and be trusted.

Successful principals are known not only for their values, vision and scope for the future, but also their optimism – manifested in high expectations and changes from a 'can't do' to a 'can do' school. We shall see later how such hope and optimism are not naïve or blind, and how successful principals engage in 'progressive trust' in which judgements about the extent and timing of the development of trust actions in schools are based not only on values and dispositions, but also contextual data about the trustworthiness of others.

A recent exploratory study of elementary school teachers' beliefs (Hoy *et al.*, 2008: 821) revealed that 'academic optimism was a general construct composed of efficacy, trust and academic emphasis'; and that four 'variables' in teachers association with this were: dispositional optimism, humanistic classroom management, student-oriented teaching and teacher citizenship behaviour (ibid.: 833). The authors suggested, also, that teachers' academic optimism is influenced, positively or negatively, by an amalgam of personal, class and school-level effects (ibid.: 323); and that 'principals who develop structures and procedures to enable the teachers to do their jobs influence the collective academic optimism of the school' (ibid.: 832). This confirms earlier research on academic optimism in schools, which had found that it was 'a collective property of the culture of schools and ... directly related to student achievement, controlling for socio-economic status, prior achievement, and other demographic characteristics' (ibid.: 822; see also Hoy *et al.*, 2006). Their research in elementary schools in the United States is confirmed by our own research in primary and secondary schools over a three-year period (Day *et al.*, 2009), which states that successful principals promote both collective and individual academic optimism, and that this results in an increased sense of individual and collective efficacy, defined as a teacher's 'judgement of his or her capability to bring about desired outcomes of student engagement and learning, even among those students who may be difficult or unmotivated' (Tschannen-Moran *et al.*, 1998: 202).

Moreover, in her later research in elementary schools, Tschannen-Moran (2004: 128) found:

Teachers with strong efficacy beliefs are likely to be more enthusiastic, more organised and devote more time to planning their teaching.... In addition

[they] are less likely to become angry, impatient or frustrated with a student who is having difficulty; will stick with that student longer; and will try more strategies to help the student understand.

Conclusions: a cause for optimism?

Recent research reports an emerging, more optimistic scenario for teachers in English schools (Day and Smethem, 2009). An investigation of the latest professional standards framework for teachers in England and Wales (TDA, 2007) also hints at a change of discourse, in an era of freeing up of the national curriculum to make 'learning relevant, engaging and irresistible' (QCA, 2008), encouragement to make the curriculum locally relevant, which enables context to be addressed, and relaxation of frameworks for teaching to become more flexible. In 2008, the DCSF also abandoned the standardised assessment tests for pupils aged 14 (initially boycotted by teachers, subsequently and ironically accepted and embedded in support materials). The same year also saw the provision of funded opportunities for teachers to gain a masters degree. Audited school self-evaluation has also become integral to the external inspection system for most schools. The beginnings of a change of discourse in England are also perhaps evident in one of the 33 standards for the Award of Qualified Teacher Status, which requires qualified teachers to 'have a creative and constructively critical approach towards innovation'. This small step may signify support for a re-emergence of teachers' individual and collective sense of autonomy, which may have been lost or partially submerged in cultures of managed compliance (Day and Smethem, 2009: 151). However, there are also to be 'Report Cards' for schools and teachers, and in the most recent Government White Paper, 21st-Century Schools, it is proposed that teaching contracts will be renewed every five years.

There is evidence, also, that under the wise leadership of heads, teachers and schools in England are not all incapacitated by the national agendas of government in the ways that much research by academics suggests. Not only are such schools able to meet and exceed pupil attainment targets imposed at national and local levels, but they are able to do so through empowering staff to make discretionary judgements. The role of the successful school leader in galvanising teacher ownership of change is clear: they and their staff are not compliant, but resilient, activist professionals (Day, 2007). There is considerable evidence that teachers across all nations are knowledgeable, pedagogically sensitive individuals who have moral purposes and are committed (Day, 1997), and who continue to make a difference to their students' lives. Although difficult to measure, moral purposes are acknowledged internationally to be important elements of the best professional practice (Hansen, 2001; Jackson, 1999; Lortie, 1975; Nias, 1989a; Noddings, 1996; Tickle, 2000). Such schools and such heads and teachers exist in all countries; and the reasons for their success in terms of pupil and staff well-being and achievement in and beyond the relatively narrow target-setting agendas of government have been well documented. They do not all work in schools that are achieving unmitigated success in terms of government agendas. Yet they are able, it seems, to exercise substantial autonomy. It is not that governments create the conditions, and crucially the culture, for transformations that lead to and are created by the schools themselves (Barber, 2001: 38), but more that these schools and the teachers' work are founded upon hope, a sense of agency, and a belief that they can continue to make a positive contribution to the learning and achievement of their pupils. They refuse to allow economic considerations to overwhelm their moral and ethical purposes, or to subordinate themselves to the 'epidemic of educational policy' (Levin, 1998, cited in Ball, 2001). As with the case reported by Woods *et al.*, (2001: 86), they have 'found a way ... of reconciling two apparently opposing discourses ... through the cultivation of their own political awareness ... [and] the refinement of their own philosophies'.

Teachers who are committed to their work are also those who are willing to learn and, where appropriate, to change. However, to do so they need support. The next chapter, therefore, examines how leaders can make a difference in teachers' lives and work.

Chapter 8

Leadership effects

Introduction

> If schools are to continue to exist well into the 21st century they need to be
> more fulfilling, more creative and more humanly attentive places than they
> have been thus far in their chequered histories, both for those who teach in
> them and for those who are required to attend them. This necessitates at
> least two things: firstly, a better understanding of the internal workings of
> organisational life and, secondly, a framework within which larger concerns
> of schools as places of learning and being can be analysed and understood.
>
> (Fielding, 2006: 350)

This chapter focuses on the contribution to the quality of the professional and
personal lives of teachers made by school leaders, in particular heads as creators
and guardians of the organisational conditions for good teaching, successful
learning and achievement and teachers who are trusted.

Research perspectives

In a debate on the search for the good life in the twenty-first century, conducted under the auspices of the Royal Society of Arts (RSA), Mulgan and
others call for organisations to attend to the wellbeing of their workers through
valuing and nurturing their talents (Zeldin, 2004: 36–39). They go on to associate this with a 'recurrent feature of almost any measure that you make of satisfaction or contentment in a society ... the degree to which people feel they have
some control over their lives and choices' (ibid.: 39). For Theodore Zeldin,
Historian and Fellow at St Anthony's College, Oxford, and participant in the
debate, the purpose of his 'The Oxford Muse' foundation is:

> To aim higher than teaching competence ... to bring a spark into everyday
> lives, to enable people to see and to say what they would not normally dare,
> to make them feel that it is possible to redesign life, but without being
> utopian.
>
> (Ibid.: 39)

For Geoff Mulgan, former head of policy at the Prime Minister's Office, and subsequently director at the Institute of Community Studies, promoting work–life balance and reducing the hours of work are not solutions to soul-destroying jobs:

> Reducing the hours of work is not enough if work is soul destroying. Nor is work–life balance the solution, because it gives us the excuse for tolerating awful jobs, with the compensation that we can recover at home. Most jobs which do not expand our talents make us into part-time slaves.
>
> (Mulgan, 2005: 38)

Research on job satisfaction among teachers over many years confirms these views (Bogler, 2001, 2002; Dinham and Scott, 1998, 2000; Evans, 1998, 2001; Kyriacou and Sutcliffe, 1979; Liu and Ramsey, 2008; Scott *et al.*, 2003; Sergiovanni, 1967; Shann, 1998; Skaalvik and Skaalvik, 2009; Zembylas and Papanastasiou, 2005). Research on schools that improve has consistently identified the importance of ongoing formal and informal staff development opportunities which emphasise the creative potential of individuals, as well as focusing on organisationally identified needs. Leaders in these schools – often referred to as 'learning communities' (Stoll and Louis, 2007) but more accurately described as 'learning and achievement communities', since good teaching must be complemented by successful learning and achievement, which is defined broadly rather than against only measurable attainment – uniformly place staff training and development, including succession planning, at the heart of their improvement strategies, since leadership is second only to classroom teaching in its influence on pupils' learning (Leithwood *et al.*, 2006).

The leadership effect on the quality of commitment and, through this, teaching and learning, is, therefore, important. In the schools in our research our teachers, the model of professional development was one which supported both individual and organisational growth needs through a range of internal and external learning and development opportunities which were designed to meet the cognitive, emotional and practical needs of staff. They were an integral rather than 'bolt-on' part of the fabric of school life and culture, defined as the way things are done and the way people behave and relate to each other. In these schools, expectations of self, trust in others and commitment to education as an individual and joint enterprise were high. Professional learning arose from – and fed back into – teachers' work and expertise. It was an integral part of the change process. It supported teachers as activists with control over the direction of their work. It enhanced their sense of commitment.

Laura's story in Chapter 3 provides a graphic example of a teacher in the later years of a professional life, who was struggling to sustain motivation, commitment and job satisfaction during a period of change in her personal and professional life and under the leadership of a head who wanted to change the school's way of working. Her children had left home to pursue their own lives at university. She was helping to fund these and so could not afford to move from full-time to part-time work, as she wished.

Whilst this general picture of decline in motivation due to her hostility to a national curriculum – which, in her view, had led to fewer opportunities for pupils to interact socially or be creative and 'put children under too much pressure, preventing them enjoying their learning' – with a decade or more of teaching ahead of her, is a concern, there is also evidence that the leadership of the school and support of colleagues can and do make a difference. Laura provides both positive and negative examples of their influence during her decade of teaching in a school. Her fluctuations to date can be divided into three periods, each coinciding with the leadership of a different head. In the first period she had felt sidelined by the leadership.

> Although I've got the title of 'coordinator' and I'm supposed to be part of the management team, I have not been involved in any decision-making.
>
> (Laura)

Her commitment to classroom teaching and the good results achieved by her pupils had kept her going:

> It's made me realise that sometimes it's not what you know, it's who you know.
>
> (Laura)

The negative experience of management had caused her to become less naive and more cynical. The period when the head had left the school and was temporarily replaced with an 'acting' head had marked a positive change:

> The support from the acting head has been very good, very different. She's been excellent. If you had any personal issues, she would listen. So there's been a huge difference. The whole school has a completely different feel about it – much more openness ... we work together as a team. Everyone is working as hard as before but feeling less threatened ... a lot happier.
>
> (Laura)

She herself had been given more responsibility and felt, 'a lot more valued than before'. She connected this with her becoming both a more effective teacher and more effective leader.

I never questioned my ability as a teacher. I knew I could do it. I've been teaching so long. I could do it with my eyes shut.

(Laura)

Teachers' work contexts can restrict or broaden the available learning experiences and knowledge growth (Scribner, 1998). Indeed, some research claims that as early as the pre-service phase, student teachers' job satisfaction and career commitment may be increased when their placement schools promote their professional concerns, especially those of 'collegial relations, teacher autonomy and freedom, and equal expectations of boys and girls' (Huang and Waxman, 2009: 242).

A recent government-funded project on the impact of leadership on student learning outcomes confirmed that for heads in successful schools in England, commitment to improving and enhancing teacher quality remained an important part of their drive to raise standards (Day *et al.*, 2009, 2010). It was evident that CPD was seen as an entitlement in these schools and that it was motivational for teachers to receive a rich variety of professional learning and development opportunities which impacted positively upon their teaching practices.

The research also showed that improving and effective schools were vigilant in the pursuit of improved teaching, learning and achievement. Teachers in such schools were encouraged to go beyond their usual teaching models and to try new or alternative approaches. Heads encouraged staff to be leaders in their own classrooms and provided an infrastructure where it was safe to take informed decisions to extend their teaching approaches. Staff responded to this opportunity positively because it affected the way they saw themselves as professionals and improved their sense of self-efficacy. This, in turn, had a positive impact on the way they interacted with pupils and other staff members in the schools. The testimonies of the teachers in this book, however, show that, unfortunately, not all school leaders provide opportunities designed to develop creativity or enhance teachers' sense of agency and autonomy.

In English schools today, as in those in many other countries, there are more out-of-classroom roles and responsibilities than ever before. Thus, fewer teachers, most but by no means exclusively in primary schools, are able to focus exclusively upon what has traditionally been their classroom teaching role. In the VITAE study (Day *et al.*, 2007) we noted that the overwhelming majority of primary school teachers held such roles. Reid *et al.* (2004: 252) found that in many secondary schools, also, 'few teachers only teach', with only 24 per cent who were without at least one significant leadership role. They suggest that this proliferation has been largely the result of the need to implement a plethora of central government policy initiatives which have placed greater accountability on schools. For some teachers in their study, this:

> Impinge[d] on my ability to plan for, monitor and assess my class effect-
> ively. I sometimes have no choice but to do the bare minimum in order to
> be able to grab time for subject coordination, because there is no allocation
> for this within my contracted hours.
>
> (Ibid.: 257–258)

For others, it caused 'lack of sleep due to overwork … even working till 10
o'clock at night doesn't get me anywhere' (ibid.: 258). Additionally, there has
been an increase in the number of meetings to be attended in the pursuit of an
increased focus upon school-to-school networking, changing curricula and pedagogies, assessment training, community collaborations and other initiatives
relating to new forms of school-based initial teacher development and training,
all of which have increased teachers' responsibilities.

The stultifying effects of the national testing regime on the work and mind
sets of many teachers are illustrated also by Jodie's experiences of teaching
14-year-olds:

> After Christmas, I focus upon teaching for the exam. It's just ridiculous
> spending nine months out of a year teaching to one exam when you don't
> know if they are going to be marked correctly anyway. All the teachers in the
> department hate this, but are working like this to try to allow the teacher to
> teach objectives but in their own way and in a way that allows kids access to
> the whole text.
>
> (Jodie)

As management and leadership roles have increased in complexity and
created multiple layers of accountability for many more classroom teachers, so
the quality of headteacher leadership has become more important as a key medi-
ator at the boundary between high challenge and high stress, between increased
productivity and decreasing efficiency. At one extreme there are the heads who
are both person- and task-centred, who support their staff's motivation, self-
efficacy and commitment through acts of care, trust and the exercise of strategies which promote taking ownership, belonging and wellbeing. In their
schools there is a low staff turnover, high expectations and success for all. At the
other extreme, are cases of stress-related absences and illness exemplified by the
award by the House of Lords of a significant sum of money to a former head of
mathematics who had lost his deputies and been given extra duties: 'The case
established that, "an autocratic and bullying style of leadership" … [that is] …
unsympathetic to complaints of occupational stress is a factor that courts can
take into account in deciding claims' (*Independent*, 16 May 2005: 16).

The impact of leadership was a significant feature, also, in the lives of teachers
in their early years, particularly in relation to pupil behaviour. Jodie's experiences illustrate:

> It is much better here, in my present school, than in my last. This is due to strong management. The SLT plays a key role in the effective school discipline. It is strict, but more important is the level of consistency. Children know what the score is and that the staff are going to back one another up. SLT are visible and respected by children and staff.
>
> (Jodie)

Where leaders do focus on supporting teachers' wellbeing and continuing quest for improvement, as the stories of Frances, Jill and Peter will show in the following chapter, it is clear that their capacities to work at levels higher than mere competence and, as important, their motivation, self-efficacy, commitment and resilience increase.

The learning and achieving school

Almost all the research into teacher motivation, commitment and their abilities and capacities to promote successful student learning and achievement through teaching to their best, suggests that attention needs to be given to both their functional, task-centred relationships (with students and adults) and those which are personal. Drawing on the work of MacMurray, a Scottish philosopher, Michael Fielding, describes the differences:

> 'Functional' or instrumental relations are typical of those encounters that help us to get things done in order to achieve our purposes. Indeed, functional relations are defined by those purposes.... In contrast, 'personal' relations exist in order to help us be and become ourselves in and through our relations with others and part of that becoming involves our mutual preparedness to be open and honest with each other about all aspects of our being.
>
> (Fielding, 2006: 351, 353)

Fielding goes on to suggest that whilst the functional and personal are interconnected, they are not equally important. Again, research on successful schools and school leadership supports his argument that:

> not only is the functional for the sake of the personal, and the personal through the functional, but the influence of the personal on the functional is transformative of it: the functional should be expressive of the personal. Ends and means must be inextricably linked; the means should themselves be transformed by the ends by which they are inspired and towards which they are aiming. The functional ways in which we work together in schools to achieve personal, communal and educational ends should be transformed by the normal and interpersonal character of what we are trying to do.
>
> (Ibid.: 353)

From this position, Fielding creates four organisational and communal orientations of schools: impersonal, affective, person-centred and high performance, which illustrates different relationships between the functional and personal and the likely consequences of these for school organisation, relationships and outcomes (Table 8.1).

The findings of a 14-country international project on successful school principals (ISSPP) provide in-depth empirical data which supports his thesis that schools that are person-centred, and where the functional is for the sake of and expressive of the personal are both morally and instrumentally successful (Day and Leithwood, 2007). Moreover, the illustrations of teachers in this book confirm their purposes and sources of motivation, commitment and identity and achievement as being reflective of Fielding's stance and that of the leadership and cultures within their schools.

Such a stance is close to that which is taken by authors of a range of research into schools as learning communities. Mitchell and Sackney (2001: 2), for example, discuss the differences in the key assumptions between learning organisations and learning communities as being that: 'The learning community is concerned with the human experience whereas the learning organisation is concerned with organisational productivity.'

For Fielding there is no dichotomy. Rather, to follow the purposes of schooling as he defines them is to ensure that the functional (organisational productivity) is for the sake of the personal (enriching the human experience).

Table 8.1 The organisational and communal orientation of schools: understanding the relation between functions and persons

Schools as impersonal organisations	Schools as affective communities	Schools as high-performance learning organisations	Schools as person-centred learning communities
The functional marginalises the personal	The personal marginalises the functional	The personal is used for the sake of the functional	The functional is for the sake of/ expressive of the personal
Mechanistic organisation	Affective community	Learning organisation	Learning community
Community is unimportant/ destructive of organisational purposes	Community has few organisational consequences or requirements	Community is useful tool to achieve organisational purposes	Organisation exists to promote community
Efficient	Restorative	Effective	Morally and instrumentally successful

Source: Fielding, 2006: 354.

Although it is not our purpose to elaborate upon the nature, purposes and characteristics of learning communities in detail (see Stoll and Louis (2007) for an international perspective), it is, nevertheless, instructive to match the experiences of organisational cultures, leadership and support reported by the teachers in this book with these and with the dilemmas which must be managed if they are to be established and sustained.

Mitchell and Sackney (2001) suggested that building personal, interpersonal and organisational capacity is the key means of developing learning communities. In Australia, for example, a 2005 Department of Education, Science and Training (DEST) study of 20 highly effective schools found that all performed as 'professional learning communities' and that in these communities it was the principals who sanctioned and were actively involved in the whole staff's development. In reporting on this study, Avenell (2007: 46–47) identified five requirements for schools to become professional learning communities:

1   principals who shared leadership and decision making;
2   a shared vision which includes an 'unswerving' commitment to student and staff learning;
3   collective learning among staff which could be applied to enhancing student learning;
4   evidence-based peer support and feedback on classroom teaching;
5   physical conditions and human capacities which support teaching and learning.

Yet some teachers experience a range of impediments to the building of personal, interpersonal and organisational capacities. The leadership may not be committed or sufficiently knowledgeable of the ways these may be developed. School structures might emphasise cultures of segregation rather than inclusivity, competition rather than collaboration, hierarchies rather than leadership diversity and distribution, disrespect rather than respect for students and their communities.

In Laura's case, a darker period was experienced on the appointment of a new, permanent head who was 'desperate to change things'. Laura felt that the changes in structures and cultures, 'the way we do things', had cast a shadow on her colleagues.

> We don't want to change. There have already been too many changes which have had a negative effect on the staff who have been here a long time.
>
> (Laura)

As part of the new head's restricting effects, Laura had lost her role as literacy coordinator and, once again, had become 'unsettled'.

Having the right leaders

On the basis of 64 detailed, multi-perspective studies of successful heads in elementary and secondary schools in Australia, Canada, Denmark, England, Norway, Sweden and the United States, the ISSPP concluded that, while all heads possessed the attributes, qualities, skills and broad moral and instrumental purposes described earlier, these were applied in five different combinations and with different emphasis at different times according to their own and their schools' phase of development and the demands of the broader policy and demographic contexts.

These combinations were:

1   *Sustaining passionate commitment and personal accountability.* High expectations; strong self-esteem; persistent; assertive; achievement oriented; learning-centred; open communication; concern for educating the whole person based on clearly articulated values; rooted in the rights of students, inclusivity, social justice, and democratic principles.

2   *Managing tensions and dilemmas and maintaining moral purposes.* Able to manage ambiguities and conflicts in ways that enhance individual and school improvement and that go beyond instrumental rationality.

3   *Being other-centred and learning focused.* Continuous improvement; individual and collective communication and capacity building; collaborative learning cultures; dispersing leadership, decision-making and responsibilities; encouraging trust; intervening strategically in ways which are relevant to personal and system contexts through community involvement; de-privatising professional practice; nurturing teacher leadership.

4   *Making emotional and rational investments.* Emotional understanding; empathy, trust; being courageous; staying close to the action; interacting on both cognitive and emotional levels with key stakeholder groups; creating safe teaching and learning environments, being innovative.

5   *Emphasising the personal and the functional.* Building person-centred communities which are functionally successful; modelling values; respecting others; exercising care with accountability.

(Leithwood and Day, 2007: 17)

Jodie valued the enormous support from her head of department and the SLT for the person in the professional:

There is a policy that families come first. That sort of support is really good, so you don't feel guilty if you are taking a day off. There doesn't seem to be any pressure if you're off ill. You can take as much time as you like. People watch out for each other. For example, I was getting fed up with having to move desks back in place and remove dirty cups from my classroom first thing

> in the morning after evening classes. The deputy head found me doing this one morning and I explained the situation to him. Later that week I found a gift on my desk, with a note saying, 'hope this makes up for these difficulties'. It makes a difference. If you're busy you can feel quite isolated.
>
> (Jodie)

In *The Six Secrets of Change: What the Best Leaders Do to Help Their Organisations Thrive and Change* (2008), Michael Fullan implicitly endorses the messages from research on teachers' work and lives in this book. For Fullan, the secrets of success are:

1 A recognition that systems will only improve if the improvements are complemented by respect for the people in the organisation, i.e. which do not create teacher fatigue or have an adverse effect on morale (love your employees).
2 Aligning the values of the school with those of the individuals in the school through collaborative work so that knowledge of effective (and ineffective) practices can be shared. Such purposeful interactions, he suggests, will counter the dangers of fragmentation of purpose and practice and lead to the development of professional learning communities (connect peers with purpose).
3 Developing individual and collective capacities among staff to learn and change (capacity building prevails).
4 Creating a balance between consistency of practice across the organisation, based upon the relentless pursuit of core objectives with the search for improvement through innovation (learning is the work).
5 Developing informed trust and corporate accountability through making judgements about progress and achievement which are based on the collection and analysis of data (transparency rules).
6 Enacting 1–5 above by identifying patterns and relationships, always seeking improvement, learning from experiences and being action oriented, investing passion and energy to achieve desired outcomes (systems learning).

(Fullan, 2008)

Trust matters

Trust has been defined as 'the assurance that one can count on the good will of another to act in one's best interests' (Baier, 1994, cited in Tschannen-Moran, 2004: 15).

Research by Ross and Gray involving over 3,000 elementary teachers in Canadian schools is one of a number of studies which have found that the quality of leadership affects teachers' individual and collective sense of efficacy and their organisational commitment (Ross *et al.*, 2008). In research into successful primary and secondary schools in England, regardless of socio-economic status, students' prior achievement and sector, staff were uniformly optimistic and efficacious about what they and their students were achieving and could achieve, worked hard willingly both in and out of the classroom, were committed and resilient, exuded a collective sense of being trusted by their heads. It was also found that the students they taught produced attainment results at or above their expected levels (Day *et al.*, 2009, 2010).

Trust and trustworthiness have been identified as key ingredients in the work of heads and essential to school improvement and success. Thus, there has been increasing interest by researchers in seeking definitions of trust in schools in particular and in society in general. This is, in part, because schools rely upon trust both from the public and internally in order to be able to function effectively; and in part because there is widespread agreement across countries and cultures that trust – usually associated with tolerance and respect – is being eroded. For schools, this is especially challenging:

> As citizens have become increasingly distrustful of their institutions and leaders, the trend away from trust creates a special challenge for schools because trust is so fundamental to their core mission. Schools need the trust of parents who send their children to school, as well as that of the communities that sponsor and fund them. In order to learn, students must trust their teachers because, for much of what is learned in schools students are asked to believe what teachers tell them and what they read without independent evidence. Students who do not trust their teachers or each other will be likely to divert energy into self-protection and away from engagement with the learning task. Moreover, students who do not feel trusted by their teachers and administrators may create barriers to learning as they distance themselves from schools and build an alienated, rebellious youth culture. They may, in fact, live down to the low expectations of a distrustful school environment.
>
> (Tschannen-Moran, 2004: 12)

Whilst researchers have not found direct cause-and-effect relationships, they have identified indirect empirical associations between trust, individual and collective efficacy, empowerment of staff through the distribution of leadership, and school improvement, including sustained improvements in student achievement and sense of achievement.

Alongside these, they have found that the head's role in creating, building and sustaining trust is paramount in establishing and sustaining such associations. In case study research in three elementary schools in urban settings, Tschannen-Moran concluded that the presence of trust is fundamental to situations of interdependence 'in which the interests of one party cannot be achieved without reliance upon another' (2004: 19). Teachers are unlikely to achieve effective teaching and sustained engagement of students in learning without the tacit, if not overt, agreement of those involved; and the same applies to the effectiveness of the work of school heads with teachers and other stakeholder groups. It is also acknowledged to be a key enabling characteristic of professional learning communities (Cummings and Worley, 2008; Hipp and Huffman, 2007). Indeed, if we regard schools as microcosms of democratic society, then a lack of presence, decline or loss of trust is likely to lead to the loss – or at the very least under-development or disruption – of the growth of social capital which is essential to problem-solving (Putnam, 1983).

Whilst trust is 'a mutual condition of a relationship' (Sockett, 1993: 117), when applied to schools, this has been allied with their moral purposes (to act for the betterment of their students) and to the increase of participation and empowerment in decision making and leadership (Fullan, 2003; Sergiovanni, 2004; Starratt, 2007).

School heads have a particular responsibility for promoting trust among all members of the school community. The data from our research shows that this is an unstated aspiration, but that it is a key component of capacity building and decisions about the extent to which leadership is distributed. Five 'facets' of leadership trust were identified consistently by colleagues inside and outside the case study schools, regardless of socio-economic status and sector. These confirm and add to those identified by Hoy and Tschannen-Moran:

- *Benevolence*: confidence that one's wellbeing will be protected by a trusted party.
- *Reliability*: the extent to which one can count on another person or group.
- *Competency*: the extent to which the trusted party has knowledge and skill.
- *Honesty*: the character, integrity and authenticity of the trusted party.
- *Openness*: the extent to which there is no withholding of information from others.

(Hoy and Tschannen-Moran, 2003)

To these qualities, we would add three others:

- *Wisdom*: the extent to which the trusted party makes timely decisions which are in the interests of the students, the school and its staff.
- *Academic optimism*: the extent to which hope and optimism are nurtured, realised and renewed by the trusted party.
- *Emotional understanding*: the extent to which the trusted party is seen to care for the emotional selves of others.

Relational trust and achievement

It is not the assurance of trust alone that will improve teaching, learning and achievement in schools (though if it is absent, there is less chance of improvement), but its manifestation through these eight facets of leadership, the quality and consistency of the leadership of actions and interactions, in particular, of relationships within and between teachers, teachers and leaders, teachers and pupils and teachers and the community.

In a much reported longitudinal study of elementary schools in Chicago, Bryk and Schneider (2002) found that: 'Trust was a critical factor in predicting which schools would make the greater gains in student achievement and which would sustain these gains over time' (cited in Tschannen-Moran, 2004: 136).

As a result of looking at 100 schools that made the greatest gains in maths and reading over a consecutive five-year period, they found that those with strong levels of trust had a 1 in 2 chance of making significant improvements in student attainment in these subjects, whilst those with lower levels of trust had a 1 in 7 chance. They defined such trust as 'relational', and suggested four essential characteristics for identifying and assessing trust in schools: respect; competence; personal regard; and integrity.

Because school life is characterised both by bureaucratic and professional relationships, it is the responsibility of the head to create and sustain the conditions in which its presence may be established and strengthened to the level that it can be observed in the interactions of three sets of relationships, in the outcomes of these, especially in terms of engagement, ownership and efficacy, and in the success of the pupils. These sets are:

- head and teacher
- teacher and teacher
- school professionals and parents.

(Bryk and Schneider, 2002: 41)

To these we may add:

- teachers and pupils.

For relational trust to be established, members within and across these four sets need to agree on understandings about obligations and expectations (about, for example, the ways teacher–student relationships should be conducted and minimum standards of teaching). The head and others need to engage in a continuing series of personal and interpersonal interactions which reinforce or reconfirm trust if it is to grow. It is clear from the heads' 'lines of success' in our research on the impact of effective leadership on pupil outcomes (Day *et al.*, 2009) that it is not only through the consistent articulation and communication of the eight facets of leadership trust (or the four aspects of relational trust identified by Bryk and Schneider) within and across the three sets of relationships in which they engage which ensures trust. The research also shows that it is the extent to which their strategic actions for organisational change are consistent with those trust values, dispositions and qualities and actions which count.

Organisational trust

Karen Seashore Louis draws attention to the importance of organisational trust in district reform contexts in her recent research in schools. In research in five high schools in the United States over a three-year period, Louis identified 'institutional' trust as a second important indicator of trust and predictor of student achievement: 'Institutional trust: the expectation of appropriate behaviour based on the norms of the institution' (Louis, 2007: 3).

Noting that relational trust itself is difficult to achieve in 'the increasingly impersonal environments of larger bureaucracies' which many secondary schools represent (ibid.) and in which there may be perceptions, if not realities, of high-power, low-power relationships, she found that the schools illustrated a range of 'high trust' or 'low trust' settings in relation to four 'quality management' values: vision, cooperation, teacher involvement and data-based decision making. These were selected in part because of their presence in the literature on change and in part because they represented the largest number of coded responses from teachers to interview questions. In addition, the research identified 'social cohesion' as an important indicator of institutional trust. Her findings are confirmed in the data from our research. We found that heads, staff, students and parents spoke of the collective sense of purpose and participation, application of common behaviour protocols, cooperation and data-informed (rather than data-based) decision making as the norms of their schools (Day et al., 2009b).

However, whilst some norms were reported to have been established in the early years of the head's tenure, others were developed over a longer period; the timing and sequencing depended on the head's judgements about the contexts they inherited and the appropriate pace of movement in its development in relation to the progressive growth of leadership structures and the organisation and form of these which demonstrated trust.

Progressive trust and the distribution of leadership: the courage of conviction

> Trust is established through a commitment period during which each partner has the opportunity to signal to the other a willingness to accept personal risk and not to exploit the vulnerability of the other for personal gain.... As participants begin to feel more comfortable with one another, there may be a tacit testing of the limits of trust and influence and attempts to arrive at a mutual set of expectations. Within eighteen months, relationships become fairly stable.
>
> (Tschannen-Moran, 2004: 42)

It is important to recognise, then, that to build trust takes time and depends upon the head establishing vision, hope and optimism, high expectations and acting with integrity. The extent and depth of initial or provisional trust will depend on a number of past, as well as present, factors. For example, if the head inherits a school whose members have a history of experiencing distrustful relationships, then it may take longer than if the reverse were the case. Tschannen-Moran (2004: 57) found: 'Discerning the proper level of trust requires wisdom and discernment on the part of the educational leader. Optimal trust is prudent, measured and conditional.'

For successful school leaders the process of trusting others is neither naive nor calculative, but rather, an expression of five factors:

1   *Values and attitudes:* beliefs that (most) people cared for their students and would work hard for their benefit if allowed to pursue objectives to which they were committed.
2   *Disposition to trust:* a history of received – and observing in others – benefits deriving from trusting relationships.
3   *Trustworthiness:* the extent to which they were able to establish trust by others in them.
4   *Repeated acts of trust:* enabling the increasing distribution of leadership roles, responsibilities and accountabilities and broadening of stakeholder participation
5   *Building and reinforcing trustworthiness:* through consistency in interactions, structures and strategies which show consistency with agreed values and vision.

The data from our interviews over the two-year period of fieldwork on the effective leadership project (Day *et al.*, 2009) confirmed the 'self-reinforcing pattern' of trust identified by Tschannen-Moran (2004: 56):

> A self-reinforcing pattern of trust emerges as repeated cycles of exchange, risk taking and successive fulfilment of expectations strengthen the willingness of trusting parties to rely on each other. A history of fulfilled expectations accumulates and leads to a reputation for trustworthiness that can then facilitate and reinforce trust in a wider context.

The provisional trust they had placed on others and others upon them had been vindicated through their demonstration of integrity and consistency of values, and their application in actions taken. On the one hand, they had fostered trust, and on the other, they had earned trust. Moreover, it is clear from their own statements and those of others that they had earned their trustworthiness through consistent exercise – over time – of care, courage and sensitivity:

> To be a trustworthy leader takes courage. It also takes sensitivity. It takes a willingness to deal with difficult situations and difficult people in a straightforward and firm manner. A caring stance does not mean that teachers are

not held accountable. On the contrary, your caring and commitment to students demand that you hold high expectations for teachers' performance. These high expectations are bolstered by the support and guidance to help teachers meet these standards.

(Tschannen-Moran, 2004: 84)

Conclusions: the leadership factor

Trustworthy, flexible, committed and passionate heads are at the heart of successful schools. These heads have a strong sense of moral purpose and are able to build their visions, actions and relationships upon a clear understanding of the schools' history, current context and development stage (Gu and Johansson, forthcoming). In other words, they are able to layer their leadership strategies over time to build capacity within the school and enable the change to be implemented (Day *et al.*, 2009).

> It is heads' selection of appropriate actions, at appropriate times, that enables them to impact on pupil outcomes. However, these actions are not discrete, or stand-alone items that diminish once a task has been completed. Rather, actions, develop, broaden and deepen over time, forming a foundation upon which further actions can be built.... It is the ability to construct, and layer leadership in this way, together with certain personal and professional values and qualities, that makes the heads in our study so successful.
>
> (Ibid.: 193)

Studies cited in this chapter on the importance of leadership support to teachers' wellbeing and continuing commitment all suggest that success is an ongoing process and that the key to success is to be able to identify, diagnose, predict and respond to problems in a contextually appropriate manner.

These studies also show that shared visions between teachers and the leadership team, focused but flexible curriculum and learning support and a school culture that promotes teachers' collective agency, efficacy and professional learning and development are necessary conditions for teachers to sustain their capacities to teach to their best in all professional life phases. As Moore Johnson (2004: 117) reminds us: 'Although a few brilliant and heroic teachers may triumph despite decrepit and dysfunctional settings, most teachers must rely on their school as a place that makes steady, good work not only possible but likely.'

Resilience counts

Introduction

> Good teaching is charged with positive emotions. It is not just a matter of knowing one's subject, being efficient, having the correct competences, or learning all the right techniques. Good teachers are not just well-oiled machines. They are emotional, passionate beings who connect with their students and fill their work and their classes with pleasure, creativity, challenge and joy.
>
> (Hargreaves, 1998: 835)

To teach, and to teach to one's best over time, requires resilience. Resilience is not an option. It is a necessary quality for all teachers. This is not to valorise the teaching profession, but rather to acknowledge the special relationship between the abilities and capacities of its members to manage its intellectual and emotional demands in order to sustain their contributions to the quality of their students' learning and achievements.

Research perspectives

Resilience is of importance in teaching for three reasons. First, it is unrealistic to expect pupils to be resilient if their teachers, who constitute their primary role models, do not demonstrate resilient qualities (Henderson and Milstein, 2003). Second, teaching is a demanding job in an emerging 'age of diversity and sustainability' (Hargreaves and Fink, 2006: 16). A shift in the focus of attention of policy makers, providers and heads from teacher stress and burnout to resilience provides a promising and more productive perspective to understand the ways that teachers manage and sustain their motivation and commitment in times of change. Third, resilience, defined as the capacity to continue to 'bounce back', to recover strengths or spirit quickly and efficiently in the face of adversity, is closely allied to a strong sense of vocation, self-efficacy and motivation to teach, which are fundamental to sustaining a commitment to promoting achievement in all aspects of students' lives.

The notion of resilience originated in the disciplines of psychiatry and developmental psychology as a result of a burgeoning attention to personal characteristics or traits that enabled some children, although having been classified as being at risk of having negative life outcomes, to adapt positively and thrive despite significant adversity (Block and Block, 1980; Howard *et al.*, 1999; Waller, 2001). The 1980s marked the paradigmatic change to the concept of resilience which, whilst recognising the pain, struggle and suffering involved in the adaptation process in the face of adversity, focused more on positive qualities and strengths (Gore and Eckenrode, 1994; Henderson and Milstein, 2003). Over the following two decades, the focus of resilience research has developed from identifying personal traits and protective factors to investigating underlying protective processes, i.e. how such factors may contribute to positive outcomes (Luthar *et al.*, 2000). We have discussed the nature of resilience in more detail in an earlier publication (Gu and Day, 2007). For the purpose of this chapter, we provide a summary of the meaning of resilience both as a psychological and a social construct.

Resilience as a psychological construct

Fredrickson's recent development of a 'broaden-and-build' theory of positive emotions (2001, 2004) provides a useful psychological conceptual framework. She (2004) observes that a subset of positive emotions – joy, interest, contentment and love – promote discovery of novel actions and social bonds, which serve to build individuals' personal resources. These personal resources, ranging from physical and intellectual resources to social and psychological resources, 'function as reserves that can be drawn on later to improve the odds of successful coping and survival' (ibid.: 1367). This theory predicts that experiences of positive emotions might, over time, broaden the scope of attention and cognition, enabling flexible and creative thinking and consequently fuel psychological resilience (ibid.; see also Aspinwall, 1998, 2001; Fredrickson and Joiner, 2002; Isen, 1990).

Fredrickson's theory, from a psychological perspective, contributes to the conceptual basis for understanding the resilient qualities of teachers who are doing a job that is itself emotional by nature; and it mirrors the work of a range of educational researchers on the emotional nature of teaching (Fried, 2001; Nias, 1989a, 1999; Nieto, 2003; Palmer, 1998).

Resilience as a multidimensional, socially constructed concept

For other authors (Walsh, 1998; see also Henderson and Milstein, 2003; Howard and Johnson, 2004; Richardson *et al.*, 1990), resilience is a multidimensional and multi-determined concept and is best understood as a dynamic within a social system of interrelationships. While the concept of resilience elaborated in the discipline of psychology helps clarify the internal factors and personal characteristics of trait-resilient people, it fails to address how the capacity to be resilient in different negative circumstances, whether these be connected to personal or professional factors, can be enhanced or inhibited by the nature of the settings in which we work, the people with whom we work and the strength of our beliefs or aspirations (Bernard, 1991; Henderson and Milstein, 2003; Luthar, 1996; Oswald et al., 2003; Day et al., 2006).

Resilient qualities can be learned or acquired (Higgins, 1994), and can be achieved through providing relevant and practical protective factors, such as caring and attentive educational settings, positive and high expectations, positive learning environments, a strong supportive social community, and supportive peer relationships (Bernard, 1991, 1995; Glasser, 1965; Johnson et al., 1999; Oswald et al., 2003; Pence, 1998; Rutter et al., 1979; Wang, 1997; Werner and Smith, 1988). Resilience, therefore, is not a quality that is innate. Rather, it is a construct that is relative, developmental and dynamic (Howard et al., 1999; Luthar et al., 2000; Rutter, 1990). It is thus both a product of personal and professional dispositions and values, influenced by organisational and personal factors and determined by individuals' capacities to manage context-specific factors. For example, teachers may respond positively or negatively in the presence of challenging circumstances depending on the quality of organisational or colleague leadership and the strength of their own commitment. The social construction of teacher resilience acknowledges, as the psychological construction does not, the importance of such combinations of personal, professional and situated factors on their capacities to sustain their emotional wellbeing and professional commitment.

The quest for teacher resilience

Whilst there is now a considerable body of research internationally which attests to the importance of emotion in teachers' work and lives (Hargreaves, 2000, 2004, 2005; Leithwood, 2007; Leithwood and Beatty, 2008; Nias, 1996; Schutz and Pekrun, 2007; Troman and Woods, 2001; Van Veen and Lasky, 2005; Zembylas, 2005; Zembylas and Schutz, 2009), there is much less that focuses on teacher resilience itself. Yet most teachers who survive the first four or five years remain in the job for a further 30; and during this period not only will they be subject, as all are, to the vagaries of the ageing process and unanticipated events that may affect the course of their personal lives (marriage, divorce, illness, the loss of a close relative or declining health), they will also need to adjust their professional lives as colleagues come and go, the demands of students and the processes of working with them become more complex, and conditions of service change.

There are three truths about teachers' emotional worlds:

1   like the vast majority of human beings, teachers' goals in life and work are to experience pleasure rather than pain as part of a continuing process of seeking adjustment to changing contexts or scenarios rather than attempting to maintain a fixed point of balance;

2   their observable behaviour (their emotions) may mask their feelings. In other words, it is impossible for others, however much 'emotional intelligence' (Goleman, 1996) they may have, to manage teachers' feelings. However, they may create conditions which either help or hinder these by the organisational structures and cultures they establish in schools and through the relationships they promote; and

3   the emotional content of teachers' lives in schools and classrooms may have short- and longer-term consequences for how they feel about themselves and others and how they behave (i.e. their experiences of interactions with pupils, colleagues, parents and, more vicariously, policy agendas from within or without the school). These may affect their self-efficacy, sense of professional identity and, ultimately, their commitment and capacity to teach to their best.

The complexities of achieving change and sustaining effectiveness are illustrated in Figure 9.1, which maps the inter-connected relationships between teachers' professional life phases, their professional identities and their wellbeing, commitment, resilience and effectiveness, both as perceived and in terms of measures of pupils' progress and attainment (Day *et al.*, 2007: 238). Among

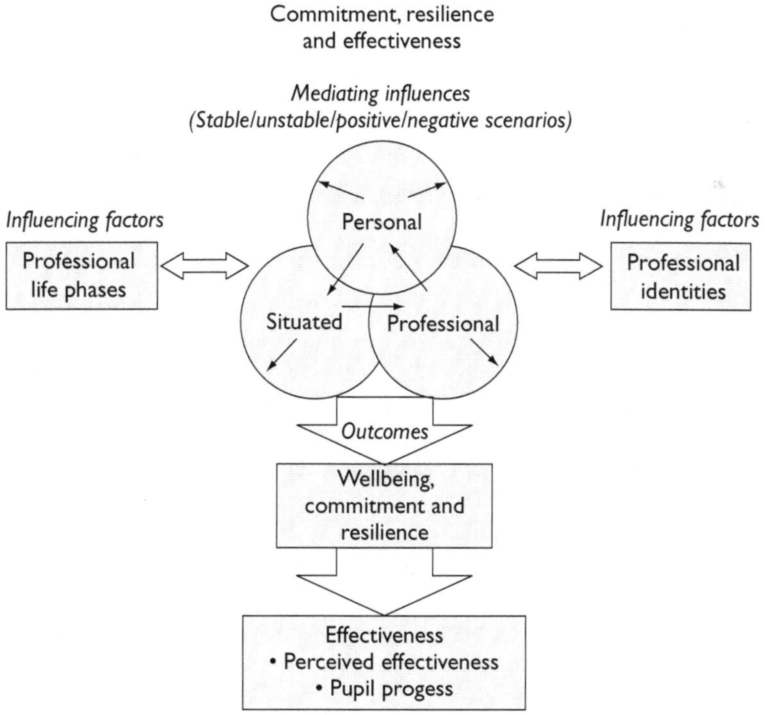

Figure 9.1 Teachers' wellbeing, commitment and effectiveness.

these interrelationships, the roles played by teachers' sense of wellbeing, commitment and resilience are fundamental. This nexus, where the combination of personal, professional and situated factors converges, impacts, positively or negatively, upon their capacity to give their best to the learning and growth of their pupils.

Research on the affective dimensions of teaching is, therefore, important, both because these dimensions reinforce the empirical association between cognition and emotion, and because they act as reminders to policy makers, teacher educators and school principals that 'teacher effectiveness' is the product of the preparation and continuing support of both the head (cognition) and the heart (emotion).

Such a reminder must, however, provide more than a means of raising awareness for it to be useful to the business of improving teaching and learning. It must also be able to be applied within the broader, as well as the narrower, contexts in which teachers' work is conducted and evaluated. At a time when teaching in the twenty-first century is rated as one of the most stressful professions (Kyriacou, 2000; Nash, 2005; PricewaterhouseCoopers, 2001), there is a particularly urgent need to investigate whether external and internal demands and challenges for teachers working in different contexts and in different professional life phases have dimmed their sense of commitment and, more important, the ways in which their resilience, and ultimately their commitment, self-efficacy and wellbeing, may be nurtured, developed and sustained over time and in different contexts. All students in all contexts, as Edwards (2003: 11) argues, 'deserve to be taught by enthusiastic, motivated individuals'.

Resilient teachers: their contexts and stories

Story 1: increasing motivation and commitment – an early years teacher

> It's a challenge, a daily challenge. We have quite difficult children. We have got quite difficult parents. It challenges your ability not only to teach but work as a classroom team. There is a lot of responsibility. You've got to do your part of the team well as what you do reflects on everyone else. I've gone from being just an ordinary classroom teacher to part of the senior management team.
>
> (Frances)

Frances, a teacher with seven years' experience, taught pupils aged 6–7 years and coordinated the work of KS1 teachers in a recently built 3–11 community school in the southwest of England, which had grown from 130 to 300+ pupils over the five years of its existence. The school had a good reputation among the people who live in this semi-rural area and was described as 'the hub' of the community. Standards of teaching and learning were judged by Ofsted to be satisfactory. The pupils were drawn from a wide range of social backgrounds and were predominantly white. The number of pupils eligible for free school meals was close to the national average. There was a high proportion of the pupils (21.4 per cent) that were classified as having SEN.

In this first example we show the important contributions that school leadership, other colleagues and the stability of teachers' personal lives can make to their ongoing resilience. It reveals how teachers may gain emotional strength from these positive influences in their personal and professional lives in order to manage the nuances and fluctuations within their professional development journey.

Sense of vocation

Frances was originally attracted to teaching because it was 'something that I had always wanted to do. I knew I could make a difference to the children.' This still applied.

> Originally, I wanted to work in business and banking, but I changed schools for sixth form and they said I wasn't clever enough for banking, I wouldn't get good enough A level results, so I looked at other options and I always liked working with the children and did a day release in a primary school one day a week and went from there really.

Growing in supportive school environments

The last three of Frances' seven years in teaching had been spent in this school where she was 'really happy – I really like it. I've been given the chance to grow professionally and personally and all the challenges I've taken on I've done', although she was 'really tired' as a result of temporarily taking over a school-wide role.

> It got to the point where the paperwork took over and the deadlines took over. It does happen to people and that's what I worry about the most. They start doubting themselves and as soon as they've got that seed of doubt, they leave.

Frances had never worked in a school where everyone got on so well together: 'Lots of social things happen where we celebrate things and we do it all together – it's like being in a family. I feel that I can rely on my colleagues.' School leadership played a 'huge' part in her enjoyment of teaching in the school: 'That's what makes the difference. It opens opportunities.'

The head, in particular, had been very supportive at the time of her grand-parent's passing.

Gaining rewards from pupils' progress

Her pupils' progress has always been the main source of Frances' motivation:

> I have a good relationship. There are times when you do doubt yourself, when you receive criticism, and it's normally from parents. You do have to justify yourself, but working as a team where people support you and they say you have done really well with this child and you do see the results and little things, not the SATs results, but the child that stops you in Tesco or the Mum that stops you and says their child has stopped crying for the first time in three years before school every morning. It's remembering these things when people do criticise you that keeps you going.

In each of the last three years, however, her classes had been quite different. First there was a bright group, which made it easy to focus on improving their standards; then there was a class with some difficult behaviour problems, which shifted the focus to improving behaviour; then a class of quieter, 'gentler' children that lacked confidence and needed gentle handing.

> Just seeing where the children are, getting to know the whole person, the background. You're almost like a social worker on some days. The root of the problem is not normally at school, it's at home. The trials and tribulations they go through before getting to school, and the relationships with the parents makes a difference.

Personal support: a necessary condition for ongoing resilience and commitment

Frances had little life outside school during the week. Her 'other half' was a 'workaholic' but not a teacher. They had agreed to both work late all week but keep weekends free. She enjoyed a happy and stable personal life and stated that she would not be able to do her job without the support at home. She intended to continue teaching but might not be as committed when starting a family or when beginning to feel that her job had strongly affected her personal life: 'The job is not everything to me. My home life is everything to me.' Frances added that teaching would become 'just a job' if her life outside began to suffer. Nevertheless, she was looking for new challenges to maintain her motivation and continue her successful teaching career trajectories.

Frances' workline illustrates the steady growth over time of her sense of self-efficacy, particularly related to the good results her pupils achieved in national

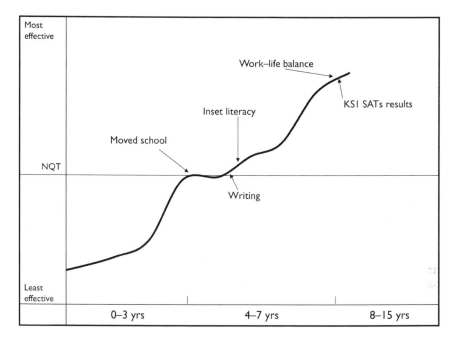

Workline 15   Frances' workline.

tests in literacy, numeracy and science. The three factors that had the most impact on her sense of effectiveness during the last three years were:

1   her relationships with her colleagues;
2   her positive professional and personal experiences; and
3   interacting with new people (e.g. working abroad).

She spent most of her school time in the classroom or on the paperwork and regretted a lack of time to work with her colleagues:

> Because my stress levels were quite high, I wasn't so nice, and was unwilling to take more things on. You don't work as much. I tried to be on the surface of things quite smiley and bubbly still. But children have a way of picking up. So I suppose I did become quite snappy for a couple of weeks and not as bubbly and bright. I really did doubt myself, not so much academically, I always knew that what I've taught the children was fine, but just generally in how I speak to people and how I handle people and my own self esteem personally. I was happier inside the classroom with the children than outside of it. So I didn't like the times when the parents came in. I didn't enjoy parents evenings and it was those times that put the stress on me.

Nevertheless, she had learned from this experience:

> I think that has made me a lot stronger and it's probably made me a little more organised and happier, I think. I feel more included and much more aware of things that are going on around me. I've become a teacher governor this year, I probably wouldn't have done if it wasn't for all the things that happened this year. Being more included in things and being part of the team has made me want to give something back to the school. I feel much more part of the family rather than somebody who's come in from the outside.

Frances had recently achieved the AST (Advanced Skills Teacher) status. She stressed that becoming an AST and a recent overseas climbing experience had been 'really positive experiences' for her because 'they are not easy to achieve'. She had become a stronger person and achieved a better work–life balance. Over three years of teaching in this school, Frances' focus had moved 'from improving standards to behaviour management to confidence building, team building': 'I've grown as a teacher. I've realised it's not all about standards and raising standards. It's about the children's own expectations, so my outlook on teaching is different.'

Story 2: sustaining high commitment despite challenges – a watershed phase

> Thinking of continuing what I am doing for the next 20 years fills me with horror: too many policies, too much paperwork!
>
> (Jill)

This second example illustrates well the dilemmas mid-career teachers face as they struggle to maintain a life outside school whilst taking on ever more extra classroom leadership and management responsibilities. It points to the important role of in-school support as they strive to sustain their commitment, sense of efficacy and wellbeing.

Jill had been teaching for 22 years. Having taught in three other schools, she had been in her present school as head of English for six years and was a well-established, well-respected teacher and colleague.

The suburban school in which she worked had 1,100 pupils aged 11–18, drawn from a socially and culturally diverse population in inner-city, suburban and semi-rural areas. It had 25 per cent of pupils who received free school meals, with above the national average (21 per cent) classified as having SEN, a high proportion (14 per cent) having English as their second language, and 33 per cent coming from ethnic minority families. Pupil attendance and behaviour were good. The school was popular with parents and was oversubscribed. In terms of academic achievement, in comparison with other schools in similar circumstances, according to its external inspection report, the school was 'well above average'. The school was also supporting a local school that had been judged as having failed to meet the minimum educational standards laid down by the government and was moving toward closure as part of the government's 'Transforming Secondary Schools' Initiative. The quality of teaching was judged to be 'satisfactory throughout the school ... frequently good and sometimes very good and excellent'. Jill's teaching fell into the latter category.

The call to teach

Jill had entered teaching, like many other secondary school teachers, out of 'love of subject' and 'the rewards of teaching the young'. She regularly attended in-service courses related to all aspects of her subject and continued to enjoy and be wholeheartedly committed to her teaching because of her continuing belief that she had a positive impact on her pupils' learning and achievement.

In her own school, pupils were 'naughty rather than bad and respond well if they know you see them as a person'. She did not have any problems in managing pupils and used different approaches according to her identification of their needs. Nevertheless, because the pupils were from diverse backgrounds, she found: 'With some students it's a constant strategy game to keep them focused and stop them disrupting the learning for other students.'

Gaining strength from leadership support

Whilst her level of commitment remained high, this had deteriorated in relative terms over the last three years. The longer she did the job, the 'more cynical' she had become about the value of initiatives which she was asked to implement. Jill regularly worked 61–65 hours each week. There were, in her view, 'too many policies and too much paperwork'. These, coupled with her management role and heavy marking load had resulted in an increasing dissatisfaction with the time she was able to give to planning her lessons, the time she was able to give to working with her departmental colleagues, providing for the needs of individual pupils and reflecting on her own teaching. The result for her was that 'the job is three times as great as the teaching contact time and my personal life is greatly affected and compromised'.

She feared, also, that her own lack of management effectiveness put pressure on her team: 'To take the pressure off my team I think I need to be more effective.'

Support and recognition from her line manager played a crucial role in restoring her sense of efficacy and her ongoing commitment. Jill described her line manager as 'brilliant' for the support she gave her as she struggled with the stress of management issues, including a high staff turnover and extended absence of her deputy head of department. This help was crucially important to her and had made her want to try harder.

Managing work–life tensions

Jill was worried that the job was taking over her life and felt guilty, also, about her contributions at home, particularly concerning the time she gave to her young child who was just beginning a new school. She felt guilty at work, also. She felt that she was never quite able to cover everything adequately and so was in a constant battle with prioritising between work directly related to her teaching and the managerial aspects of her role as head of department: 'I'm tired of always dealing with three or four things at a time.'

She was 'constantly beating myself up' about this, though she still saw herself as an 'idealist'. She spoke of how she had worked for 72 hours during a school spring holiday break, causing her partner extreme irritation – and even then she had not managed to meet the deadline. For Jill, being a teacher was a key part of her self-identity, so if she felt she was not doing a good job at school, she brought her sense of despondency home: 'You either draw a line and not do what you know needs doing and spend time with your family and go out or you do work and lock yourself away. I do a combination of both.'

Jill's workline shows graphically the fluctuations experienced by this teacher as she strove to manage work–life tensions and sustain her commitment and

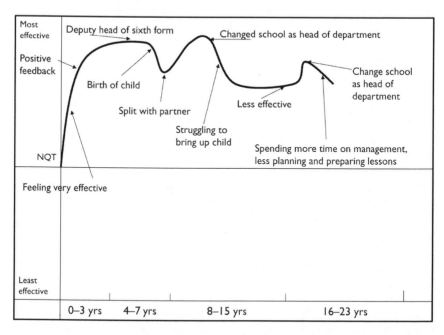

Workline 16 Jill's workline.

sense of efficacy both as a teacher and as a middle manager. Support and recognition made important contributions to her ability to restore mastery and control over the course of her professional life.

Jill continued to enjoy working with the other members of her department and others in the school, in which there was considerable support for staff and opportunities for career development. However, the head and SLT seemed to have become 'remote'. She attributed this to the growth of the school numbers, possibly the price of popularity, and to the takeover of the nearby failing school. More recently, Jill decided to become an AST rather than continue to pursue a role in the SLT, thus ensuring that her love of subject and classroom teaching would continue to be prioritised and remain the cause of her sustained commitment.

Story 3: sustaining commitment

> My motivation's reasonably high. I'm not flagging although there's a considerable amount of work to be done, although I do feel because of personal issues I have a little more time to devote to what I want to do.... When I come to work I still don't see it as work. I get on with the job and I enjoy my job.... The main enjoyment of the job has always been in the classroom.
>
> (Peter)

In the third example we show how positive emotions derived from teaching, together with supportive school environments, may contribute to a veteran teacher's ongoing commitment, motivation and a strong sense of efficacy in the final phase of his professional life.

Enjoyment in teaching: fuelling commitment with emotional strength

Peter 'followed' his sister and 'fell into' teaching, but had never regretted it. He found classroom teaching, which 'brings out the closet entertainer in me', the most enjoyable part of the job. He liked the variety: 'Very rarely you get two days that are the same.' He believed that he was a good teacher and enjoyed a high level of self-efficacy and commitment.

> Peter was 48 years old and had taught for 26 years. He had been teaching at his current school of 800+ pupils aged 11–16, set in a rural area and drawing from a diverse, principally white indigenous population with a mix of working- and middle-class parents, for nine years, having previously worked at three others. Peter was head of mathematics, enjoyed teaching and felt that he was effective.
>
> I think children enjoy my classes. There are always areas where you can improve or bring a variety of styles. I know one or two parents that have

given me very nice compliments from things that the child has already said to them.... I'm committed to the job because as a parent I would like to think the teachers that are in charge of my children would be committed to the job and I think the whole feeling towards the job when I did have children, coming to it from a parental angle rather than just an educational one, does make a difference. You see them in a different light.

Sustaining motivation and commitment in a supportive work environment

Peter enjoyed the 'nice atmosphere' in his current school and described the overall behaviour of the pupils as 'good'. He thought that his school was less challenging than others in which he had worked, that pupils did well, and that he experienced stress in his work only 'occasionally'. He described the senior management at his school as 'strong' and 'effective'. School policies on pupil behaviour had the biggest positive impact on his work as a teacher:

We've got a supportive senior management; the pupils are not allowed in many respects to get away with little things. The emphasis upon making sure the little things are right means they're not moving onto the next stage where they become particularly difficult.

Peter thought his school also benefited from 'quite a sociable staff', but regretted that the time spent on staff relaxing and meeting up after school 'seems to have become less and less' over the years. However, he had remained positive about the ethos at his current school: 'We work on the principle that everyone's treated fairly. We don't have a particular hit list. They get the same attitude and approaches from the staff throughout the years.'

Learning to prioritise: managing work–life tensions

Peter was 'a very private person' who did not bring personal issues to work.

There have been personal issues, but wherever possible I've tried to keep that to the outside and bare minimum. I know myself motivational wise. You take your eyes off the goal a little when you have personal issues going on in your life but I would like to think that they're now less influential than they were.

Peter had been head of department in his previous school, where he had to 'work every evening and every weekend with a view to getting things ready and sorted', but 'then certain things change and so you start doing them the year after'. He had been able to prioritise more at his current school: 'If I need to spend a weekend doing it I will, but I won't do everything all over the weekend.' He was particularly pleased with the current policy, which provided him with more non-class contact to fulfil his departmental leadership responsibilities.

Peter felt that he was managing his work–life tensions and that he would continue to maintain his work–life balance because he was happy with his present position and had no intention of pursuing further career advancement. He welcomed new ideas and wanted to continue to improve his teaching in the classroom, though he 'wouldn't rush into new things any more'. Rather, he would reflect on them and seek to develop them into existing practices. He enjoyed his job 'too much' and was not looking forward to retirement.

Peter's workline illustrates the fluctuations, continuities and discontinuities that may challenge teachers' sense of self-efficacy, commitment and effectiveness over a career span. Note the combination of workplace- and age-related highs and lows. Importantly for Peter, his latest school experience coupled with his own high sense of self-efficacy and his decision not to move further on the career ladder, but to maintain a secure sense of wellbeing in life and work, had ensured that, barring unforeseen events, he was likely to remain committed throughout the final phases of his teaching.

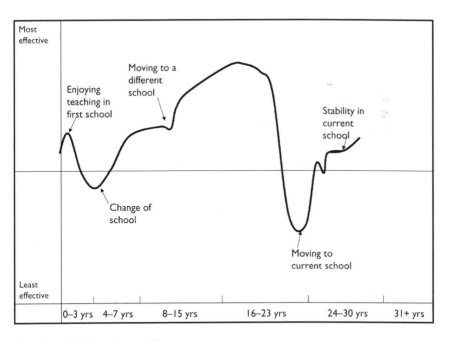

Workline 17 Peter's workline.

Mapping the territory: teacher resilience in three interrelated settings

Teachers' work takes place in complex individual, relational and organisational settings. Whilst these do not necessarily influence their levels of subject knowledge or technical competencies, together with the broader social and cultural structures in which these are located, they inevitably influence their sense of professional self, wellbeing and capacities to teach to their best. They may also challenge their ability to sustain the educational values and sense of vocation with which they entered teaching, as shown in the stories of our three resilient teachers.

Resilience in the teaching self: the 'inner landscapes' of teaching

In Chapter 2, we suggested that a sense of vocation is at the heart of many teachers' work and lives. The stories of teachers in this and other chapters demonstrate the importance of this sense of vocation to their sense of self – the 'inner landscapes' of teaching. It is an important asset of teachers, fuelling their personal resources with 'determination, courage and flexibility, qualities that are in turn buoyed by the disposition to regard teaching as something ... to which one has something significant to offer' (Hansen, 1995: 12). Both Frances and Jill had a strong calling to teach and continued to enjoy the pleasure of being able to make a difference to the learning and lives of their pupils. For Peter, the joy he derived from working with children played a key role in his sustained commitment in the final phase of his professional life.

The testimony of the four teachers in Hansen's classic study (ibid.) also suggests that teaching as a vocation presupposes many of the meanings 'characteristically associated with helping others learn and improve themselves intellectually and morally' (ibid.: 15). Margolis (2008) also, in a study which sought to make sense of the complexities of teachers' professional lives in light of changes in social and economic forces, concluded that opportunities which promote teachers' learning and enable them to share their gifts with others in the profession are what keep 'good teachers' teaching (ibid.: 160–161). Teachers' inner vocational drive 'turns the focus of perception in such a way that the challenges and the complexities in teaching become sources of interest in the work, rather than barriers or frustrating obstacles to be overcome' (Hansen, 1995: 144).

Palmer (1998) proposed three important interwoven paths in the inner landscape of the teaching self: intellectual, emotional and spiritual. He explained that the teacher's inner quest to help pupils learn, the way that they feel about the act of teaching and their heart's longing to be connected with the work of teaching form the essence of their inner terrain. A key notion that connects these three paths of the teacher's inner world is that of 'vocation' or 'calling'; and the embodiment of a sense of vocation and self-efficacy in teachers' professional identity provides the foundation for teachers' positive emotions. Their sense of vocation, especially, provides a sense of purpose for their actions, and their management of their experiences, commitment and wellbeing.

To maintain their vocational drive, teachers need an enduring 'optimistic sense of personal efficacy' (Bandura, 1989: 1176) – as in the cases of all three teachers illustrated in this chapter. Hoy and Spero (2005: 343) locate teachers' sense of efficacy in their confidence about 'their abilities to promote students' learning'. These self-judgements and beliefs 'affect the effort teachers invest in teaching, their level of aspiration, the goals they set' (ibid.: 345). Bandura (1997: 71) postulates that 'turning visions into realities is an arduous process with uncertain outcomes'. He argues that 'people must have a robust sense of personal efficacy to sustain the perseverant effort needed to succeed' (1989: 1176): 'When faced with obstacles, setbacks, and failures, those who doubt their capabilities slacken their efforts, give up, or settle for mediocre solutions. Those who have a strong belief in their capabilities redouble their effort to master the challenges' (Bandura, 2000: 120).

For Frances, Jill and Peter, an immediate consequence of their exercise of self-efficacy was their feelings of regaining control, self-esteem, confidence and, ultimately, wellbeing, commitment and capacity to teach to their best.

Relational resilience: drawing strength from each other

Close relationships in the workplace act as important 'social glue', which helps people 'deal with the uncertainties of their changing world' (Goodwin, 2005: 615, cited in Edwards, 2007: 8); and in positive psychology, particular attention has been given to the importance of relationship-based assets and their contribution to resilience (Gorman, 2005; Luthans *et al.*, 2007; Masten, 2001). Neuroscientists' discovery of the social brain reveals that 'we are wired to connect' (Goleman, 2007: 4). This revelation provides a biological basis for understanding the nature and confirming the importance of good-quality relationships in maintaining a sense of positive identity, wellbeing and effectiveness in our daily work and lives:

> Surely much of what makes life worth living comes down to our feelings of wellbeing – our happiness and sense of fulfilment. And good quality relationships are one of the strongest sources of such feelings.... In a sense, resonant relationships are like emotional vitamins, sustaining us through tough times and nourishing us daily.
>
> (Ibid.: 312)

An important feature of the three teachers in this chapter, as of those of many other teachers in this book, is the role of supportive and collaborative relationships within the workplaces in facilitating the formation of social ties. It is through these that expertise, knowledge and information, and ultimately teachers' sense of efficacy and resilience, can be nurtured, strengthened and shared (Penuel *et al.*, 2007). We have, therefore, coined the term *relational resilience* to acknowledge that teachers' capacity to perform to their best in the face of adversity can be developed through membership of communities of practice in their workplaces. Relational resilience resonates with the central thesis of social capital: 'relationships matter' (Field, 2008: 1):

> By making connections with one another, and keeping them going over time, people are able to work together to achieve things they either could not achieve by themselves, or could only achieve with great difficulty. People connect through a series of networks and they tend to share common values with other members of these networks; to the extent that these networks constitute a resource, they may be seen as forming a kind of capital.
>
> (Ibid.: 1)

Thus, trusting and open communities of practice may function as a valuable asset, or 'capital', which not only provide intellectual, spiritual and emotional resources for teachers' professional development, but also enable them to build a sense of belonging in the school community. Bryk and Schneider (2002: 20) argue that teachers' interpersonal worlds are organised around a distinct set of role relationships: 'Teachers with students, teachers with other teachers, teachers with parents and with their school principal.' Among these, a trusting relationship between teachers is of vital importance in building their sense of collective resilience. A lack of social support from colleagues could, on the other hand, lead to teachers' emotional exhaustion and depersonalisation (Schaufeli and Bakker, 2004). Nieto (2003) stresses that in the contemporary contexts for teaching, schools need to become places where teachers find community and engage in intellectual work because a learning community is an important incentive that keeps teachers going. Communities of practice exist within such learning communities and these are claimed to enhance teachers' sense of belonging and shared responsibility, sustain morale and perceived efficacy, develop aspects of resilient qualities, and thrive and flourish socially and professionally (Wenger, 1998). For Frances, for example, the feelings of being able to rely on her colleagues at the outset of her professional life made an important contribution to her positive professional trajectory.

In contrast to teachers' individual resilient qualities, relational resilience is developed through the many and varied interactions which characterise their work. The presence, quality and range of opportunities that promote relationships of trust and shared values and visions amongst the staff can foster the strength of a collective capacity for joint work. For teachers working in schools in socio-economically challenging circumstances in particular, staff collegiality and mutual trust and support are of profound importance in sustaining their morale, sense of efficacy, wellbeing and effectiveness (Day *et al.*, 2007; see also Peterson *et al.*, 2008). Positive relational bonds in such circumstances help to build collective efficacy beliefs amongst teachers, in which a 'robust sense of group capability' establishes expectations (cultural norms) for success which encourage 'organisational members to work resiliently toward desired ends' (Goddard *et al.*, 2004: 8). In education, these desired ends have to be related to students' progress and achievement. Moreover, the importance of building collective strength and confidence in communities of teachers in the reality of teaching is that they are able to 'interact knowledgeably and assertively with the bearers of innovation and reform' (Hargreaves, 1994: 195).

Organisational resilience: leadership matters

The concept of organisational resilience has been developed largely outside education. Hamel and Välikangas (2003), writing in the context of business, define organisational resilience as the ability to reinvent strategies dynamically in response to changes in circumstances. They describe a truly resilient organisation as a workplace that is filled with excitement and argue that strategic renewal, i.e. 'creative reconstruction', 'must be the natural consequence of an organisation's innate resilience' (ibid.: 2–3). Horne and Orr (1998) proposed seven 'Cs' to describe key features of resilient organisations: community, competence, connections, commitment, communication, coordination and consideration. These characteristics are also used in the educational research literature to portray schools as learning communities in which both pupils and teachers are able to experience enriched relationships with others, enhanced efficacy and commitment and increased job fulfilment (Stoll and Louis, 2007). At a time when the contemporary landscape of teaching is littered with successive and persisting government policy reforms that have increased teachers' external accountabilities, work complexity and emotional workload, such learning communities promote and nurture organisational resilience – a necessary condition for schools to sustain their sense of collective identities and continue to work for improvement.

In contrast to the nature of individual and relational resilience, organisational resilience places an importance on the effectiveness of the organisational context, structure and system; on how the system functions as a whole to create supportive environments for individuals' professional learning and development. In such environments, as our stories show, trusting relationships amongst staff and a collective sense of efficacy and resilience may be built which enable the organisation to sustain continuing development and, where necessary, transformation in times of change. Key to organisational resilience is the presence of good leadership.

Committed and trustworthy leaders are at the heart of resilient schools. The qualities of school principals and the contextually sensitive strategies they enact over time (Leithwood, 2007) are key to building and retaining the commitment, engagement and collective loyalty of teachers – as in the case of all three teachers. Jill's and Peter's experiences, in particular, illustrate the critical role of organisational arrangements, recognition and support in helping teachers in their middle and late professional life phases exercise their resilience and sense of efficacy as they strive to manage work–life tensions and continue to enjoy the pleasure of giving their best to the progress and achievement of their pupils. Knoop (2007: 223) argues: 'Considering the present pace of sociocultural change, it is difficult to imagine a time in history when good leadership was more important than it is today, and when the lack of it was more dangerous.'

> Leaders are the stewards of organisational energy [resilience] ... they inspire or demoralise others, first by how effectively they manage their own energy and next by how well they manage, focus, invest and renew the collective energy [resilience] of those they lead.
>
> (Loehr and Schwartz, 2003: 5)

Similarly, Henry and Milstein (2006: 8) argue: 'Teachers, students, parents, support personnel are the fabric of the school. Leaders are weavers of the fabric of resiliency initiatives.'

Examples of such leadership may also be found in a mixed-methods national study of the impact of school leadership on pupil outcomes, the largest and most extensive study of contemporary school leadership to be conducted in England (Day *et al.*, 2009). Principals' professional values and leadership strategies and practices were shown to have had a profound influence on the development of individual, relational and organisational capacity and trust in a group of effective and improved primary and secondary schools. Context-sensitive interactions, structures and strategies which secured individual and collective consistency with values and vision in the school were identified as fundamental to establishing and sustaining relationships within the school community – a key contributory factor in teachers' sense of individual, relational and organisational resilience. As Peter, our veteran teacher, commented:

> The one thing that I've found here, the support and the actual discipline within the school allows me to think about my own teaching.... I think it goes right through.
>
> (Peter)

Conclusions: resilience counts

It is clear that resilience is a multi-faceted and unstable construct. Its nature and sustainability throughout teachers' different professional life phases will be determined by the interaction between the strength of the vocation of individual teachers, those whom they meet as part of their daily work and the collective resilience of the organisation in its internal and external environments. Their capacities to manage unanticipated, as well as anticipated, events effectively will be mediated by these.

The portraits of the teachers in this chapter (as of those in the other chapters) suggest resilience is necessary on a daily basis to:

1 meet the often unpredictable challenges posed by students who may not always be highly motivated to learn, and whose problems outside the school are likely to form part of their behaviour in school;
2 manage the tensions inherent in meeting externally identified, narrowly defined sets of academic standards whilst simultaneously caring for the personal and citizenship needs of students;
3 respond to changes in the curriculum;
4 maintain the physical, psychological and emotional energy needed to engage others in learning for sustained periods of time; and
5 collaborate with colleagues in planning and evaluating in order to improve.

In the case of Frances and Peter, the leadership of their school heads, supportive school cultures, staff collegiality and positive teacher–pupil relationships were found to be contributing influences to their ability to gather intellectual and emotional strengths in the face of setbacks and challenges (e.g. work–life tensions and national school inspection), and through these, sustain their sense of efficacy, commitment and their capacity to teach to their best and continue to fulfil their passion for teaching. Attempts to reduce teachers' working time and improve their work–life balance alone are, unfortunately, unlikely to increase teacher resilience:

> People need one another and, above all, they need encouragement, but that encouragement is best when it is personal, taking account of their unique history and hopes, coming from somebody who inspires trust.
>
> (Zeldin, 2004: 38)

It is the complexities and subtleties of the emotions that many teachers experience and manage in every school day – including teaching increasing numbers of those who have behavioural problems, those who find it difficult to engage in learning and those who are emotionally anxious and troubled because of unhappy family relationships at home – that makes what they do unique. It is the ongoing demands on their intellectual energy, competence and capacity to connect 'self and subject and students in the fabric of life' (Palmer, 1998: 11) that distinguishes the teaching self from the selves of other professionals. Many teachers would argue that coping with adverse circumstances in the minefields of every school day, although at its best immensely rewarding, is also emotionally draining and physically exhausting. In times when organisational and professional change is inevitable in order to meet new local, national and global social and economic challenges, it is those who are supported in managing connections between their educational values, beliefs and deepest callings with those of their colleagues and organisations through the exercise of individual, relational and organisational resilience who are most likely to overcome setbacks in different work settings. It is they who will most enjoy the happiness, joy and fulfilment derived from the differences that they make to the lives and achievements of their pupils and, through them, the wellbeing of tomorrow's society.

Chapter 10

Teachers who make a difference

New lives, old truths

Introduction

> Eric Hanushek, an economist from Stanford, estimates that the students of
> a very bad teacher learn, on average, half a year's worth of material in one
> school year. The students in the class of a very good teacher will learn a year
> and a half's worth of material. That difference amounts to a year's worth of
> learning in a single year.... After years of worrying about issues like school
> funding levels, class size and curriculum design, many reformers have come
> to the conclusion that nothing matters more than finding people with the
> potential to be great teachers. But there's a hitch: no one knows what a
> person with the potential to be a great teacher looks like.
>
> (Gladwell, 2008)

There is now a considerable body of research that points to associations between
teachers' content and pedagogical knowledge, commitment, resilience and a
stable sense of positive professional identity and self-efficacy and their classroom
effectiveness. As the evidence in this book has shown, however, experience of
teaching does not necessarily lead to expertise and, over the span of personal
and professional lives, as contexts change, without support so, also, do the challenges to teachers to sustain their capacities to strive always to teach to their
best. Emotional and intellectual work may become emotional and intellectual
labour (Hochschild, 1983) as commitment becomes eroded as a result of time
and circumstance. Yet, in an age of mass education, increasing economic competition and challenges to the harmony and traditional social fabric of life,
ensuring the high quality of teachers and teaching and learning in schools is of
paramount importance. That quality is related not only to the knowledge, skills
and dispositions that may be developed during training and improved during
the course of a career, but also to the passion the best teachers bring to their
work and their continuing capacity to teach to their best. This final chapter discusses connections between the quality of teachers and pupil outcomes, the
complex relations between the quality of teaching and successful learning, why
teaching in this century is more stressful than ever, and why passion matters in
the new lives of teachers.

Research perspectives

Research on school effectiveness acknowledges that teacher and classroom variables and between-teacher and between-class variables have much more effect on student learning than school effects (Scheerens *et al.*, 1989; Tymms, 1993). In other words, teacher quality matters. Whilst the quality of teaching is not the only ingredient in successful learning, it is 'a key determinant of students' experiences and outcomes of schooling' (Rowe, 2003: 21) (see also Figure 10.1).

Moreover, there is sufficient research evidence now to argue strongly that

> attempts to describe the knowledge base of teachers in terms of subject knowledge and general and subject-specific pedagogical knowledge may offer tools for analysing particular aspects of practice, but fail to provide an adequate account of what is required to function effectively minute by minute in the classroom.
>
> (Ainley and Luntley, 2007: 1127)

'The effect of poor quality teaching on student outcomes is debilitating and cumulative.... The effects of quality teaching on educational outcomes are greater than those that arise from students' backgrounds.... A reliance on curriculum standards and state-wide assessment strategies without paying

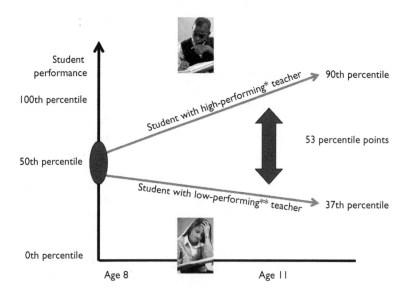

Figure 10.1 Teachers make an extraordinary difference (source: Sanders and Rivers (1996)).

Notes
* Among the top 20 per cent of teachers.
** Among the bottom 20 per cent of teachers.

due attention to teacher quality appears to be insufficient to gain the improvements in student outcomes sought.... The quality of teacher education and teaching appear to be more strongly related to student achievement than class sizes, overall spending levels or teacher salaries'.

(Darling-Hammond, 2000: 3)

Others who have estimated, through research, the value of good teachers to schools conclude that:

1   Having three consecutive years of teachers who are judged to be 'good' (i.e. in the top 15 per cent) can reverse the average deficit in achievement between disadvantaged students (drawn from low-income families) and others (Hanushek, 2002; Hanushek and Rivkin, 2004);
2   Students aged 10–11 years (fifth grade) who had experienced poor teachers for three years were likely to score 50 percentile points below their peers who were taught by good teachers over the same period (Rivers and Sanders, 2002).

(cited in Smith, 2008: 612)

Although these researchers did not find any 'systematic link between teacher characteristics and student outcomes' (Hanushek and Rivkin, 2004: 7), this is likely to be a function of the research paradigm through which they collected school-level data against performance in state-wide tests. They did not include close-up observation of teachers' work, nor extensive interviewing, nor consideration of the positive and/or negative influences of their work environment. Teacher quality was measured by a number of 'proxies', i.e. demonstration of qualifications and subject knowledge, not pedagogical skills or personal qualities or values. Thus 'quality' of teachers was defined by these researchers in terms of student attainment outcomes. In determining teacher quality it is important, also, however, to examine teaching and learning processes and the 'ingredients' that influence these.

Quality teaching, quality learning?

Other research concludes that 'it is clear that the factors most closely linked to school outcomes are not related to the quality of teachers at all', and that 'it is the nature of the school student population that is most likely to determine how a school performs' in terms of accountability testing regimes (Smith, 2008: 620). There is certainly evidence that in terms of attainment and educational achievement, students attending schools in highly disadvantaged communities perform less well than others (Department for Education and Employment, 1997; Joseph Rowntree Foundation, 2007; Malacova et al., 2009). However, there is also counter evidence that some schools in such areas are able to 'buck the trend' and perform well above expectations based on students' socio-economic background and prior attainment (Day *et al.*, 2009, 2010; Gorard, 1998; Gorard and Smith, 2004; Gu *et al.*, 2008). Moreover, emphasising establishing quality through investigating only the relationships between teacher knowledge and qualification and student test scores, by default, fails to acknowledge the processes of teaching and learning, the multiple academic, social citizenship and moral purposes of schooling and the ongoing effects of communities' social, economic and well-being environments upon students themselves as they attend (or do not attend) schools.

A second issue, connected with teachers' own learning, is embedded in the language of many policy documents which imply a causal connection between good teaching and successful pupils. Two distinguished American authors question this:

> There is currently a considerable policy focus on quality teaching, much of it rooted in the presumption that the improvement of teaching is a key element in improving student learning. We believe that this policy focus rests on a naïve conception of the relationship between teaching and learning. This concept treats the relationship as a straightforward causal connection, such that if it could be perfected, it could then be sustained under almost any conditions, including poverty, vast linguistic, racial, or cultural differences, and massive differences in the opportunity factors of time, facilities and resources. Our analysis suggests that this presumption of simple causality is more than naïve; it is wrong ... good teaching is but one of four ingredients in the mix. The others are that the learner desires to learn and expends the necessary effort to do so; that the social surround of family, community, and peer culture support all assist in learning; and that there are sufficient facilities, time and resources (opportunities) to accomplish the learning that is sought.
>
> (Fenstermacher and Richardson, 2005: 3)

With these words, Fenstermacher and Richardson capture the real and ever present complexity of the conditions in which teachers work to provide the best education for their pupils. Their four ingredients are, in effect, conditions for learning and so may be used as a means of appraising the quality of teaching. It is perhaps no accident that they have been shown to be the priorities of successful school principals in a range of national and international research (Day and Leithwood, 2007; Day *et al.*, 2009, 2010; Leithwood *et al.*, 2006). Good leaders and good teachers recognise that their work may not always result in successful learning. Forces outside of the control of the teacher may be too powerful. They work, therefore, to minimise the negative effects of such forces and maximise the positive effects. They know that good teaching that is person and task centred and context sensitive is more likely to result in increasing the desire of pupils to engage in learning and acknowledge its significance for them. Where this happens, a feedback loop is created between teacher, subject and learner, and a 'virtuous cycle' of mutual success is established (Palmer, 2007).

For Palmer, the capacity for connectedness distinguishes good teachers from bad teachers:

> Good teachers possess a capacity for connectedness. They are able to weave a complex web of connections among themselves, their subjects, and their students so that students can learn to weave a world for themselves.... The connections made by good teachers are held not in their methods but in their hearts – meaning *heart* in its ancient sense, as the place where intellect and emotion and spirit and will converge in the human self.
>
> (Ibid.: 11)

In a similar vein, Fenstermacher and Richardson (2005: 4) observe that 'When teaching in the task sense is done well, we called it good teaching. When teaching results in learning, we called it successful learning.'

They identify 'good' teaching as 'learner sensitive' pedagogy in order to distinguish it from 'successful' teaching, which is learning dependent. Good teaching, they suggest, is a combination of three elements: logical acts (teaching activities of, for example, explaining, interpreting, correcting, demonstrating); psychological acts (encompassing, for example, motivating, encouraging, rewarding, punishing); and moral acts (in which the teacher expresses and fosters, for example, honesty, courage, tolerance, compassion, respect and fairness). These three elements are present in the work of successful classroom and school leaders, and their enactment is a key part in dynamic – and sometimes uncertain – growth of expertise.

Why passion matters

> There are strong empirical grounds for believing that teachers can and do make a difference and that consistent high quality teaching, supported by strategic professional development, can and does deliver dramatic improvements in student learning.
>
> (Rowe, 2003: 27)

Five key observations about the qualities evident in good teaching and teachers have been made in this book. They correspond closely with those identified by other researchers over the years. First, good teaching is recognised by its combination of technical and personal competencies, deep subject knowledge and empathy with the learners (Hargreaves, 1998, 2001; Palmer, 1998). Teachers as people (the person in the professional, the being within the action) cannot be separated from teachers as professionals (Nias, 1989a). Teachers invest themselves in their work. Teaching at its best, in other words, is a passionate affair (Day, 2004).

Second, good teachers are universally identified by students as those who care. They care for them as part of their exercise of their professional duty and their care about them is shown in the connectiveness of their everyday class-room interactions, as well as their concern for their general wellbeing and achievement (Ashley and Lee, 2003; Fletcher-Campbell, 1995a, 1995b; Nod-dings, 1992).

Third, teachers' sense of identity and agency (the means by which they respond, reflect upon and manage the interface between their educational ideals, beliefs, work environments and broader social and policy contexts) are crucial to their own motivation, commitment, wellbeing and capacity to teach to their best. It is how they define themselves as 'teacher'.

Fourth, the extent to which teachers are able to understand emotions within themselves and others is related to their ability to lead and manage teaching and learning. Good teaching 'requires the connection of emotion with self-knowledge' (Denzin, 1984; see also Zembylas, 2003: 213).

Fifth, to be a good and effective teacher over time requires hopefulness and resilience, the ability to bounce back in challenging circumstances and changing contexts (Gu and Day, 2007).

It is the successful management by teachers of the combination of external policy, workplace and internal factors that enables them to teach to their best. A recent study of teachers who had received awards for their outstanding per-formance affirms that 'success' is likely to be a consequence of positive per-sonal, professional and contextual factors, confirming that, 'even though the teachers themselves possess both personal and professional qualities, one cannot guarantee that they will be successful in the work environment if the contextual support does not exist' (Cheung Lai-man et al., 2008: 633). As Chapter 8 shows, one of the qualities identified in a range of research about successful school leadership is a focus on the development of staff and whole-school cultures of care and achievement (Day et al., 2000; Day and Leithwood, 2007). Indeed, in some research studies, staff development has been estimated to have the biggest single effect upon teacher quality (Robinson, 2007).

However, despite this overwhelming evidence that good teaching that results in successful learning requires both the sustained and renewed personal and pro-fessional investment of teachers, care for and about learning and learners, com-binations of technical competencies, deep subject knowledge and empathy, and the maintenance of a strong sense of identity (agency) and commitment with an emotional understanding of self and others, these qualities and commitments are still, as the portraits of the 18 teachers in this book demonstrate, 'largely neglected in educational policy and teacher standards' (O'Connor, 2008: 117) and, sometimes also, in the potentially mediating structures and cultures of schools themselves as well as those in their personal lives (Day et al., 2007; Zembylas, 2003).

In examining what quality means, and how it might grow or decline during teachers' careers, we make three evidence-informed observations. First, teachers and learners benefit when their intellectual needs – their knowledge of subject area and pedagogical content knowledge – are able to be reviewed, refined and updated through tailored combinations of formal development programmes and in-school learning through mentoring, coaching and critical friendship. Second, good teaching and successful learning require the intellectual and emotional commitment of good teachers. Third, what marks teachers out as good or better than good is more than their mastery of content knowledge and pedagogical skills – it is their passion for teaching, for students and for learning. Sustaining such passion is intimately connected with their ongoing commitment, which itself is related to their sense of professional identity, to their belief that they can make a difference in the motivation, engagement and achievements of all their students, day in, day out, year in, year out. Such ongoing commitment is mediated by school leadership, conditions for teaching and learning and colleagues.

Is anything really different now? Workload and stress

Gary Cooper, an eminent researcher in the field of stress at work, made the following observation:

> Teachers are under far more stress than they were 20 years ago. They are at the mercy of demands from managers and parents. They have to meet more rigorous criteria, with more exams and higher expectations. They are working longer hours, many marking homework late into the night. They also have to cope with more bad, aggressive and abusive behaviour from children.
>
> (Cooper, cited in Brennan, 2009: 9)

The effects of stress at work on life outside the workplace have been well exemplified by teachers across all professional life phases. Faith, a veteran teacher, provides another fascinating insight:

> What's more important is that I spend time worrying about school and sleepless nights and that affects me – my personality and the way I am at home with my husband – irritable, etc., when I'm well aware that I'm irritable because I haven't slept. In the last week I only slept more than six hours on two nights – the rest of the time my mind buzzing with school which another teacher says is 'classic stress'.
>
> (Faith)

In the early phase of teaching it seems to be difficult for most teachers to achieve a balance between the time and effort they feel able to give to their lives outside teaching; and for some, there comes a point of decision in the middle years, the 'watershed' phase of their professional lives. Rosa, a primary school teacher who was moving towards this watershed phase, provides a good illustration of this dilemma:

> Having a life outside school hinders your effectiveness as a teacher! It's making that decision and having confidence about what you do in the classroom enables you to have a life outside school. It's always been weighted to school but over the seven years I've learnt to have a life outside school – I take the holidays and I take most weekends now but I work all during the week, all night long, but I've stopped myself to take holidays and take time out. I feel better for it and more effective but it hasn't helped in the paperwork so I've had to prioritise – but it has helped my general approach to life and my general stress levels.
>
> (Rosa)

Christine, a secondary teacher who had to manage a number of personal and professional stresses over three of her first five years of teaching made this comment about its impact upon life outside school:

> I don't know how people cope with somebody else (a partner) who has got a demanding job. It did make me realise what the workload is at weekends where perhaps a lot of people are going out and I think it makes you realise that things in this job are a lot more demanding.
>
> (Christine)

The influential Teacher Workload Study (PricewaterhouseCoopers, 2001), commissioned by the UK government, was concerned with issues of recruitment and retention. It concurred with Fullan's (2001) findings that teachers also experience a lack of professional trust. The study reported that, although some teachers welcomed the spirit of government initiatives to improve teaching and learning, they felt a lack of support, and that the pace and manner of implementation intensified their work; teachers felt a lack of ownership of change (PricewaterhouseCoopers, 2001). The report identified a need to 'reduce teacher workload' and thereby achieve 'improved teacher morale and better retention rates' (ibid.: 2) with the following recommendations among their six key proposals:

- Improve teachers' ownership and control of their work.
- Improve ways of government and agencies bringing in change.

(Ibid.: 1–6)

The levels of stress teachers experience in twenty-first-century schools, and the negative effects of these on their work, have begun to be recognised nationally in England through the work of the Teacher Support Network (TSN). Its website offers a variety of support and provides the latest research on the felt consequences of stress upon significant numbers of teachers. Its chief executive, Julian Stanley, observed, for example: 'Every year we come across teachers who have turned to alcohol as a coping mechanism. Far too many teachers are experiencing difficult emotional challenges at work because of the pressures heaped upon them' (http://teachersupport.info/news/in-the-press/Spirit-measure-TES.php).

The organisation also provides 24/7 free and confidential support and each year receives more than 17,000 requests from teachers for help and support. In a survey (completed by 777 people) it developed a 'snapshot' of the state and wellbeing of teachers in 2008, finding that:

- 87 per cent had suffered from stress in the last two years;
- over 60 per cent reported that issues in the workplace were responsible for these feelings;
- 82 per cent experienced problems such as trouble sleeping and 53 per cent reported lack of concentration.

Figure 10.2 shows the damaging impact of these symptoms on their work performance. Issues were, in rank order: excessive workload; rapid pace of change; pupil behaviour; unreasonable demands from managers; bullying by colleagues; and problems with pupils' parents. Professor Dame Carol Black (2009), the National Director for Health and Work, commented:

This report highlights the worrying levels of avoidable or needlessly prolonged health and wellbeing problems among those who work in

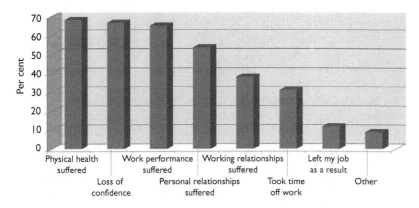

Figure 10.2 The detrimental effects of health and wellbeing problems on teachers' work performance (source: TSN (http://teachersupport.info/ news/policy-and-public-affairs/better-health-and-wellbeing.php).

education, particularly the high levels of common mental health problems, and the fact that teachers often feel they lack adequate support from their line managers to help them cope with the demands of their work. Such problems cause clear distress to individuals and their families, as well as having a profound impact on school communities and society in general.

(Black, 2009)

These findings would seem to be a response by a significant number of teachers which substantiate today those reported by Market & Opinion Research International (MORI), who surveyed all serving teachers registered with the General Teaching Council for England in 2002. Their analysis of over 70,000 respondents choosing their three greatest demotivating factors in their work found that:

- 56 per cent of respondents cited workload;
- 39 per cent cited initiative overload;
- 35 per cent cited target-driven culture;
- 31 per cent cited pupil behaviour and discipline.

(General Teaching Council, 2002: 5)

The effects of disruptions in classrooms

> As with many other more experienced teachers, Sam observed deterioration in pupils' attitudes to school-based learning:
>
> > It's the attitudes of the kids that is changing and, rather than generational, it seems to be more marked year by year. The general work ethic seems to be missing in quite a number of children. It's all down to peer pressure and street cred. It's not 'cool' to be seen to be good at science. That makes it more of a struggle for us to pull those kids around.
> >
> > (Sam)

Alongside (though not necessarily associated with) this, there has been a rise in dissatisfaction with their school experiences by a significant number of pupils, expressed in increases in absenteeism, behavioural problems in classrooms and in the less easily measurable but well-documented alienation from formal learning of many who remain.

In a survey of members of the National Association for Schoolmasters and Union of Women Primary School Teachers in 2008, half of the respondents claimed that 'low level' disruption in classrooms occurred on a daily basis, with almost two-thirds claiming that behaviour had deteriorated in recent years, and one in five that they had to deal with physical aggression at least once each week.

Significantly, teachers with more than 20 years' experience were 'most likely to report significantly more challenging behaviour' (*Daily Telegraph*, 2008: 10). On the same day as this, a report was filed that illustrates the very different perspectives that teachers' representatives and government spokespersons hold, this time in relation to statistics that showed that 15,000 teachers were absent from schools each day and that, in 2007–8, teachers in England took 2.9 million working days off school, as against 2.3 million in 1999. On the one hand, the acting general secretary of the largest teachers' organisations in England, (National Union of Teachers) claimed that 'Given the enormous pressures that teachers are working under, it is remarkable that they have so little sick leave on average', whilst on the other, a government employer spoke of working hard 'to reduce the pressures on teachers' (Paton, 2008: 2). The same report noted that teachers received more than 6,000 pages of government paperwork in 2008. Whilst these examples are drawn from the English context, they are, to a greater or lesser extent, replicated elsewhere also (Day and Smethem, 2009).

> We have kids from diverse backgrounds and some are a delight to teach and others are very challenging. They lack the self-esteem to recognise the boundaries of appropriate behaviour. With some students it's a constant strategy game to keep them focused and stop them disrupting the class for other students.
>
> (Jane)

A lesson from the teachers in this book and the larger number in the original VITAE study (Day *et al.*, 2007) is that passion may grow or die according to changes in personal and work circumstances. Without organisational support, bringing a passionate and resilient self to teaching every day of every week of every school term and year can be stressful, not only to the body but also to the heart and soul, for the processes of teaching and learning are rarely smooth, and the results are not always predictable. Thus, the commitment, hope and optimism with which many teachers still enter the profession, unless supported within the school, may be eroded as battles with those who don't wish to learn or cannot, or disrupt others' opportunities to learn, increasing media criticism and lack of work–life balance take their toll.

Teachers have hearts and bodies, as well as heads and hands, though the deep and unruly nature of their hearts is governed by their heads, by the sense of moral responsibility for students and the integrity of their subject matter which is at the core of their professional identity. They cannot teach well if any part of them is disengaged for long. Increasingly, social and political pressures give precedence to head and hand, but if the balance between feeling, thinking and doing is disturbed too much or for too long, teaching becomes distorted, teachers' responses are restricted, they may even cease to be able to teach. Teachers are emotionally committed to many different aspects of their jobs. This is not an indulgence; it is a professional necessity. Without feeling, without the freedom to 'face themselves', to be whole persons in the classroom, they implode, explode – or walk away.

(Nias, 1996: 305)

Passion is not a luxury, a frill, a quality possessed by just a few teachers or a personality trait that some teachers have and others lack:

Passion and practicality are not opposing notions; good planning and design are as important as caring and spontaneity in bringing out the best in students. Although not the whole story, passion, uncomfortable as the word may sound, is at the heart of what teaching is or should be.

(Fried, 1995: 6)

Being passionate about others' learning and achievement creates energy and fuels determination, conviction and commitment. Passion should not be regarded only as a disposition – people are not born, nor do they die, passionate.

As we have shown, there are many factors that help or hinder good teaching and successful learning. Not least among these are the family histories and circumstances of the parents, the students, the leadership and learning culture of the school, the effects of government policies, the perceived relevance and value of the curriculum, behaviour in the classroom and staff room, relationships with students, parents and the wider community, and teachers' knowledge, skills and competencies. Yet the primary factors that drive committed teachers are much more than these. They are the inner qualities of the teacher; a continuing striving for excellence (in herself and others); a caring for and fascination with growth; and, throughout external challenges, the 'bumpy moments' and 'discontinuities' of the new lives of teachers, a deep and abiding commitment to providing the best possible opportunities for each pupil.

Three inner qualities

Three inner qualities are central to being, behaving and sustaining a passion for teaching:

1   relationships with pupils
2   moral purposes: care, courage and hopefulness
3   emotional identities.

Relationships with pupils

Just as teachers may make a positive difference, so they may achieve the reverse. Twenty years ago, John Goodlad wrote of 1,000 classrooms which he and his colleagues had visited, saying they were:

> almost completely devoid of outward evidences of effect. Shared laughter, overt enthusiasm, or angry outbursts were rarely observed. Less than 3 percent of classroom time was devoted to praise, abrasive comments, expressions of joy or humor, or somewhat unbridled outbursts such as 'wow' or 'great'.
>
> (Goodlad, 1984: 229–230)

Today there are still stories of humiliation, fear and disconnection in classrooms.

> One student ... said she could not describe her good teachers because they differed so greatly.... But she could describe her bad teachers because they were all the same: 'Their words float somewhere in front of their faces, like the balloon speech in the cartoons.'
>
> (Palmer, 1998: 11)

A survey by the Campaign for Learning in England found that a high proportion of 14–16-year-old students claimed that 'poor teaching' – associated with teachers who were distant, patronising and who were not interested in them as people – was a cause for their underachievement:

> 'The teachers never explain anything, they're always on people's backs like that's wrong, that's pathetic, you're thick.'
> 'Teachers favour the more intelligent students in our class and don't help us less intelligent students enough.'
> 'Basically, we are patronised and treated as though we are little kids.'
> 'The teachers don't even try to understand us.'
>
> (Bentley, 1998: 80)

> 'The good teachers are the ones who know how to listen as well as talk, who don't make you feel that your opinion isn't worth anything. It's not age that's important, it's their attitude to young people. There are some who don't seem to enjoy what they're doing, and there are others who seem so enthusiastic about their subjects. It's brilliant being with those sort of teachers.'
>
> (Gillian, in White, 2000: 18)

> 'My teacher ... was the catalyst for my interest in the teaching profession as well as the match that lit my fiery passion for European history.... He was

so full of knowledge ... that ... he would just tell us stories off the top of his head.... He was the first teacher to ever make me feel as though I was as intelligent as the other students in the class ... he seemed to really value what I had to say ... he was a very kind and intelligent man as well as an excellent teacher.'

(Sandra, in ibid.: 159–160)

'What matters is that they have a passion for their subject and a way of motivating you. Some teachers have the ability to motivate people, to know just how far they can push it, how provoking they can be to make you this close to giving up, but then you decide: "I'm going to show this teacher."'

(Julia, in ibid.: 159)

As we have discussed earlier in this book, the nature of good teaching presupposes a care for the one taught as well as respect for the integrity of what is taught (Sergiovanni and Starratt, 1993). Teachers and students alike work better when they are cared 'about': an expression of teachers' personal beliefs and emotional commitment that goes beyond the contractual obligation of caring 'for' (Fletcher-Campbell, 1995b). Children, especially, are 'emotionally attuned to be on the look out for caring, or lack thereof, and they seek out and thrive in places where it is present' (Elias *et al.*, 1997). Yet to care for someone, teachers need to know who they are, their strengths and limitations, how they can grow in order to respond to their needs. Teachers who are passionate about their work know, also, that who they are as well as what they teach must connect emotionally with each student.

Moral purposes: care, courage and hopefulness

Whilst it is important not to 'sentimentalize' (Jackson, 1999: 88), it is necessary to acknowledge that moral purposes are an essential part of the identity and efficacy of many effective teachers. They are what keep teachers going. They contribute to their commitment, hope and resilience, positive emotions and capacity to teach to their best. For passionate teachers, professional accountability is about far more than satisfying externally imposed bureaucratic demands or annually agreed targets for action linked to government and school improvement agendas. They understand that the nature of teaching, the terms of their work, oblige them to 'place the intellectual and moral wellbeing of students first and foremost' through their actions and interactions (Hansen, 1998: 651). The study of values, ethics and moral purposes on which the actions of teachers will be based, should be, then, not only a key part of the content of teacher education programmes, but regularly revised and, where appropriate, refined throughout the teaching career.

Sockett (1993) and others (Falkenberg, 2007; Osguthorpe, 2008; Zembylas and Barker, 2007) argue that techniques of teaching are always subservient to a moral end and, therefore, that the moral character of the teacher is of prime importance. He identifies five major virtues: honesty, care, courage, fairness and practical wisdom.

Courage is a particularly necessary virtue in teaching. Sockett defines courage as 'a virtue that describes how a person, often selflessly, behaves in difficult and adverse circumstances that demand the use of practical reason and judgement in pursuit of long term commitments that are morally desirable' (Sockett, 1993: 74). Where curricula are closely scripted and where school cultures inhibit the expression of certain kinds of emotion, there may be less room for spontaneity, risk-taking, or improvisation in teaching. More importantly, there may be less room for attention to individual pupils' needs. To put it another way, in results-driven classroom contexts, teachers need to be courageous if they are to diverge from pre-planned pathways for the purposes of meeting the pupil learning needs they have identified. Additionally, in classrooms where the behaviour of some pupils is problematic, to be warm and encouraging requires courage to persist in caring for every student in the class, those who are able, those who are not, those who are interested and those who are alienated. It takes courage to continue to believe in and be actively engaged in one's moral purposes and not to default or care less due to the pressure of effort and energies required to fulfil instrumentally dominated agendas.

Central to this is 'academic optimism' (Hoy *et al.*, 2008), defined as

> a teacher's positive belief that he or she can make a positive difference in the academic performance of students by emphasizing academics and learning, by trusting parents and students to co-operate in the process, and by believing in his or her own capacity to overcome difficulties and react to failure with resilience and perseverance.
>
> (Ibid.: 822)

Seligman (2003) suggests that optimism is as important to success and achievement as talent or motivation and that it can be learned.

Morally based courageous and optimistic relationships between teachers and students, then, are fundamental to good teaching and successful learning; and whilst optimism is the glue that binds the two together and creates rich learning opportunities, the more powerful indicator of teachers' commitment is *hope*: 'An orientation of the spirit, an orientation of the heart.... It is not the conviction that something will [by definition] turn out well, but the certainty that something makes sense, regardless of how it turns out' (Havel, 1990: 181).

Teaching is, by definition, a journey of hope based on a set of ideals – for example – that I, as a teacher, can and will make a difference to the learning and the lives of the students I teach and the colleagues with whom I work – despite an acute awareness of obstacles to motivation and commitment (my own and others), the socio-economic circumstances of students, resource constraints and policy factors over which I have no control. Teachers who are passionate about what, how and who they teach remain hopeful. Arguably, it is our ideals that sustain us through difficult times and challenging environments; and it is our ideals that commit us to changing and improving our practice as the needs of students and the demands of society change. From the perspective of emotional intelligence,

> having hope means that one will not give in to overwhelming anxiety.... Indeed, people who are hopeful evidence less depression that others as they manoeuvre through life in pursuit of their goals, are less anxious in general, and have fewer emotional distresses.
>
> (Goleman, 1995: 87)

Emotional identities

Emotions play a key role in the construction of identity (Zembylas, 2003). They are the necessary link between the social structures in which teachers work and the ways they act. The evidence in this book provides an affirmation of teaching as work in which emotions are central (Day and Gu, 2009; Fineman, 1993; Hargreaves, 1994, 1998, 2004; Nias, 1996; Van Veen and Lasky, 2005; Zembylas and Barker, 2007). Thus, because teachers' work is a principal source for their sense of self-esteem and personal, as well as professional, satisfaction, it is inevitable that they will have deeply felt emotions. Maintaining an awareness of the tensions in managing our emotions is part of the safeguard and joy of teaching. The messages are clear and unequivocal:

1   Emotions are indispensable to rational decision making (Damasio, 1994, 2000; Sylwester, 1995).
2   Emotional understanding and intelligence are at the heart of good professional practice (Denzin, 1984; Goleman, 1995).
3   Emotional and cognitive health are affected by personal biography, career, social context (of work and home) and external (policy) factors (Kelchtermans, 1996; Nias, 1989a, 1996).
4   Emotional health is crucial to effective teaching over a career (Day et al., 2007).

Teaching calls for and, at its best, involves daily, intensive and extensive use of both emotional labour (e.g. smiling on the outside whilst feeling anything but happy on the inside) and emotional work, which enables teachers to manage the challenges of teaching classes that contain students with a range of diverse motivations, personal histories and learning capacities (Hochschild, 1983). However, too much of the former leads to a disengagement with the complexities of teaching and learning, and a loss of trust by students; and too much investment of one's emotional self may lead to personal vulnerability, feelings of inadequacy at being unable to engage everyone in learning all the time and, in extreme cases, overwork and breakdown. It may lead teaching to become predominantly 'emotional labour', where the smile of communication is about business, not the person, where 'How are you today?' does not require a response, and where even acts of care are understood as devices to progress rather than emanating from genuine respect: 'When we sell our personality in the course of selling goods or services we engage in a seriously self-estranging process' (ibid.: ix).

However, research that focuses on the passion of vocation in relation to the person as well as the professional remains scarce. In many instances, emotions are managed and regulated only in order to ensure the efficient and effective running of the organisation and achievement of its goals. Even in this century, they:

> are usually talked about only insofar as they help administrators and reformers 'manage' and offset teachers' resistance to change or help them set the climate or mood in which the really important business of cognitive learning or strategic planning can take place.
>
> (Hargreaves, 1998: 837)

As we have seen, there are unavoidable interrelationships among teachers, also, between their professional and personal identities. The overwhelming evidence is that teaching demands significant personal investment.

Identities are not always stable, and it is likely that mild fluctuations may enhance teachers' learning and development. However, such relative stability can be subject to discontinuities and challenges, even crises, as times, contexts and people change. Today's professional has been described by some as 'mobilizing a complex of occasional identities in response to shifting contexts' (Stronach *et al.*, 2002: 117). Such mobilisations occur in the space between the 'structure' (of the relations between power and status) and 'agency' (the influence we and others can have). As the lives and work of teachers portrayed in this book show, it is the management of the interaction between these that influences how teachers maintain, revisit and renew (or do not renew) their personal and professional identities and, within this, their belief that they are able to make a difference to the learning and achievement of their pupils.

Conclusions: new lives, old truths

> The people who develop ... are those who love to learn, who seek new challenges, who enjoy intellectually stimulating environments, who are reflective, who make plans and set goals, who take risks, who see themselves in the large social contexts of history and institutions and broad cultural trends, who take responsibility for themselves and their environs.
>
> (Rest, 1986: 174–175)

Good teaching has never been easy. It has always required more than content knowledge and classroom competencies, more than 'a sophisticated understanding of, and the capacity to move between, the multiple dimensions and perspectives within education' (Crosswell, 2006: 222). In the new lives of teachers there are old truths. If they are to meet the demands of today's standards, and the expectations of today's and tomorrow's pupils, parents and politicians, their inner passion for their work and their pupils, their sense of positive emotional identity and wellbeing and their sense of hope in themselves as professionals who may be trusted to raise standards of care and achievement must be supported and sustained. For teachers to be and continue to be committed, resilient and to teach to their best, they need to work in environments that are less alienating, less bureaucratically managerial, less reliant on crude measures of performativity – for we know from countless studies that this saps rather than builds their capacities to teach well. To teach to their best, they need to work in schools in which leadership is just, supportive, clear and passionately committed to challenging them to sustain the quality of their commitment. They need a strong and enduring sense of efficacy. They need to believe, and have reason to believe, that they are making a difference.

Passion is fundamental to commitment, resilience and wellbeing. If teachers are to sustain these – they and those responsible for their training, education and leadership will need to build understandings of the cognitive and emotional contexts in which they work in order to increase their capacities to manage these. It is in everyone's interest to ensure that the inner values, qualities and purposes that form the foundation for passion among effective teachers, and which find their expression in the vision, knowledge, expectations and practices that children and young people experience, are developed and nurtured.

The environments in which teaching and learning take place will continue to change and, if they are to sustain their capacities to teach to their best, teachers will have to learn to live new lives. Yet, if they are to succeed, the quality of their new lives must be characterised by the care, passion, integrity, energy, wellbeing, commitment and resilience that has always infused the work of good teachers; and they must be supported by high-quality leadership that supports the creativity, efficacy, resilience and wellbeing of staff in the certain knowledge that unless they do so, for many teaching may become just a job.

Appendix

The workline chart

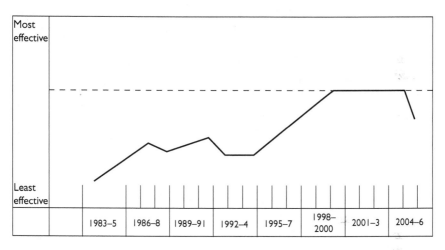

Figure A.1 The workline chart.

Notes

1 The book has grown out of a large-scale, mixed-methods study of variations in teachers' work, lives and their effects on pupils over a three-year period, which has been reported elsewhere (Day *et al.*, 2007). The study, with 300 teachers in 100 schools over a three-year period, focused on two kinds of teacher effectiveness – that which the teachers themselves perceived and that which was measured by the year-long progress and value-added test results of their pupils. The study found, not surprisingly, that teacher commitment was a key factor in their perceived effectiveness. In addition, it provided statistically significant empirical associations between teacher commitment and measured effectiveness.

2 Huberman identified five phases. The last two, 26–33 and 34–40, are very similar to the VITAE final phases of 24–30 and 31+ years.

Bibliography

Aaronson, D. (2008) The impact of baby boomer retirements on teacher labor markets. Chicago Fed Letter 254, September. Retrieved from www.chicagofed.org/publications/fedletter/cflseptember2008_254.pdf.

Achinstein, B. (2006) New teacher and mentor political literacy: Reading, navigating and transforming induction contexts. *Teachers and Teaching: Theory and Practice*, 12 (2): 123–138.

Acker, S. (1999) *The Realities of Teachers' Work: Never a Dull Moment*. London: Cassell.

Ainley, J. and Luntley, M. (2007) Towards an articulation of expert classroom practice. *Teaching and Teacher Education*, 23 (7): 1127–1138.

Allen, J. M. (2009) Valuing practice over theory: how beginning teachers re-orient their practice in the transition from the university to the workplace. *Teaching and Teacher Education*, 25: 647–654.

Appadurai, A. (1996) *Modernity at Large: Cultural Dimensions of Globalisation*. Minneapolis and London: University of Minnesota Press.

Apple, M. W. (1986) *Teachers and Texts: A Political Economy of Class and Gender Relations in Education*. London: Routledge.

Arthur, M., Inkson, K. and Pringle, J. (1999) *The New Careers: Individual Action and Economic Change*. Thousand Oaks, CA: Sage.

Ashley, M. and Lee, J. (2003) *Women Teaching Boys: Caring and Working in the Primary School*. Stoke on Trent: Trenthan Books.

Aspin, D. (1996) The liberal paradox. In Chapman, J., Boyd, W. and Lands, R. (eds), *The Reconstruction of Education: Quality, Equality and Control* (pp. 47–72). London: Cassell.

Aspinwall, L. G. (1998) Rethinking the role of positive affect in self-regulation. *Motivation and Emotion*, 22: 1–32.

Aspinwall, L. G. (2001) Dealing with adversity: Self-regulation, coping, adaptation, and health. In Tesser, A. and Schwarz, N. (eds) *The Blackwell Handbook of Social Psychology*, Vol. 1 (pp. 591–614). Malden, MA: Blackwell.

Aubusson, P., Steele, F., Dinham, S. and Brady, L. (2007) Action learning in teacher learning community formation: Informative or transformative? *Teacher Development*, 11 (2): 133–148.

Avenell, K. (2007) Common themes on learning communities. *The Australian Educational Leader*, 29 (1): 46–47.

Baier, A. C. (1994) *Moral Prejudices: Essays on Ethics*. Cambridge: Harvard Business Press.

Ball, S. J. (1993) Education markets, choice and social class: The market as a class strategy in the UK and the USA. *British Journal of Sociology of Education*, 14 (1): 3–19.

Ball, S. J. (2001) *The Teachers' Soul and the Terrors of Performativity*. University of London: Institute of Education.

Ball, S. J. (2003) Professionalism, managerialism and performativity. *Professional Development and Educational Change*. Paper presented at a conference organised by the Danish University of Education, 14 May.

Ball, S. and Goodson, I. (1985) Understanding teachers: Concepts and cultures. In Ball, S. and Goodson, I. (eds), *Teachers' Lives and Careers*. Lewes: Falmer Press.

Bandura, A. (1989) Human agency in social cognitive theory. *American Psychologist*, 44: 1175–1184.

Bandura, A. (1997) *Self-efficacy: The Exercise of Control*. New York: Freeman.

Bandura, A. (2000) Cultivate self-efficacy for personal and organisational effectiveness. In Locke, E. A. (ed.), *Handbook of Principles of Organisation Behaviour* (pp. 120–136). Oxford: Blackwell.

Barber, B. R. (2001) The 'engaged university' in a disengaged society: Realistic goal or bad joke? Retrieved 1 October 2003, from www.diversityweb.org/Digest/Sm01/engaged.html.

Barth, R. (1976) A principal and his school. *The National Elementary Principal*, 56 (November/December): 9–21.

Beijaard, D. (1995) Teachers' prior experiences and actual perceptions of professional identity. *Teachers and Teaching: Theory and Practice*, 1: 281–294.

Beijaard, D., Meijer, P. C. and Verloop, N. (2004) Reconsidering research on teachers' professional identity. *Teaching and Teacher Education*, 20 (2): 107–128.

Benjamin, K. and Wilson, S. (2005) Facts and misconceptions about age, health status and employability. Report HSL/2005/20. Buxton: Health and Safety Laboratory.

Benner, P. E. (1984) *From Novice to Expert: Excellence and Power in Clinical Nursing Practice*. Menlo Park: Addison Wensley.

Bentley, T. (1998) *Learning Beyond the Classroom: Education for a Changing World*. London: Routledge.

Bereiter, C. and Scardamalia, M. (1993) *Surpassing Ourselves: An Inquiry into the Nature and Implications of Expertise*. La Salle, IL: Open Court.

Berliner, D. (1994) Expertise: The wonder of exemplary performances. In Manglere, J. N. and Block, C. C. (eds), *Creating Powerful Thinking in Teachers and Students: Diverse Perspective* (pp. 161–186). Ft. Worth, TX: Holt, Rinehart & Winston.

Bernard, B. (1991) *Fostering Resiliency in Kids: Protective Factors in the Family, School, and Community*. San Francisco: WestEd Regional Educational Laboratory.

Bernard, B. (1995) Fostering resilience in children. Retrieved from http://resilnet.uiuc.edu/library/benard95.html.

Bernstein, B. (1996) *Pedagogy, Symbolic Control and Identity*. London: Taylor & Francis.

Betoret, F. D. (2006) Stressors, self-efficacy, coping resources, and burnout among secondary school teachers in Spain. *Educational Psychology*, 26: 519–539.

Biesta, G., Field, J., Goodson, I., Hodkinson, P. and Macleod, F. (2008) Strategies for improving learning through the life-course. The Learning Lives Project, July 2008. Retrieved 1 November 2009, from www.learninglives.org/articles/Learning%20Lives%20Pamphlet%20July%202008.pdf.

Bingham, C. (1991) Teachers' terms and conditions: A view from the schools. In Grace,

G. and Lawn, M. (eds), *Teacher Supply and Teacher Quality: Issues for the 1990s* (pp. 47–53). Clevedon: Multilingual Matters.

Black, D. C. (2009) Comment from the National Director for Health and Work. Retrieved 1 November 2009, from http://teachersupport.info/news/policy-and-public-affairs/better-health-and-wellbeing.php.

Block, J. H. and Block, J. (1980) The role of ego-control and ego resiliency in the organization of behaviour. In Collins, W. A. (ed.), *Minnesota Symposium on Child Psychology*, Vol. 13 (pp. 39–101). Hillsdale, NJ: Erlbaum.

Blumer, H. (1969) *Symbolic Interactionism: Perspective and Method*. Englewood Cliffs, NJ: Merrill.

Bobbitt, S. A., Faupel, E. and Burns, S. (1991) *Characteristics of Stayers, Movers, and Leavers: Results from the Teacher Follow-up Survey, 1988–89*. Washington, DC: Office of Educational Research and Improvement.

Boe, E. E., Bobbitt, S. A., Cook, L. H., Whitener, S. D. and Weber, A. L. (1997) Why didst thou go? Predictors of retention, transfer, and attrition of special and general education teachers from a national perspective. *The Journal of Special Education*, 30 (4): 390–411.

Bogler, R. (2001) The influence of leadership style on teacher job satisfaction. *Educational Administration Quarterly*, 37 (5): 662–683.

Bogler, R. (2002) Two profiles of schoolteachers: A discriminant analysis of job satisfaction. *Teaching and Teacher Education*, 18 (6): 665–673.

Bogler, R. and Somech, A. (2004) Influence of teacher empowerment on teachers' organizational commitment, professional commitment and organizational citizenship behavior in schools. *Teaching and Teacher Education*, 20 (3): 277–289.

Bolam, R. and McMahon, A. (2004) Literature, definitions and models: Towards a conceptual map. In Day, C. and Sachs, J. (eds), *International Handbook on the Continuing Professional Development of Teachers* (pp. 33–63). Maidenhead: Open University Press.

Bottery, M. (2005) The individualization of consumption: A Trojan horse in the destruction of the public sector? *Educational Management, Administration and Leadership*, 33 (3): 267–288.

Bouffard-Bouchard, T., Parent, S. and Larivee, S. (1991) Influence of self-efficacy on self-regulation and performance among junior and senior high-school age students. *International Journal of Behavioral Development*, 14 (2): 153–164.

Brennan, M. (1996) *Multiple Professionalisms for Australian Teachers in an Important Age*. New York: American Educational Research Association.

Brennan, Z. (2009) Ready to explode. *Sunday Times*. Retrieved from www.timesonline.co.uk/tol/news/uk/education/article6945824.ece.

Brookfield, S. (1995) Adult learning: An overview. In Tuinjman, A. (ed.), *International Encyclopaedia of Education*. Oxford: Pergamon Press. Retrieved 20 November 2006, from www3.nl.edu/academics/cas/ace/facultypapers/StephenBrookfield_AdultLearning.cfm.

Brown, S. and McIntyre, D. (1992) *The Craft of Teaching*. Buckingham: Open University Press.

Brundage, S. E. (1996) What kind of supervision do veteran teachers need? An invitation to expand collegial dialogue and research. *Journal of Curriculum and Supervision*, 12 (1): 90–94.

Bryk, A. S. and Schneider, B. L. (2002) *Trust in Schools: A Core Source for Improvement*. New York: Russell Sage Foundation Publications.

Bryk, A. S., Lee, V. E. and Holland, P. B. (1993) *Catholic Schools and the Common Good*. Cambridge, MA: Harvard University Press.

Bullock, A. and Thomas, H. (1997) *Schools at the Centre? A Study of Decentralisation*. London: Routledge.

Bullough, R. and Knowles, G. (1991) Teaching and nurturing: Changing conceptions of self as teacher in a case study of becoming a teacher. *International Journal of Qualitative Studies in Education*, 4: 121–140.

Campbell, R. and Neill, S. (1994) *Primary Teachers at Work*. London: Routledge.

Castells, M. (2004) *The Power of Identity* (2nd edn). Malden, MA: Blackwell Publishing.

Certo, J. L. and Engelbright Fox, J. (2002) Retaining quality teachers. *The High School Journal*, 86 (1): 57–75.

Chambers, D. (2002) The real world and the classroom: Second career teachers. *The Clearinghouse*, 75 (4): 212–217.

Chan, D. W. (2007) Burnout, self-efficacy, and successful intelligence among Chinese prospective and in-service school teachers in Hong Kong. *Educational Psychology*, 27: 33–49.

Cherubini, L. (2009) Reconciling the tensions of new teachers' socialisation into school culture: A review of the research. *Issues in Educational Research*, 19 (2): 83–99.

Cheung Lai-man, E., Cheng May-hung, M. and Pang King, C. (2008) Building a model to define the concept of teacher success in Hong Kong. *Teaching and Teacher Education*, 24: 623–634.

Chevalier, A. and Dolton, P. (2004) Teacher shortage: Another impending crisis? *CentrePiece*, Winter: 15–21. Retrieved from http://cep.lse.ac.uk/pubs/download/CP164.pdf.

Child Poverty Action Group (2009) *Child Wellbeing and Child Poverty*. London: Child Poverty Action Group.

Chitty, C. (1992) *The Education System Transformed*. Manchester: Baseline Books.

Cinamon, R. and Rich, Y. (2005) Work–family conflict among female teachers. *Teaching and Teacher Education*, 21: 365–378.

Clarke, J. and Newman, J. (1997) *The Managerial State: Power, Politics and Ideology in the Remaking of Social Welfare*. London: Sage.

Cohen, R. M. (1988) After 35 years: Ethnographic portraits of three veteran teachers. Unpublished dissertation, Teachers College, Columbia University.

Crosswell, L. (2006) Understanding teacher commitment in times of change. Unpublished EdD thesis submitted to Queensland University of Technology, Brisbane, Australia.

Csikszentmihalyi, M. (1990) *Flow: The Psychology of Optimal Experience*. New York: Harper & Row.

Cummings, T. and Worley, C. (2008) *Organization Development and Change*. Mason, OH: South-Western Cengage Learning.

Daily Mail (2009) Only six in ten children share a home with both parents (13 October). Retrieved 1 November 2009, from www.dailymail.co.uk/news/article-1219953/Only-children-share-home-parents.html.

Daily Telegraph (2008) Parents blamed for primary pupils' bad behaviour (December 29), p. 10

Damasio, A. (1994) *Descartes Error: Emotion, Reason and the Human Brain*. New York: Grosser/Putnan.

Damasio, A. (2000) *The Feeling of What Happens: Body and Emotion in the Making of Consciousness*. New York: Harcourt Brace.

Danielewicz, J. (2001) *Teaching Selves*. Albany, NY: State University of New York.

Darling-Hammond, L. (1990) Teacher professionalism: Why and how? In Lieberman, A. (ed.), *Schools as Collaborative Cultures: Creating the Future Now*. London: Falmer Press.

Darling-Hammond, L. (1997) *Doing What Matters Most: Investing in Quality Teaching*. New York: National Commission on Teaching & America's Future.

Darling-Hammond, L. (1999) *Solving the Dilemmas of Teacher Supply, Demand, and Standards: How we can Ensure a Competent, Caring, and Qualified Teacher for Every Child*. Kutztown, PA: National Commission on Teaching & America's Future.

Darling-Hammond, L. (2000) Teacher quality and student achievement. *Education Policy Analysis Archives*, 8 (1): n.p. Retrieved from http://epaa.asu.edu/epaa/v8n1.

Day, C. (1997) Teachers in the twenty-first century: Time to renew the vision. In Hargreaves, A. and Evans, R. (eds), *Beyond Educational Reform: Bringing Teachers Back In* (pp. 44–61). Buckingham: Open University Press.

Day, C. (1999) *Developing Teachers: The Challenges of Lifelong Learning*. London: Falmer Press.

Day, C. (2000a) Stories of change and professional development: The costs of commitment. In Day, C., Fernandez, A., Hauge, T. and Møller, J. (eds), *The Life and Work of Teachers: International Perspectives in Changing Times* (pp. 109–129). London: Falmer Press.

Day, C. (2000b) Effective leadership and reflective practice. *Reflective Practice*, 1 (1): 113–127.

Day, C. (2004) *A Passion for Teaching*. London and New York: Routledge Falmer.

Day, C. (2007) Sustaining success in challenging contexts. In Day, C. and Leithwood, K. (eds), *Successful Principal Leadership in Times of Change: An International Perspective* (pp. 59–70). Dordrecht: Springer.

Day, C. and Gu, Q. (2007) Variations in the conditions for teachers' professional learning and development: Sustaining commitment and effectiveness over a career. *Oxford Review of Education*, 33 (4): 423–443.

Day, C. and Gu, Q. (2009) Teacher emotions: Well being and effectiveness. In Zembylas, M. and Schutz, P. (eds), *Teachers' Emotions in the Age of School Reform and the Demands for Performativity* (pp. 15–31). Dordrecht: Springer.

Day, C. and Leithwood, K. (eds) (2007) *Successful School Principal Leadership in Times of Change: International Perspectives*. Dordrecht: Springer.

Day, C. and Smethem, L. (2009) The effects of reform: Have teachers really lost their sense of professionalism? *Journal of Educational Change*, 10 (2–3): 141–157.

Day, C., Elliot, B., and Kington, A. (2005) Reforms, standards and teacher identity: Challenges of sustaining commitment. *Teaching and Teacher Education*, 21, 563–577.

Day, C., Harris, A., Hadfield, M., Tolley, H. and Beresford, J. (2000) *Leading Schools in Times of Change*. Buckingham: Open University Press.

Day, C., Sammons, P., Harris, A., Hopkins, D., Leithwood, K., Gu, Q. and Brown, E. (2010) *Ten Strong Claims for Successful School Leadership in English Schools*. Nottingham: National College for Leadership of Schools and Children's Services.

Day, C., Sammons, P., Hopkins, D., Harris, A., Leithwood, K., Gu, Q., Brown, E., Ahtaridou, E. and Kington, A. (2009) *The Impact of School Leadership on Pupil Outcomes*. London: Department for Children, Schools and Families.

Day, C., Sammons, P., Stobart, G., Kington, A. and Gu, Q. (2007) *Teachers Matter: Connecting Lives, Work and Effectiveness*. Maidenhead: Open University Press.

Day, C., Stobart, G., Sammons, P., Kington, A., Gu, Q. and Smees, R. (2006) *Variation in Teachers' Work, Lives and Effectiveness*. London: DfES.

Denzin, N. (1984) *On Understanding Emotion*. San Francisco: Jossey-Bass.

Department for Children, Schools and Families (2008) The national strategies: Secondary. Retrieved 27 August 2009, from www.standards.dcsf.gov.uk/secondary/framework.

Department for Children, Schools and Families (2009) *Deprivation and Education*. London: Department for Children, Schools and Families.

Department for Education and Employment (1997) *Excellence in Schools*. London: HMSO.

Department for Education and Skills (2003) *School Teachers' Pay and Conditions Document*. London: HMSO.

Dinham, S. and Scott, C. (1996) *The Teacher 2000 Project: A Study of Teacher Satisfaction, Motivation and Health*. Sydney: University of Western Sydney, Nepean.

Dinham, S. and Scott, C. (1998) A three domain model of teacher and school executive satisfaction. *Journal of Educational Administration*, 36: 362–378.

Dinham, S. and Scott, C. (2000) Moving into the third, outer domain of teacher satisfaction. *Journal of Educational Administration*, 38 (3): 379–394.

Dorman, J. P. (2003) Relationships between school and classroom environment and teacher burnout: A LISREL analysis. *Social Psychology of Education*, 6: 107–127.

Dreyfus, H. L. and Dreyfus, S. E. (1986) *Mind Over Machine: The Power of Human Intuition and Expertise in the Era of the Computer*. New York: The Free Press.

Dworkin, A. G. (1980) The changing demography of public schools teachers: Some implications for faculty turnover in urban areas. *Sociology of Education*, 53: 65–73.

Ebmeier, H. and Nicklaus, J. (1999) The impact of peer and principal collaborative supervision on teachers' trust, commitment, desire for collaboration, and efficacy. *Journal of Curriculum and Supervision*, 14 (4): 351–378.

Education Reform Act (1988) London: HMSO.

Edwards, A. (2007) Relational agency in professional practice: A CHAT analysis. *Actio: An International Journal of Human Activity Theory*, 1: 1–17.

Edwards, E. A. (2003) Retention and motivation of veteran teachers: Implications for Schools. Unpublished dissertation presented to the Faculty of the Department of Educational Leadership and Policy Analysis, East Tennessee State University.

Egyed, C. J. and Short, R. J. (2006) Teacher self-efficacy, burnout, experience and decision to refer a disruptive student. *School Psychology International*, 27: 462–474.

Elias, M. J., Zins, J. E., Weissberg, R. P., Frey, K. S., Greenberg, M. T., Haynes, N. M., Kessler, R., Schwab-Stone, M. E. and Shriver, T. P. (1997) *Promoting Social and Emotional Learning*. Alexandra, VA: Association for Supervision and Curriculum Development.

Eliot, G. (1871–2 [1985]) *Middlemarch*. Harmondsworth: Penguin Books.

Elliott, B. and Crosswell, L. (2001) Commitment to teaching: Australian perspectives on the interplays of the professional and the personal in teachers' lives. Paper presented at the International Symposium on Teacher Commitment at the European Conference on Educational Research, Lille, France.

Eraut, M., Maillardet, F., Miller, C., Steadman, S., Ali, A., Blackman, C. and Furner, J. (2004) Learning in the professional workplace: Relationships between learning factors and contextual factors. AERA Conference paper, San Diego, 12 April.

Eraut, M., Steadman, S., Maillardet, F., Miller, C., Ali, A., Blackman, C., Furner, J. and

Caballero, C. (2007) Early career learning at work: Insights into professional development during the first job. Teaching and Learning Research Briefing, 25 March. Retrieved 1 November 2009, from www.tlrp.org/pub/documents/Eraut%20RB%20 25%20FINAL.pdf.

Etzioni, A. (ed.) (1969) *The Semi-professions and their Organization*. London: Collier-Macmillan.

Evans, K., Hodkinson, P., Rainbird, H. and Unwin, L. (2006) *Improving Workplace Learning*. London: Routledge.

Evans, L. (1998) *Teacher Morale, Job Satisfaction and Motivation*. London: Paul Chapman Publishing.

Evans, L. (2001) Delving deeper into morale, job satisfaction and motivation among education professionals: Re-examining the leadership dimension. *Educational Management Administration*, 29: 291–306.

Evans, M. (2009) Prevention of mental, emotional, and behavioral disorders in youth: The Institute of Medicine report and implications for nursing. *Journal of Child and Adolescent Psychiatric Nursing*, 22 (3): 154–159.

Every Child Matters: Change for Children (2004) London: Department for Children, Schools and Families.

Falkenberg, T. (2007) On the grounding of teacher education in the human condition. *Journal of Educational Thought*, 41 (3): 245–262.

Farber, B. A. (1991) *Crisis in Education: Stress and Burnout in the American Teacher*. San Francisco, CA: Jossey-Bass.

Farkas, S., Johnson, J. and Foleno, T. (2000) *A Sense of Calling: Who Teaches and Why*. New York: Public Agenda.

Feiman-Nemser, S. (2003) What new teachers need to learn. *Educational Leadership*, 60 (8): 25–29.

Fenstermacher, G. D. and Richardson, V. (2005) On making determinations of quality in teaching. *Teachers College Record*, 107 (1): 186–213.

Field, J. (2008) *Social Capital*. London and New York: Routledge.

Fielding, M. (2004) Transformative approaches to student voice: Theoretical underpinnings, recalcitrant realities. *British Educational Research Journal*, 30 (2): 295–311.

Fielding, M. (2006) Leadership, personalization and high performance schooling: Naming the new totalitarianism. *School Leadership and Management*, 26 (4): 347–369.

Fineman, S. (ed.) (1993) *Emotions in Organizations*. London: Sage.

Firestone, W. A. (1996) Images of teaching and proposals for reform: A comparison of ideas from cognitive and organizational research. *Educational Administration Quarterly*, 32 (2): 209–235.

Flanagan, J. C. (1954) The critical incident technique. *Psychological Bulletin*, 51 (4): 327–359.

Fletcher-Campbell, F. (1995a) Values and values education. *International Review of Education*, 44 (1): 113–114.

Fletcher-Campbell, F. (1995b) Caring about Caring? *Pastoral Care*, September: 26–28.

Floden, R. and Huberman, M. (1989) Teachers' professional lives: The state of the art. *International Journal of Educational Research*, 13 (4): 455–466.

Flores, M. A. (2006) Being a novice teacher in two different settings: Struggles, continuities, and discontinuities. *Teachers College Record*, 108 (10): 2021–2052.

Flores, M. A. and Day, C. (2006) Contexts which shape and reshape new teachers' identities: A multi-perspective study. *Teaching and Teacher Education*, 22: 219–232.

Foresight Mental Capital and Wellbeing Project (2008) *Final Project Report*. London: The Government Office for Science.

Fredrickson, B. L. (2001) The role of positive emotions in positive psychology: The broaden-and-build theory of positive emotions. *American Psychologist*, 56 (3): 218–226.

Fredrickson, B. L. (2002) Postive emotions. In Snyder, C. R. and Lopez, S. J. (eds), *Handbook of Positive Psychology* (pp. 120–134). Oxford: Oxford University Press.

Fredrickson, B. L. (2004) The broaden-and-build theory of positive emotions. *The Royal Society*, 359 (1449): 1367–1377.

Fredrickson, B. L. and Joiner, T. (2002) Positive emotions trigger upward spirals toward emotional well-being. *Psychological Science*, 13: 172–175.

Freidus, H. (1994) Supervision of second career teachers: What's our line? Paper presented at the annual meeting of the *American Educational Research Association*, New Orleans.

Fried, R. L. (1995) *The Passionate Teacher: A Practical Guide*. Boston, MA: Beacon Press.

Fried, R. (2001) *The Passionate Teacher: A Practical Guide*, 2nd edn. Boston, MA: Beacon Press.

Friedman, T. L. (2005) *The World is Flat*. London: Penguin Books.

Friedson, E. (1983) The theory of professions: The state of the art. In Dingwall, R. and Lewis, P. (eds), *The Sociology of Professions*. London: Macmillan.

Friedson, E. (2001) *Professionalism: The Third Logic*. Cambridge: Polity.

Fullan, M. (1993) *Changing Forces*. London: Cassell.

Fullan, M. (2001) *Leading in a Culture of Change*. San Francisco, CA: Jossey-Bass.

Fullan, M. (2003) *The Moral Imperative of School Leadership*. California: Corwin Press.

Fullan, M. (2008) *What's Worth Fighting for in the Principalship?* New York: Teachers College Press.

Gabarro, J. (1978) The development of trust, influence, and expectations. In Athos, A. and Gararro, J. (eds), *Interpersonal Behavior: Communication and Understanding in Relationships* (pp. 290–303). Englewood Cliffs, NJ : Prentice-Hall.

Gallo-Fox, J. (2009) Transferring schema or transforming cultures? *Cultural Studies of Science Education*, 4: 449–460.

Galton, M., Hargreaves, L., Comber, C., Pell, T. and Wall, D. (1999) *Inside the Primary Classroom: 20 Years On*. London: Routledge.

General Teaching Council for England (2002) *Teachers on Teaching: A Survey of the Teaching Profession*. London: GTCE/*Guardian*/MORI.

Gilroy, P. and Day, C. (1993) The erosion of INSET in England and Wales: Analysis and proposals for a redefinition. *Journal of Education for Teaching*, 19 (2): 151–157.

Gladwell, M. (2008) Most likely to succeed: How do we hire when we can't tell who's right for the job? *The New Yorker*, 15 December. Retrieved from www.newyorker.com/reporting/2008/12/15/081215fa_fact_gladwell.

Glasser, W. (1965) *Schools Without Failure*. New York: Harper & Row.

Goddard, R. D. (2002) A theoretical and empirical analysis of the measurement of collective efficacy: The development of a short form. *Educational and Psychological Measurement*, 93: 467–476.

Goddard, R. and O'Brien, P. (2003) Beginning teachers' perceptions of their work, well-being and intention to leave. *Asia-Pacific Journal of Teacher Education and Development*, 6 (2): 99–118.

Goddard, R. D., Hoy, W. K. and Woolfolk Hoy, A. (2004) Collective efficacy: Theoretical developments, empirical evidence, and future directions. *Educational Researcher*, 33 (3): 3–13.

Gold, Y. (1996) Beginning teacher support: Attrition, mentoring, and induction. In Sikula, J., Buttery, T. J. and Guyton, E. (eds), *Handbook of Research on Teacher Education*, 2nd edn (pp. 548–594). New York: Simon & Schuster.

Goleman, D. (1995) *Emotional Intelligence: Why It can Matter More than IQ,* London: Bloomsbury.

Goleman, D. (1996) *Emotional Intelligence.* London: Bloomsbury Publishing.

Goleman, D. (2007) *Social Intelligence.* New York: Arrow Books.

Goodlad, J. I. (1984) *A Place Called School.* New York: McGraw-Hill.

Goodson, I. and Hargreaves, A. (1996) *Teachers' Professional Lives.* London: Falmer Press.

Goodson, I., Moore, S. and Hargreaves, A. (2006) Teacher nostalgia and the sustainability of reform: The generation and degeneration of teachers' missions, memory, and meaning. *Educational Administration Quarterly*, 42 (1): 42–61.

Goodwin, R. (2005) Why I study relationships and culture. *The Psychologist*, 18 (10): 614–615.

Gorard, S. (1998) Schooled to fail? Revisiting the Welsh school-effect. *Journal of Education Policy*, 13 (1): 115–124.

Gorard, S. (2006) Value-added is of little value. *Journal of Educational Policy*, 21 (2): 233–241.

Gorard, S. and Smith, E. (2004) What is 'underachievement' at school? *School Leadership and Management*, 24 (2): 205–225.

Gore, S. and Eckenrode, J. (1994) Context and process in research on risk and resilience. In Haggerty, R., Sherrod, L. R., Garmezy, N. and Rutter, M. (eds), *Stress, Risk and Resilience in Children and Adolescents: Process, Mechanisms and Interventions* (pp. 19–63). New York: Cambridge University Press.

Gorman, C. (2005) The importance of resilience. *Time*, 165 (3): A52–A55.

Gould, J. D. (1978) How experts dictate. *Journal of Experimental Psychology: Human Perception and Performance*, 4 (4): 648–661.

Grier, J. and Johnston, C. (2009) An inquiry into the development of teacher identities in STEM career changers. *Journal of Science Teacher Education*, 20: 57–75.

Griffiths, A. (2007a) Improving with age. *Safety and Health Practitioner*, 25 (4): 53–55.

Griffiths, A. (2007b) Healthy work for older workers: Work design and management factors. In Loretto, W., Vickerstaff, S., and White, P. (eds) *The Future for Older Workers: New Perspectives* (pp. 121–137). Bristol: Policy Press.

Grissmer, D. and Kirby, S. N. (1997) Teacher turnover and teacher quality. *Teachers College Record*, 99 (1): 57–61.

Grossman, P., Wineburg, S. and Woolworth, S. (2001) Toward a theory of teacher community. *Teachers College Record*, 103 (6): 942–1012.

Groundwater-Smith, S. and Mockler, N. (2009) *Teacher Professional Learning in an Age of Compliance: Mind the Gap.* Rotterdam: Springer.

Gu, Q. and Day, C. (2007) Teachers resilience: A necessary condition for effectiveness. *Teaching and Teacher Education*, 23: 1302–1316.

Gu, Q. and Day, C. (forthcoming) Emotional Journeys: Teacher resilience counts. *Teaching and Teacher Education*.

Gu, Q. and Johansson, O. (forthcoming) Understanding school performance: Two interactive dimensions. *International Journal of Leadership in Education*.

Gu, Q., Sammons, P. and Mehta, P. (2008) Leadership characteristics and practices in schools with different effectiveness and improvement profiles. *School Leadership and Management*, 28 (1): 43–63.

Guardian (2003) Workload hits teacher morale. Report on General Teaching Council/ *Guardian*/Mori Teacher Survey.

Guardian (2007) British children: Poorer, at greater risk and more insecure. 14th February, p. 1.

Guardian (2009) Stressed teachers suffer breakdowns (13 April). Retrieved 1 December 2009, from www.guardian.co.uk/education/2009/apr/13/stressed-teachers-face-burn-out/print.

Guttman, C. (2001) A hard sell for teaching. *The UNESCO Courier*, 54 (10): 13.

Haberman, M. (2004) Can star teachers create learning communities? *Educational Leadership*, 61 (8): 52–56.

Halpin, D. (2003) *Hope and Education: The Role of the Utopian Education*. London: Routlege-Falmer.

Hamachek, D. (1999) Effective teachers: What they do, how they do it, and the importance of self-knowledge. In Lipka, R. P. and Brinthaupt, T. M. (eds), *The Role of Self in Teacher Development* (pp. 189–224). Albany, NY: State University of New York Press.

Hamel, G. and Välikangas, L. (2003) The quest for resilience. *Harvard Business Review*, September: 1–13.

Hamon, H. and Rotman, P. (1984) *Tam yu'ily aura desprofs*. Paris: Editions du Seuil.

Handy, C. (1989) *The Age of Unreason*. London: Business Books Ltd.

Hansen, D. T. (1995) *The Call to Teach*. New York: Teachers College Press.

Hansen, D. T. (1998) The moral is in the practice. *Teaching and Teacher Education*, 14 (6): 643–655.

Hansen, D. T. (2001) *The Moral Heart of Teaching: Towards A Teacher's Creed*. New York: Teachers College Press.

Hanushek, E. A. (2002) Teacher quality. In Izumi, L. T. and Evers, W. M. (eds), *Teacher Quality*. Hoover Institution Press, Publication No. 505.

Hanushek, E. A. and Rivkin, S. G. (2004) How to improve the supply of high-quality teachers. In Ravitch, D. (ed.), *Brookings Papers on Education*. Washington, DC: Brookings Institution Press.

Hargreaves, A. (1994) *Changing Teachers, Changing Times: Teachers' Work and Culture in the Postmodern Age*. New York: Teachers College Press.

Hargreaves, A. (1998) The emotional practice of teaching. *Teaching and Teacher Education*, 14 (8): 835–854.

Hargreaves, A. (2000) Four ages of professionalism and professional learning. *Teachers and Teaching: Theory and Practice*, 6: 151–182.

Hargreaves, A. (2001) The emotional geographies of teaching. *Teachers College Record*, 103 (6): 1056–1080.

Hargreaves, A. (2003) *Teaching in the Knowledge Society: Education in the Age of Insecurity*. New York: Teachers College Press.

Hargreaves, A. (2004) Inclusive and exclusive educational change: Emotional responses of teachers and implications for leadership. *School Leadership & Management*, 24: 287–309.

Hargreaves, A. (2005) Educational change takes ages: Life career and generational factors in teachers' emotional responses to educational change. *Teaching and Teacher Education*, 21: 967–983.

Hargreaves, A. (2007) Sustainable professional learning communities. In Stoll, L. and Louis, K. S. (eds), *Professional Learning Communities: Divergence, Depth and Dilemmas* (pp. 181–196). Maidenhead: Open University Press/McGraw-Hill.

Hargreaves, A. and Fink, D. (2006) *Sustainable Leadership*. San Francisco, CA: Jossey-Bass.

Hargreaves, A. and Goodson, I. (1996) Teachers' professional lives: Aspirations and actualities. In Goodson, I. and Hargreaves, A. (eds), *Teachers' Professional Lives* (pp. 1–27). London: Falmer Press.

Hargreaves, D. H. (1994) The new professionalism: The synthesis of professional and institutional development. *Teaching and Teacher Education*, 10 (4): 423–438.

Havel, V. (1990) *Disturbing the Peace*. London: Faber & Faber.

Helsby, G. (1999) *Changing Teachers' Work: The Reform of Secondary Schooling*. Buckingham: Open University Press.

Helsby, G. and McCulloch, G. (1996) Teacher professionalism and curriculum control. In Goodson, I. and Hargreaves, A. (eds), *Teachers' Professional Lives* (pp. 56–74). London: Falmer Press.

Henderson, N. and Milstein, M. (2003) *Resiliency in Schools: Making it Happen for Students and Educators*. Thousand Oaks, CA: Corwin Press.

Henry, D. A. and Milstein, M. (2006) Building leadership capacity through resiliency. Paper presented at the Commonwealth Council for Educational Administration and Management, Lefcosia, Cyprus.

Herzberg, F., Mausner, B. and Snyderman, B. B. (1959) *The Motivation to Work*, 2nd edn. New York: John Wiley.

Higgins, G. O. (1994) *Resilient Adults: Overcoming a Cruel Past*. San Francisco, CA: Jossey-Bass.

Hipp, K. and Huffman, J. (2007) Using assessment tools as frames for dialogue to create and sustain professional learning communities. In Stoll, L. and Seashore Louis, K. (eds), *Professional Learning Communities: Divergence, Depth and Dilemmas* (pp. 119–131). Maidenhead: Open University Press/McGraw-Hill.

Hobson, A., Malderez, A., Tracey, L., Homer, M., Ashby, P., Mitchell, N., McIntyre, J., Cooper, D., Roper, T., Chambers, G. and Tomlinson, P. (2009) *Becoming a Teacher: Final Report*. London: Department for Children, Schools and Families.

Hochschild, A. R. (1983) *The Managed Heart: Commercialisation of Human Feeling*. London: University of California Press Ltd.

Horne, J. and Orr, J. E. (1998) Assessing behaviors that create resilient organizations. *Employment Relations Today*, 24 (4): 29–39.

Howard, S. and Johnson, B. (2004) Resilient teachers: Resisting stress and burnout. *Social Psychology of Education*, 7 (3): 339–420.

Howard, S., Dryden, J. and Johnson, B. (1999) Childhood resilience: Review and critique of literature. *Oxford Review of Education*, 25 (3): 307–323.

Hoy, A. W. and Spero, R. B. (2005) Changes in teacher efficacy during the early years of teaching: A comparison of four measures. *Teaching and Teacher Education*, 21: 343–356.

Hoy, W. K. and Tschannen-Moran, M. (2003) The conceptualisation and measurement of faculty trust in schools. In Hoy, W. K. and Miskel, C. (eds), *Studies in Leading and Organising Schools* (pp. 191–207). New York: Information Age Publishing.

Hoy, H. W., Hoy, W. K. and Kurz, N. M. (2008) Teacher's academic optimism: The development and test of a new construct. *Teaching and Teacher Education*, 24: 821–835.

Hoy, W. K., Tarter, C. J. and Woolfolk Hoy, A. (2006) Academic optimism: A second order confirmatory analysis. In Hoy, W. K. and Miskel, C. G. (eds), *Contemporary Issues in Educational Policy and School Outcomes* (pp. 135–149). Greenwich, CT: Information Age Publishing.

Huang, S. L. and Waxman, H. C. (2009) The association of school environment to student teachers' satisfaction and teaching commitment. *Teaching and Teacher Education*, 25 (2): 235–243.

Huberman, M. (1989a) The professional life cycle of teachers. *Teachers College Record*, 91 (1): 31–57.

Huberman, M. (1989b) On teachers' careers: Once over lightly, with a broad brush. *International Journal of Educational Research*, 13 (4): 347–362.

Huberman, M. (1993) *The Lives of Teachers*. London: Cassell.

Huberman, M. (1995a) Professional careers and professional development. In Guskey, T. and Huberman, M. (eds), *Professional Development in Education: New Paradigms and Practices* (pp. 193–224). New York: Teachers College Press.

Huberman, M. (1995b) Networks that alter teaching. *Teachers and Teaching: Theory and Practice*, 1 (2): 193–221.

Huberman, M. and Vandenberghe, R. (1999) Introduction: burnout and the teaching profession. In Vandenberghe, R. and Huberman, M. (eds), *Understanding and Preventing Teacher Burnout* (pp. 1–11). Cambridge: Cambridge University Press.

Independent (2005) Five million UK workers 'suffer extreme stress' (16 May). Retrieved 1 November 2009, from www.independent.co.uk/life-style/health-and-families/health-news/five-million-uk-workers-suffer-extreme-stress-490856.html.

Ingersoll, R. (2001) Teacher turnover and teacher shortages: An organisational analysis. *American Educational Research Journal*, 38 (3): 499–534.

Ingersoll, R. (2002) The teacher shortage: A case of wrong diagnosis and wrong prescription. *NASSP Bulletin*, 86: 16–31.

Ingersoll, R. (2003) Is there really a teacher shortage? Research report. The Consortium for Policy Research in Education and the Center for the Study of Teaching and Policy. Philadelphia, PA. Retrieved 17 July 2007, from: http://depts.washington.edu/ctpmail/PDFs/Shortage-RI-09-2003.pdf.

Isen, A. M. (1990) The influence of positive and negative affect on cognitive organization: Some implications for development. In Stein, N., Leventhal, B. and Trabasso, T. (eds), *Psychological and Biological Approaches to Emotion* (pp. 75–94). Hillsdale, NJ: Erlbaum.

Jackson, P. (1999) Teaching as a moral enterprise. In Lang, M., Olson, J., Hensen, H. and Bünder, W. (eds), *Changing Schools of Changing Practices: Perspectives on Educational Reform and Teacher Professionalism*. Louvain: Garant.

Jackson, P., Boostrom, R. and Hansen, D. (1993) *The Moral Life of the Schools*. San Francisco, CA: Jossey-Bass.

James-Wilson, S. (2001) The influence of ethnocultural identity on emotions and teaching. Paper presented at the annual meeting of the American Educational Research Association, New Orleans, April.

Johnson, B. and Down, B. (2009) Re-conceptualising early career teacher resilience: A critical alternative. Paper presented at the European Conference on Educational Research, University of Vienna, Austria, 28 September.

Johnson, B., Howard, S. and Oswald, M. (1999) Quantifying and prioritising resilience-promoting factors: Teachers' views. Paper presented at the Australian Association for

Research in Education and New Zealand Association for Research in Education conference, Melbourne, 29 November–2 December.

Johnson, S., Cooper, C., Cartwright, S., Donald, I., Taylor, P. and Millet, C. (2005) The experience of work-related stress across occupations. *Journal of Managerial Psychology*, 20 (2): 178–187.

Joseph Rowntree Foundation (2007) Young children see poverty holding them back at school. Retrieved 1 November 2009, from www.jrf.org.uk/media-centre/young-children-see-poverty-holding-them-back-school.

Kardos, S. M. and Moore Johnson, S. (2007) On their own and presumed expert: New teachers' experience with their colleagues. *Teachers College Record*, 109 (9): 2083–2106.

Kauffman, D., Moore Johnson, S., Kardos, S. M., Liu, E. and Peske, H. (2002) 'Lost at sea': New teachers' experiences with curriculum and assessment. *Teachers College Record*, 104 (2): 273–300.

Kelchtermans, G. (1993) Getting the stories, understanding the lives: From careers stories to teachers' professional development. *Teaching and Teacher Education*, 9 (5/6): 443–456.

Kelchtermans, G. (1996) Teacher vulnerability: Understanding its moral and political roots. *Cambridge Journal of Education*, 26 (3): 307–324.

Kelchtermans, G. (2004) CPD for professional renewal: Moving beyond knowledge for practice. In Day, C. and Sachs, J. (eds), *International Handbook on the Continuing Professional Development of Teachers* (pp. 217–237). Maidenhead: Open University Press.

Kelchtermans, G. (2009) Who I am in how I teach is the message: Self-understanding, vulnerability and reflection. *Teachers and Teaching: Theory and Practice*, 15 (2): 257–272.

Kelchtermans, G. and Vandenberghe, R. (1994) Teachers' professional development: A biographical perspective. *Journal of Curriculum Studies*, 26 (1): 47.

King, R. (1983) *The Sociology of School Organization*. London: Methuen and Co. Ltd.

Knoop, H. H. (2007) Control and responsibility. In Gardener, H. (ed.), *Responsibility at Work*. San Francisco, CA: Jossey-Bass.

Korthagen, F. A. (2004) In search of the essence of a good teacher: Towards a more holistic approach in teacher education. *Teaching and Teacher Education*, 20: 77–97.

Korthagen, F. and Vasalos, A. (2005) Levels in reflection: Core reflection as a means to enhance professional growth. *Teachers and Teaching: Theory and Practice*, 11 (1): 47–71.

Kossek, E. E. and Ozeki, C. (1998) Work–family conflict, policies, and the job–life satisfaction relationship: A review and direction for organizational behavior–human resources research. *Journal of Applied Psychology*, 83: 139–149.

Kushman, J. W. (1992) The organisational dynamics of teacher workplace commitment: A study of urban elementary and middle schools. *Educational Administration Quarterly*, 28 (1): 5–42.

Kyriacou, C. (1987) Teacher stress and burnout: An international review. *Educational Research*, 29 (2): 146–152.

Kyriacou, C. (2000) *Stress Busting for Teachers*. Cheltenham: Stanley Thornes Ltd.

Kyriacou, C. and Kunc, R. (2007) Beginning teachers' expectations of teaching. *Teaching and Teacher Education*, 23: 1246–1257.

Kyriacou, C. and Sutcliffe, J. (1979) Teacher stress and satisfaction. *Educational Research*, 21: 89–96.

Larson, M. S. (1977) *The Rise of Professionalism: A Sociological Analysis*. Berkeley, CA: University of California Press.

Lasch, C. (1991) *True and Only Heaven: Progress and Its Critics*. New York: Norton.

Lave, J. and Wenger, E. (1991) *Situated Learning: Legitimate Peripheral Participation*. Cambridge: Cambridge University Press

Lawn, M. (1996) *Modern Times? Work, Professionalism and Citizenship in Teaching*. London: Falmer Press.

Layard, R. and Dunn, J. (2009) *A Good Childhood: Searching for Values in a Competitive Age*. London: Penguin Books.

Learning and Skills Council (2007) *Skills in England 2007: Volume 1: Key Messages*. Coventry: Learning and Skills Council.

Lee, V. E., Bryk, A. S. and Smith, J. B. (1993) The organization of effective secondary schools. In Darling-Hammond, L. (ed.), *Review of Research in Education*, 19 (pp. 171–267). Washington, DC: American Education Research Association.

Leithwood, K. (2007) The emotional side of school improvement: A leadership perspective. In Townsend, T. (ed.), *The International Handbook on School Effectiveness and Improvement* (pp. 615–634). Dordrecht: Springer.

Leithwood, K. and Beatty (2008) *Leading with Teacher Emotions in Mind*. Thousand Oaks, CA: Corwin Press.

Leithwood, K. and Day, C. (2007) What we learned: A broad view. In Day, C. and Leithwood, K. (eds), *Successful School Leadership in Times of Change* (pp. 189–203). Toronto: Springer.

Leithwood, K., Day, C., Sammons, P., Harris, A. and Hopkins, D. (2006) *Seven Strong Claims about Successful School Leadership*. Nottingham: National College for School Leadership.

Leshem, S. (2008) Novices and veterans journeying into real-world teaching: How a veteran learns from novices. *Teaching and Teacher Education*, 24: 204–215.

Levin, B. (1998) An epidemic of education policy: (What) can we learn from each other? *Comparative Education*, 34 (2): 131–141.

Lieberman, A. and Miller, L. (1992) *Teachers – Their World and Their Work: Implications for School Improvement*. New York: Teachers College Press.

Lindeman, E. C. (1926) *The Meaning of Adult Education*. New York: New Republic. Republished in a new edition in 1989 by The Oklahoma Research Center for Continuing Professional and Higher Education.

Lindsey, S. (2007) Retention and intention in teaching careers: Will the new generation stay? *Teachers and Teaching: Theory and Practice*, 13 (5): 465–480.

Liu, X. S. and Ramsey, J. (2008) Teachers' job satisfaction: Analyses of the Teacher Follow-up Survey in the United States for 2000–2001. *Teaching and Teacher Education*, 24 (5): 1173–1184.

Loehr, J. and Schwartz, T. (2003) *The Power of Full Engagement*. New York: Free Press.

Lortie, D. C. (1975) *Schoolteacher: A Sociological Study*, 2nd edn. Chicago: University of Chicago Press.

Loughran, J. J. (2004) Learning through self-study. In Loughran, J. J., Hamilton, M. L., LaBoskey, V. K. and Russell, T. L. *The International Handbook of Self-Study of Teaching and Teacher Education Practices* (Vols 1–2, pp. 151–192). Dordrecht: Kluwer Academic Publishers.

Louis, K. S. (1998) Effects of teacher quality worklife in secondary schools on commitment and sense of efficacy. *School Effectiveness and School Improvement*, 9 (1): 1–27.

Louis, K. S. (2007) Trust and improvement in schools. *Journal of Educational Change*, 8: 1–24.

Luthans, F., Avolio, B. J., Avey, J. B. and Norman, S. M. (2007) Positive psychological capital: Measurement and relationship with performance and satisfaction. *Personnel Psychology*, 60: 541–572.

Luthar, S. (1996) Resilience: A construct of value? Paper presented at the 104th Annual Convention of the American Psychological Association, Toronto.

Luthar, S., Cicchetti, D. and Becker, B. (2000) The construct of resilience: A critical evaluation and guidelines for future work. *Child Development*, 71 (3): 543–562.

Lyotard, J. (1979) *The Postmodern Condition: A Report on Knowledge*. Manchester: Manchester University Press.

McGowan, K. R. and Hart, L. E. (1990) Still different after all these years: Gender differences in professional identity formation. *Professional Psychology: Research and Practice*, 21: 118–123.

McLaughlin, C. and Clarke, B. (2009) Relational matters: A review of the impact of school experience on mental health in early adolescence. Unpublished research paper.

McLaughlin, M. (2005) Listening and learning from the field: Tales of policy implementation and situated practice. In Liberman, A. (ed.), *The Roots of Educational Change*. Dordrecht: Springer.

McLaughlin, M. and Talbert, J. (1993) *Contexts that Matter for Teaching and Learning*. Stanford, CA: Stanford University.

McRae, H. (1995) The privilege of unemployment. *Independent on Sunday* (26 February), p. 4.

Madfes, T. J. (1989) Second careers, second challenges: Meeting the needs of the older teacher education student. Paper presented at the annual meeting of the American Educational Research Association, San Francisco, CA.

Madfes, T. J. (1990) Second career, second challenge: What do career changes say about the work of teaching. In Risacher, B. (ed.), *Scientists and Mathematicians Become Teachers* (pp. 25–33). New York: National Executive Service Corps.

Malacova, E., Blair, J. L., Mattes, E., de Klerk, N. and Stanley, F. (2009) Neighbourhood socioeconomic status and maternal factors at birth as moderators of the association between birth characteristics and school attainment: A population study of children attending government schools in Western Australia. *Journal of Epidemiology and Community Health*, 63: 842–849.

Mancini, V., Wuest, D., Vantine, K. and Clark, E. (1984) Use of instruction in interaction analysis on burned out teachers: Its effects on teaching behaviors, level of burnout and academic learning time. *Journal of Teachers in Physical Education*, 3 (1): 29–46.

Margolis, J. (2008) What will keep today's teachers teaching? Looking for a hook as a new career cycle emerges. *Teachers College Record*, 110 (1): 160–194.

Martin, L. A., Chiodo, J. J. and Chang, L. (2001) First year teachers: Looking back after three years. *Action in Teacher Education*, 23: 55.

Maslach, C., Shaufeli, W. B. and Leiter, M. P. (2001) Job burnout. *Annual Review of Psychology*, 52, 397–422.

Masten, A. S. (2001) Ordinary magic: Resilience process in development. *American Psychologist*, 56: 227–239.

Matheson, I. (2007) Current demographics in the school teacher population in Scotland. Paper presented at the Scottish Educational Research Association Conference.

Maurer, T. J. and Tarulli, B. A. (1994) Investigation of perceived environment, perceived outcomes and personal variables in relationship to voluntary development activity by employees. *Journal of Applied Psychology*, 79 (1), 3–14.

Mayotte, G. (2003) Stepping stones to success: Previously developed career competencies and their benefits to career switchers transitioning to teaching. *Teaching and Teacher Education*, 19: 681–695.

Measor, L. (1985) Critical incidents in the classroom: Identities, choices and careers. In Ball, S. J. and. Goodson, F. (eds), *Teachers' Lives and Careers* (pp. 61–77). Lewes: Falmer Press.

Meijer, P., Korthagen, F. and Vasalos, A. (2009) Supporting presence in teacher education: The connection between the personal and professional aspects of teaching. *Teaching and Teacher Education*, 25 (2): 297–308.

Merrow, J. (1999) The teacher shortage: Wrong diagnosis, phony cures. *Education Week*, 38: 64.

Ministry of Education (1991) Year 2000: A framework for learning: Enabling learners. Report of the Sullivan Commission. British Columbia, Canada.

Mitchell, C. and Sackney, L. (2001) Building capacity for a learning community. *Canadian Journal of Educational Administration and Policy*, 19. Retrieved from www.umanitoba.ca/publications/cjeap/issues/issues_online.html.

Mitchell, C. and Sackney, L. (2007) Extending the learning community: A broader perspective embedded in policy. In Stoll, L. and Louis, K. S. (eds), *Professional Learning Communities: Divergence, Depth and Dilemmas* (pp. 30–44). Maidenhead: Open University Press/McGraw-Hill.

Mitchell, S. N., Reilly, R. C. and Logue, M. E. (2009) Benefits of collaborative action research for the beginning teacher. *Teaching and Teacher Education*, 25: 344–349.

Moore Johnson, S. M. and Kardos, S. M. (2002) Keeping new teachers in mind. *Educational Leadership*, 59 (6): 12–16.

Moore Johnson, S., with The Project on the Next Generation of Teachers (2004) *Finders and Keepers: Helping New Teachers Survive and Thrive in Our Schools*. San Francisco, CA: John Wiley & Sons.

Mulgan, G. (2005) *Learning to Serve: The Longest Skills Challenges for Public Services and Government and What Can Be Done about It*. London: Learning and Skills Development Agency.

Munn, P. (1999) *Promoting Positive Discipline*. Edinburgh: Scottish Office.

Naisbitt, J. (1994) *Global Paradox*. New York: Avon Books.

Nash, P. (2005) Speech to Worklife Support Conference, London Well Being Conference, London, 21 April.

National Center on Education and the Economy (2009) Commission news releases: 'Tough choices' education coalition grows with three additional states pledged to reinvent their education systems. Retrieved 1 November 2009, from www.skillscommission.org/commission_news2_3-10-09.htm.

National Research Council and Institute of Medicine (2009) *Preventing Mental, Emotional, and Behavioral Disorders among Young People: Progress and Possibilities*. Washington, DC: The National Academies Press.

Neville, K. S., Sherman, R. H. and Cohen, C. E. (2005) *Preparing and Training Professionals: Comparing Education into Six Other Fields*. Washington, DC: Finance Project.

New Economics Foundation (2009) *National Accounts of Well-being: Bringing Real Wealth onto the Balance Sheet*. London: New Economics Foundation.

Nias, J. (1981) Commitment and motivation in primary school teachers. *Educational Review*, 33 (3): 181–190.

Nias, J. (1989a) *Primary Teachers Talking: A Study of Teaching as Work*. London and New York: Routledge.

Nias, J. (1989b) Subjectively speaking: English primary teachers' careers. *International Journal of Educational Research*, 13 (4): 391–402.

Nias, J. (1996) Thinking about feeling: The emotions in teaching. *Cambridge Journal of Education*, 26 (3): 293–306.

Nias, J. (1999) Teachers' moral purposes: Stress, vulnerability, and strength. In Vandenberghe, R. and Huberman, A. M. (eds), *Understanding and Preventing Teacher Burnout: A Sourcebook of International Research and Practice* (pp. 223–237). Cambridge: Cambridge University Press.

Nias, J., Southworth, G. and Campbell, P. (1992) *Whole School Curriculum Development in Primary Schools*. London: Falmer Press.

Nieto, S. (2003) *What Keeps Teachers Going?* New York: Teachers College Press.

Nieto, S. (2005) Quality of caring and committed teachers. In Nieto, S. (ed.), *Why We Teach* (pp. 203–220). New York: Teachers College Press.

Noddings, N. (1992) *The Challenge to Care in Schools: An Alternative Approach to Education*. New York: Teachers College Press.

Noddings, N. (1996) Stories and affect in teacher education. *Cambridge Journal of Education*, 26 (3): 435–447.

Noddings, N. (2003) *Happiness and Education*. New York: Cambridge University Press.

Noddings, N. (2005) *The Challenge to Care in Schools*. New York: Teachers' College Press.

Noddings, N. (2007) *Philosophy of Education*, 2nd edn. Cambridge, MA: Westview Press.

O'Connor, K. E. (2008) 'You choose to care': Teachers, emotions and professional identity. *Teachers and Teacher Education*, 24 (1): 117–126.

OECD (2004) *Learning for Tomorrow's World: First results from PISA 2003*. Paris: OECD.

OECD (2005) *Teachers Matter: Attracting, Developing and Retaining Effective Teachers*. Paris: OECD.

Office for National Statistics (2004) *Child Health Report*. Retrieved 1 November 2009, from www.statistics.gov.uk/children/downloads/mental_health.pdf.

Osguthorpe, R. D. (2008) On the reasons we want teachers of good disposition and moral character. *Journal of Teacher Education*, 59 (4): 288–299.

Oswald, M., Johnson, B. and Howard, S. (2003) Quantifying and evaluating resilience-promoting factors: Teachers' beliefs and perceived roles. *Research in Education*, 70: 50–64.

Oxford English Dictionary (2006) Oxford: Oxford University Press.

Ozga, J. (1995) Deskilling a profession: Professionalism, deprofessionalisation and the new managerialism. In Busher, H. and Saran, R. (eds), *Managing Teachers as Professionals in Schools* (pp. 21–37). London: Kogan Page.

Pajares, F. (1996) Self-efficacy beliefs in academic settings. *Review of Educational Research*, 66 (4): 543–578.

Pajeres, F. (1997) Current directions in self-efficacy research. In Maehr, M. L. and Pintich, P. R. (eds), *Advances in Motivation and Achievement* (vol. 10, pp. 1–49). Greenwich: Jai Press Inc.

Palmer, P. J. (1998) *The Courage to Teach: Exploring the Inner Landscape of a Teacher's Life*. San Francisco, CA: Jossey-Bass.

Palmer, P. (2004) *A Hidden Wholeness*. San Francisco, CA: Jossey-Bass.

Palmer, P. (2007) *The Courage to Teach: Exploring the Inner Landscape of a Teacher's Life*. San Francisco, CA: John Wiley & Sons.

Paton, G. (2008) 15,000 teachers are off sick each day. *Daily Telegraph* (29 December), p. 2.

Patterson, D. (1991) The eclipse of the highest in higher education. *The Main Scholar: A Journal of Ideas and Public Affairs*, 3: 7–20.

Pels, P. (1999) Professions of duplexity: A prehistory of ethical codes in anthropology. *Current Anthropology*, 40 (2): 101–136.

Pence, A. R. (ed.) (1998) *Ecological Research with Children and Families: From Concepts to Methodology*. New York: Teachers' College Press.

Penuel, W. R., Fishman, B. J., Yamaguchi, R. and Gallagher, L. P. (2007) What makes professional development effective? Strategies that foster curriculum implementation. *American Educational Research Journal*, 44 (4): 921–958.

Peterson, C., Park, N. and Sweeney, P. (2008) Group well-being: Morale from a positive psychology perspective. *Applied Psychology: An International Review*, 57: 19–36.

Peterson, K. D. and Deal, T. (2009) *The Shaping School Culture Fieldbook*, 2nd edn. San Francisco, CA: John Wiley & Sons.

Pomson, A. D. M. (2005) One classroom at a time? Teacher isolation and community viewed through the prism of the particular. *Teachers College Record*, 107 (4): 20.

PricewaterhouseCoopers (2001) *Teacher Workload Study*. London: DfES.

Prick, L. (1986) *Career Development and Satisfaction among Secondary School Teachers*. Amsterdam: Vrije Universiteit Amsterdam.

Putnam, R. P. (1983) *Bowling Alone: The Collapse and Revival of American Community*. New York: Simon & Schuster.

Qualifications and Curriculum Authority (QCA) (2008) Teaching of new secondary curriculum begins. Retrieved 27 August 2009, from http://curriculum.qca.org.uk/News-and-updates-listing/News/Teaching-of-new-secondary-curriculum-begins.aspx.

Ramsay, P. (1993) *Teacher Quality: A Case Study Prepared for the Ministry of Education as part of the OECD Study on Teacher Quality*. Hamilton, NZ: University of Waikato.

Randall, J. (2009) How we all lose in the lottery of Labour's education system. *Daily Telegraph* (6 March), p. 10.

Reid, I., Brain, K. and Boyes, L. C. (2004) Teachers or learning leaders? Where have all the teachers gone? Gone to be leaders, everyone. *Educational Studies*, 30 (3): 251–264.

Rest, J. (1986) *Moral Development: Advances in Research and Theory*. New York: Praeger.

Rhodes, S. (1983) Age-related differences in work attitudes and behaviour: A review and conceptual analysis. *Psychological Bulletin*, 93 (2): 328–367.

Rich, Y. and Almozlino, M. (1999) Educational goal preferences among novice and veteran teachers of sciences and humanities. *Teaching and Teacher Education*, 15: 613–629.

Richardson, G. E., Neiger, B. L., Jenson, S. and Kumpfer, K. L. (1990) The resiliency model. *Health Education*, 21 (6): 33–39.

Richardson, V. and Placier, P. (2001) Teacher change. In Richardson, V. (ed.), *Handbook of Research on Teaching*, 4th edn (pp. 905–947). Washington, DC: American Educational Research Association.

Riehl, C. and Sipple, J. W. (1996) Making the most of time and talent: Secondary school organizational climates, teaching task environment, and teacher commitment. *American Educational Research Journal*, 33: 873–901.

Rinke, C. (2008) Understanding teachers' careers: Linking professional life to professional path. *Educational Research Review*, 3: 1–13.

Rivera-Batiz, F. L. and Marti, L. (1995) *A School System at Risk: A Study of the Consequences of Overcrowding in New York City Public Schools*. New York: Institute for Urban and Minority Education, Teachers College, Columbia University.

Rivers, J. C. and Sanders, W. L. (2002) Teacher quality and equity in educational opportunity: Findings and policy implications. In Izumi, L. T. and Eders, W. M. (eds), *Teacher Quality* (pp. 13–24). Stanford, CA: Hoover Institution Press.

Robertson, S. L. (1996) Teachers' work, restructuring and postfordism: Constructing the new professionalism. In Goodson, I. and Hargreaves, A. (eds), *Teachers' Professional Lives*. London: Falmer Press.

Robinson, V. M. J. (2007) School leadership and student outcomes: Identifying what works and why. Australian Council for Educational Leaders, Monograph 41.

Rodgers, F. R. and Raider-Roth, M. B. (2006) Presence in teaching. *Teachers and Teaching: Theory and Practice*, 12 (3): 265–287.

Roehrig, A. D., Presley, M. and Talotta, D. (eds) (2002) *Stories of Beginning Teachers: First-Year Challenges and Beyond*. Notre Dame, IN: University of Notre Dame Press.

Romano, M. E. (2006) 'Bumpy moments' in teaching: Reflections from practicing teachers. *Teaching and Teacher Education*, 22: 973–985.

Rosenholtz, S. (1984) *Myths: Political Myths about Reforming Teaching*. Denver, CO: The Commission.

Rosenholtz, S. J. and Simpson, C. (1990) Workplace conditions and the rise and fall of teachers' commitment. *Sociology of Education*, 63: 241–257.

Ross, J. A., Gray, P. and Sibbald, T. (2008) The student achievement effects of comprehensive school reform: A Canadian case study. Presented at the annual meeting of the American Educational Research Association, New York.

Rowe, K. (2003) The importance of teacher quality as a key determinant of students' experiences and outcomes of schooling. Background paper to keynote address presented at the ACER Research Conference 2003, Carlton Crest Hotel, Melbourne, 19–21 October 2003. Retrieved from www.acer.edu.au/documents/Rowe_ACER_Research_Conf_2003_Paper.pdf.

Russell, T. (1997) Teaching teachers: How I teach is the message. In Loughran, J. and Russell, T. (eds), *Teaching about Teaching: Purpose, Passion and Pedagogy in Teacher Education* (pp. 32–47). New York: Falmer Press.

Rutter, M. (1990) Psychosocial resilience and protective mechanisms. In Rolf, J., Masten, A., Cicchetti, D., Neuchterlein, K. and Weintraub, S. (eds), *Risk and Protective Factors in the Development of Psychopathology*. New York: Cambridge University Press.

Rutter, M., Maughan, B., Mortimer, P. and Ousten, J. (1979) *Fifteen-thousand Hours: Secondary Schools and Their Effects on Children*. Cambridge, MA: Harvard University Press.

Sachs, J. (2000) Rethinking the practice of teacher professionalism. In Day, C., Fernandez, A., Hauge, T. and Møller, J. (eds), *The Life and Work of Teachers: International Perspectives in Changing Times* (pp. 109–129). London: Falmer Press.

Sachs, J. (2003) The activist professional. *Journal of Educational Change*, 1: 77–95.

Sanders, W. L. and Rivers, J. C. (1996) Cumulative and residual effects of teachers on future student academic achievement. Research progress report, University of Tennessee.

Schaufeli, W. B. and Bakker, A. D. B. (2004) Job demands, job resources, and their relationship with burnout and engagement: A multi-sample study. *Journal of Organisational Behaviour*, 25: 293–315.

Schaufeli, W. B. and Enzmann, D. (1998) *The Burnout Companion to Study and Practice: A Critical Analysis*. Washington, DC: Taylor & Francis.

Scheerens, J., Vermeulen, C. J. A. J. and Pelgrum, W. J. (1989) Generalizability of instructional and school effectiveness indicators across nations. *International Journal of Educational Research*, 13 (7): 789–799.

Schutz, P. A. and Pekrun, R. (2007) *Emotion in Education*. San Diego, CA: Academic Press.

Science Daily (2009) Mental, emotional and behavioral disorders can be prevented in young people. Retrieved 1 November 2009, from www.sciencedaily.com/releases/2009/07/090729144028.htm.

Schön, D. A. (1983) *The Reflective Practitioner: How Professionals Think in Action*. New York: Basic Books.

Scott, C., Dinham, S. and Brooks, R. (2003) The development of scales to measure teacher and school executive occupational satisfaction. *Journal of Educational Administration*, 41: 74–86.

Scribner, J. P. (1998) Teacher efficacy and teacher professional learning: What school leaders should know. Paper presented at the Annual Convention of the University Council for Educational Administration, St. Louis.

Seligman, M. (2002) *Authentic Happiness*. London: Nicholas Brealey Publishing.

Seligman, M. (2003) *Learned Optimism: How to Change Your Mind and Your Life*, 2nd edn. New York: Pocket Books.

Sergiovanni, T. (1967) Factors which affect satisfaction and dissatisfaction of teachers. *Journal of Educational Administration*, 5: 66–81.

Sergiovanni, T. J. (1992) Why we should seek substitutes for leadership. *Educational Leadership*, 5: 41–45.

Sergiovanni, T. J. (2004) *The Lifeworld of Leadership: Creating Culture, Community, and Personal Meaning in Our Schools*. San Francisco, CA: Jossey-Bass.

Sergiovanni, T. J. and Starratt, R. J. (1993) *Supervision: A Redefinition*. Singapore: McGraw-Hill.

Shann, M. (1998) Professional commitment and satisfaction among teachers in urban middle schools. *The Journal of Educational Research*, 92: 67–73.

Shulman, L. S. (1987) Knowledge and teaching. *Harvard Educational Review*, 57: 1–22.

Sikes, P., Measor, L. and Woods, P. (1985) *Teacher Careers: Crises and Continuities*. Lewes: Falmer Press.

Siskin, L. (2003) Colleagues and 'Yutzes': Accountability inside schools. *Voices in Urban Education*, Spring: 24–31.

Skaalvik, E. M. and Skaalvik, S. (2009) Does school context matter? Relations with teacher burnout and job satisfaction. *Teaching and Teacher Education*, 25 (3): 518–524.

Skies, P., Measor, L. and Woods, P. (1985) *Teacher Careers: Crises and Continuities*. Lewes: Falmer Press.

Sleegers, P. and Kelchtermans, G. (1999) Inleiding op het themanummer: Professionele identiteit van leraren (professional identity of teachers). *Pedagogish Tijdschrift*, 24: 369–374.

Smith, E. (2008) Raising standards in American schools? Problems with improving teacher quality. *Teaching and Teacher Education*, 24: 610–622.

Smithers, A. and Robinson, P. (2003) Factors affecting teachers' decisions to leave the profession. Research report 430. London: Department for Education and Skills.

Smithers, A. and Robinson, P. (2004) Teacher training profiles 2004. University of Buckingham, Centre for Education and Employment Research. Retrieved 1 November 2009, from www.buckingham.ac.uk/education/research/ceer/pdfs/ittprofiles2004. pdf.

Smithers, A. and Robinson, P. (2005) Teacher turnover, wastage and movements between schools. Research report 640. London: Department for Education and Skills.

Smylie, M. A. (1995) Teacher learning in the workplace: Implications for school reform. In Guskey, T. R. and Huberman, M. (eds), *Professional Development in Education: New Paradigms and Practices*. New York: Teachers College Press.

Snoeyink, R. and Ertmer, P. (2002) Thrust into technology: How veteran teachers respond. *Journal of Educational Technology Systems*, 30 (1): 85–111.

Sockett, H. (1993) *The Moral Base for Teacher Professionalism*. New York: Teachers' College Press.

Somech, A. and Drach-Zohary, A. (2000) Understanding extra-role behavior in schools: The relationships between job satisfaction, sense of efficacy and teachers' extra-role behavior. *Teaching and Teacher Education*, 16 (5/6): 649–659.

Sparks, D. and Loucks-Horsley, S. (1990) Models of staff development. In Robert Houston, W., Haberman, M. and Sikula, J. (eds), *Handbook of Research on Teacher Education*. New York: Macmillan Publishing Company.

Starratt, R. (2007) Leading a community of learners. *Educational Management, Administration, and Leadership*, 35 (2): 165–183.

Stoll, L. and Louis, K. S. (eds) (2007) *Professional Learning Communities: Divergence, Depth and Dilemmas*. Maidenhead: Open University Press/McGraw-Hill.

Stronach, I., Corbin, B., McNamara, O., Stark, S. and Warne, T. (2002) Towards an uncertain politics of professionalism: Teacher and nurse identities in flux. *Journal of Educational Policy*, 17 (1): 109–138.

Strauss, A. L. (1959) *Mirrors and Masks: The Search for Identity*. New Brunswick: Transaction Publishers.

Sumsion, J. (2002) Becoming, being and unbecoming an early childhood educator: A phenomenological case study of teacher attrition. *Teaching and Teacher Education*, 18: 869–885.

Sutton Trust, The (2009) *Attainment Gaps between the Most Deprived and Advantaged Schools*. London: The Sutton Trust.

Sylwester, B. (1995) *A Celebration of Neurons: An Educator's Guide to the Human Brain*. Alexandra, VA: ASCD.

Szreter, S. (2001) Social capital roundtable, Glasgow, November.

Talbert, J. and McLaughlin, M. (1996) Teachers' professionalism in local school contexts. In Goodson, I. and Hargreaves, A. (eds), *Teachers' Professional Lives* (pp. 127–154). London: Falmer Press.

Teachers' Educational Supplement (2006) Standards drive falters, say studies (31 March). Retrieved 1 November 2009, from www.tes.co.uk/article.aspx?storycode=2216288.

Teachers' Educational Supplement (2009) There's always one (16 October). Retrieved 1 November 2009, from www.tes.co.uk/article.aspx?storycode=6025187.

Teaching and Learning Research Programme (TLRP) Research Briefing (2004) Improving learning in the workplace. 7 March. Retrieved from www.tlrp.org/pub/documents/no7_rainbird.pdf.

Teitelbaum, T. L. (2008) You gotta shake your own bushes: How veteran teachers remain highly invested in their careers. Paper presented at the annual meeting of the American Educational Research Association, New York.

Terry, P. (1997) Teacher burnout: Is it ideal? Can we prevent it? Paper presented at the annual meeting of the North Central Association of Colleges and Schools, Chicago, IL, 8 April.

Tickle, L. (2000) *Teacher Induction: The Way Ahead.* Buckingham: Open University Press.

Times, The (2005a) Class of '04 fearful and consumed by worries. *The Times* (April 22), p. 17.

Times, The (2005b) Almost 10,000 pupils expelled as violence against teachers escalates. *The Times* (June 4), p. 9.

Training and Development Agency for Schools (TDA) (2007) *Professional Standards for Teachers: Why Sit Still in Your Career?* London: TDA.

Travers, C. J. and Cooper, C. L. (1996) *Teachers Under Pressure: Stress in the Teaching Profession.* London: Routledge.

Tripp, D. (1993) *Critical Incidents in Teaching: Developing Professional Judgement.* London: Routledge.

Troman, G. (2008) Primary teacher identity, commitment and career in performative school cultures. *British Educational Research Journal,* 34 (5): 619–633.

Troman, G. and Woods, P. (2001) *Primary Teachers' Stress.* London: Routledge.

Tschannen-Moran, M. (2004) *Trust Matters: Leadership for Successful Schools.* San Francisco, CA: Jossey-Bass.

Tschannen-Moran, M., Woolfolk-Hoy, A. and Hoy, W. (1998) Teacher efficacy: Its meaning and measure. *Review of Educational Research,* 68 (2), 202–248.

Tsui, K. T. and Cheng, Y. C. (1999) School organisational health and teacher commitment: A contingency study with multi-level analysis. *Educational Research and Evaluation,* 5 (3): 249–265.

Tymms, P. (1993) Accountability: Can it be fair? *Oxford Review of Education,* 19 (3): 291–299.

Tymms, P., Merrell, C., Heron, T., Jones, P., Albone, S. and Henderson, B. (2008) The importance of districts. *School Effectiveness and School Improvement,* 19 (3): 261–274.

Ulvik, M., Smith, K. and Helleve, I. (2009) Novice in secondary school: The coin has two sides. *Teaching and Teacher Education,* 25: 835–842.

United States Census Bureau (2005) The living arrangements of children in 2005. Retrieved 1 November 2009, from www.census.gov/population/www/pop-profile/files/dynamic/LivArrChildren.pdf.

van den Berg, R. (2002) Teacher's meanings regarding educational practice. *Review of Educational Research,* 72 (4): 577–625.

Van Veen, K. and Lasky, S. (2005) Emotions as a lens to explore teacher identity and change: Different theoretical approaches. *Teaching and Teacher Education,* 21: 895–898.

Waldman, D. and Avolio, B. (1986) A meta-analysis of age differences in job performance. *Journal of Applied Psychology,* 71 (1): 33–38.

Waller, M. (2001) Resilience in ecosystemic context: Evolution of the concept. *American Journal of Orthopsychiatry*, 7 (3): 290–297.

Wallis, C. and Steptoe, S. (2006) How to bring our schools out of the 20th century. *Time* (9 December). Retrieved from www.time.com/time/nation/article/0,8599, 1568429,00.html.

Walsh, F. (1998) *Strengthening Family Resilience*. New York: Guildford Press.

Wang, M. (1997) Next steps in inner city education: Focusing on resilience development and learning success. *Education and Urban Society*, 29 (3): 255–276.

Warr, P. (1994) Age and job performance. In Snel, J. and Cremer, R. (eds), *Work and Age: A European Perspective* (pp. 309–322). London: Taylor & Francis.

Wassell, B. and LaVan, S. (2009) Tough transitions? Mediating beginning urban teachers' practices through coteaching. *Cultural Studies of Science Education*, 4: 409–432.

Webb, R., Vulliamy, G., Hämäläinen, S., Sarja, A., Kimonen, E. and Nevalainen, R. (2004) Pressures, rewards and teacher retention: A comparative study of primary teaching in England and Finland. *Scandinavian Journal of Educational Research*, 48 (2): 169–188.

Wenger, E. (1998) *Communities of Practice*. New York: Cambridge University Press.

Werner, E. and Smith, R. (1988) *Vulnerable but Invincible: A Longitudinal Study of Resilient Children and Youth*. New York: Adams Bannister & Cox.

White, R. C. (2000) *The School of Tomorrow: Values and Vision*. Buckingham: Open University Press.

Whitty, G., Power, S. and Halpin, D. (1998) *Devolution and Choice in Education: The School, the State and the Market*. Buckingham: Open University Press.

Williams, S. (2009) The winnowing out of happiness. *Guardian* (3 March). Retrieved from www.guardian.co.uk/education/2009/mar/03/teaching-shirley-williams.

Woods, P., Jeffery, B. and Troman, G. (1997) *Restructuring Schools, Reconstructing Teachers*. Buckingham: Open University Press.

Woods, P., Jeffrey, B. and Troman, G. (2001) The impact of New Labour's educational policy on primary schools. In Fielding, M. (ed.), *Taking Education Really Seriously: Four Years Hard Labour* (pp. 84–95). London: RoutledgeFalmer.

World Health Organisation Report (2008) Primary health care now more than ever. Non-serial publication. Geneva: World Health Organisation Press.

Zeldin, T. (2004) Richer not happier: A 21st century search for the good life. *RSA Journal*, July: 36–39.

Zembylas, M. (2001) Constructing genealogies of teachers' emotions in science teaching. Paper presented at the annual meeting of the American Educational Research Association, Seattle.

Zembylas, M. (2003) Emotional teacher identity: A post structural perspective. *Teachers and Teaching: Theory and Practice*, 9 (3): 213–238.

Zembylas, M. (2005) Beyond teacher cognition and teacher beliefs: The value of the ethnography of emotions in teaching. *International Journal of Qualitative Studies in Education*, 18 (4): 465–487.

Zembylas, M. and Barker, H. (2007) Teachers' spaces for coping with change in the context of a reform effort. *Journal of Educational Change*, 8: 235–256.

Zembylas, M. and Papanastasiou, E. G. (2005) Modelling teacher empowerment: The role of job satisfaction. *Educational Research and Evaluation*, 11 (5): 433–459.

Zembylas, M. and Schutz, P. (eds) (2009) *Teachers' Emotions in the Age of School Reform and the Demands for Performativity*. Dordrecht: Springer.

Index